What Do You Buy the Children of the Terrorist Who Tried to Kill Your Wife?

What Do You Buy the Children of the Terrorist Who Tried to Kill Your Wife?

A Memoir

David Harris-Gershon

ONEWORLD

A Oneworld Book

First published by Oneworld Publications 2013

A CIP record for this title is available from the British Library

ISBN: 978-1-85168-996-5
Ebook ISBN: 978-1-78074-222-9

Cover design by Michel Vrana
Printed and bound in the UK by Page Bros Ltd.

Oneworld Publications
10 Bloomsbury Street
London
WC1B 3SR

For my friends and foes – our hope is not yet lost.

Contents

Part 1

The Bombing

1

The force of the blast tore through the ceiling, blew out doors, tossed tables across the cafeteria. Salt shakers, plastic trays, and barbed nails were sent flying. And after the flying, there was wailing. And after the wailing, anarchy, as students in torn khakis and hijabs scrambled over the splintered tables. After that, they say people began stuffing pages from their Hebrew exercise books into the wounds.

Three weeks before the bombing, a Palestinian man from East Jerusalem named Mohammad Odeh had scouted the campus of Hebrew University perched high atop Mount Scopus. Odeh noted students' patterns of activity. He noted their eating behaviors, where they congregated, always checking the clock, calculating precise times and places. Then, as he approached the cafeteria entrance – the doors invitingly propped open – he watched those seated within and listened to a mix of Hebrew and the Western tongues of summer exchange students. He considered the oblivious mass of humanity, nodded internally and decided, yes, this is the place where it will occur.

Nobody noticed. Nobody noticed the day before Odeh struck, when he hid behind a bank of bushes, scaled one of the university's barrier fences, and buried a backpack stuffed with explosives, nails, and quarter-inch bolts under some brush. And the next morning, nobody noticed as he flashed his Jerusalem identity card, passed through security wearing cologne to mask the scent of explosives, retrieved the backpack and slung it over his shoulder.[1]

He intended to kill Jews and Americans. We were both, far from home, newly married, living in Jerusalem. Graduate students being stalked.

They say we were targets.

The moment the bomb's rippling rings expanded past the cafeteria's broken frame – the reverberations widening, traveling along electromagnetic waves reaching for T.V. antennas, hopping from house to house until reaching mine – the moment it was learned, this thing, this bombing, everything changed. Words shifted and language folded in upon itself. There was nothing anyone could have done. 'Pesto' became blood. 'Cafeteria' became detached limbs, a head face down. 'Capri pants' turned into third-degree burns, percentages of the body covered, skin grafts, recoveries.

This is what I mean:

Capri pants: On the morning of July 31, 2002, a Wednesday morning, a summer morning in Jerusalem, Jamie awoke and quietly put on her Capri pants, trying not to disturb my insomnia-induced stupor. Curiously, she did not choose shorts that morning, though outside it would reach 95 degrees Fahrenheit before 10 a.m., and she didn't choose jeans, despite being accustomed to dressing rather modestly. Instead, she chose this pair of cropped trousers, the material appearing to have been inadvertently shrunk in the dryer, a hybrid article of clothing I'd always found slightly absurd.

The evening before, Tuesday evening, Marla had come to our apartment carrying Hebrew workbooks and a concerned look. It was a look Jamie mirrored. The two were taking a Hebrew language class at the university during its summer session, and were bracing for a pivotal exam the next day, an exam they would need to pass in order to graduate with an M.A. in Jewish Education.

Still, that evening felt strangely buoyant and light, the air unusually crisp for a Jerusalem summer. A breeze carried the cries of stray cats and kids cursing in Hebrew through our open window as we sat at a large oak table, Hebrew dictionaries strewn everywhere, studying. Watching them, I thought, *They are beautiful.* And they were. Jamie with her straight, sandy brown hair occasionally falling across her face, obscuring green eyes moving right to left, eyes that trapped me immediately the first time I saw them. And Marla, with her dark curls unfurling around a radiant smile. They were both glowing.

But the Capri pants. While I slept, Jamie dressed and caught a taxi, something she did every morning that summer. It was quicker than public transportation; it saved time. At least, this is what we told ourselves. In truth, we were nervous that a bus might suddenly explode. We'd seen it so many times on the news, the frame buckling, the steel skeleton exposed and scorched, the television crews swarming, the spotlights, the ambulances flashing red.

So she took a taxi.

Class convened at 8 a.m., a final session before the exam that afternoon. Jamie and Marla decided to cram over a hot meal during the break and headed toward the Frank Sinatra Cafeteria near the university's Rothberg International School. It was the first time they had eaten on campus that summer, being accustomed to returning home each day after class for lunch and an afternoon of conjugating verbs. *Hayah.* It was. *Y'hiyeh.* It will be.

Just after 1 p.m., with their test slowly encroaching, Jamie and Marla waited in a crowded line, grumpy and frazzled. They spotted Ben, a stout friend who learned Torah by day and spun records as a DJ by night in darkened, West Jerusalem clubs, his body bouncing to jungle rhythms that pulsed until dawn, his *tzitzit* (tassels) swaying from his waist amidst the filtered light.

They grabbed three trays of kosher food and sat near the front to eat, not far from the cash register, centrally located.

Cafeteria: Mohammad Odeh lived in East Jerusalem's Silwan neighborhood, just south of the Old City's Western Wall and Al-Aqsa Mosque, where he shared a home with his wife, five-year-old son, and infant daughter.

That Wednesday at dawn, Odeh must have awoken to the muezzin's amplified adhan – the Muslim call to prayer – as it echoed through the Gihon Valley. He then likely washed his face and kissed his sleeping children before donning a pair of jeans and a polo button-down shirt, clothes that gave him the appearance of a university student. Suitably disguised, he then trekked to Shchem Gate just outside the Old City and waited for Wa'al Kassam, the leader of a Hamas cell composed solely of Jerusalemites who would take him to Hebrew University.

Weeks earlier, Kassam had arranged a private meeting between Odeh and the terror cell's general, Abu Moaz. The general, impressed, recruited Odeh into the fold and asked that he suggest a target for the cell's next attack: a test for the new recruit. It was a test Odeh passed. He mentioned he had previously worked as a contract painter at Hebrew University – that he knew the campus well. He even still had in his possession an official entry card. Immediately, Moaz approved plans for an attack, and Odeh was ordered to fix upon an exact time and place to strike.

After several days spent testing the entry card and scouting the university grounds, Odeh set his sights upon a cafeteria, adjacent to the Rothberg International School, frequented by Israelis and a significant population of foreign students, mostly American.

It was a place Palestinian students, of which there were many, would be less likely to dine. He then walked along the university's barrier fence, noticed a section facing the village of K'far Issiva that was unusually low, and lingered for a bit. After a time, with no security visible and very little traffic, Odeh decided it would be the ideal place to move a bomb onto campus.

On July 30, a bomb was prepared in Ramallah and placed in a black backpack. It was then transferred to East Jerusalem, where that evening Odeh picked it up, traveled to the university, jumped the barrier fence, and hid the bomb under some shrubs. He worked quickly in the dark. And just as quickly, he was gone.

The next morning around 8 a.m., when Kassam arrived at Shchem Gate in his car to pick up Odeh, the two stopped briefly at a kiosk to buy two items: a Hebrew-language newspaper and cologne. Odeh sprayed his hands and arms with the cologne as they skirted the eastern edge of the Old City in Kassam's car, the Dome of the Rock rising to their left, mirroring in miniature the Mount of Olives to their right. They passed through Wadi al-Joz and climbed Mount Scopus – the university at its summit – the car struggling, downshifting toward the campus's western entrance.

When they arrived, Odeh hopped out and walked toward university security – a booth surrounded by chain-link fence and barbed wire – where officials waited with metal detectors and wands. Having handled explosives the previous evening, he must have been nervous. I imagine Odeh fidgeted with his scented hands, moving them in and out of his pockets while standing there, waiting with a collection of students, some of whom he would soon tear open. His skin was steeped in the cologne to mask the scent of any explosive residue that might remain – residue the wands wanted, residue the wands failed to find.

It was early, perhaps around 8:30 a.m., when Odeh entered campus. He headed straight for the bushes, grabbed the bag, walked quickly to a utility closet, and set it down among cans of paint and rollers. Shielding his activity by closing the door slightly, he opened the bag and wired a cell phone to the bomb. Finished, he sprayed the bag with cologne, closed the closet, and "passed time."[2]

Around 1 p.m., Odeh returned to the closet, grabbed the backpack, and walked directly to the cafeteria's main entrance, newspaper in hand. It was probably not his intention to drape the day's edition over the bag, shielding it from view under a mound of newsprint; that would have drawn attention, been conspicuous. Instead, he must have thought, *Fold it*, knowing that a newspaper resting upon an abandoned backpack indicated an item to which one would soon return. He hoped nobody would notice the bag perched alone, unattended. Hoped nobody would think, *Hefetz hashud* – suspicious object.

After entering the cafeteria, he looked around – the bag slung over his shoulder – and spotted an empty table near the front. The place was full. Bustling. It was easy to blend in. Gliding past students he placed the bag on a table unnoticed, the folded newspaper balanced on top.

Then, he was gone, disappearing into Kassam's car, where he fingered the cell phone and hit "send." The phone ringing.[3]

Capri pants: After finishing their meals and failing to notice the abandoned backpack on the table next to them, Jamie and Marla decided to hang out and study. Only there was little motivation to do so, full as they were from the meal, and fatigued, with Ben still finishing up his lunch before heading to the gym. Finally, after procrastinating for as long as possible, Jamie decided to cram in one last study session, bent over, reached for her workbook on the floor, her head shielded below the table's flat, Formica surface as she reached and reached and – when the bomb exploded, Jamie was thrown against the floor. Her clothes and skin scorched by the explosion's flash. Her body punctured by shards of metal as people screamed and ran through the shattered glass, stepping over bodies and fettuccini and downed picture frames.

Jamie shook her head, sitting on the ground, dazed.

Cafeteria: Odeh pressed send, called the bag. And the world ended. Began again.

Pesto: When the phone rang at home, I was eating spaghetti with sun-dried tomato pesto. Red-tinged olive oil dripped down the strands of steaming pasta, my lips greasy. Smacking.

I paused and answered, "Hello?"

"David? This is Esther. Jamie's here with me. There was an explosion at the university, but I just want you to know she's fine. Okay? She's fine." [Click.]

I was still chewing, twirling the fork, and knew I didn't know an Esther, didn't know what she was talking about. After a few seconds, puzzled, I thought, *That was nice of her*; thought, *There must have been some kind of electrical explosion*; thought, *Keep eating.*

Although I'd lived in Israel for two years, had been anticipating this, fearing it, I was oblivious. *An electrical explosion.* As though people routinely called strangers to alert them of transformers on the fritz or wires sparking overhead. But as I continued to eat lunch, the beginning of unease, the sense that something was off, crouched silently.

I turned on the T.V.

Nothing. Channel 2 was showing its daily Spanish soap opera with Hebrew subtitles. I ate.

Then, ten minutes later, the news broke in. A man saying the word *piguah* – terrorist attack. Then a map. A star in the center. The words, Frank Sinatra Cafeteria, the words, Hebrew University. Ceasing to chew, I thought, *Not an electrical explosion*; thought, *She's fine. She's fine*; thought, *Why didn't Jamie call herself?*

Then the phone rang again.

"Hello?"

"David. This is Esther. Jamie's okay. But she's lightly hurt. They're taking her to the university hospital. She wants you to meet her there." [Click.]

Lightly hurt. She was still fine, I thought, probably just some cuts and bruises. A scrape here or there. Skinned knee. Sprained ankle. I didn't rush. I called our program's dean to let him know what had happened, gathering some clothes, saying into the phone, "Lightly."

The dean's voice was quiet on the other end. He knew, after living in Israel for decades, that the word "lightly" when conjoined with "injured" did not mean "she's fine." Finally, he asked, "David, what does that mean, 'lightly'? What did they say?"

"I don't know," I answered as tears suddenly welled and stuck in the back of my throat, feeling the fight, the flight. I was lost. In over my head. Clueless. I hung up the phone, threw it against a wall, and began packing. Frantic, I sprinted down a flight of stairs, ran to the street, and flagged down a cab.

The driver rolled down a window, leaned over, and smiled through a cigarette.

"Where to?"

"The university."

"Sorry. Impossible. Place is blocked off."

I opened the door and got in anyway. Slammed it shut. "Look. My wife was injured in the attack. She's at the hospital. I don't care how you do it. But you get me there. Now. Drive on the sidewalk.

Down one-way streets. I don't fucking care. You just get me there. Understand?"

"No problem."

Capri pants: Jamie shook her head on the floor, blinded temporarily by the blast, then heard the movement of feet and realized what must have happened – *terrorist attack.* She followed the shuffling sounds around her, first stepping, then running over broken glass with bare feet, her shoes having been blown off by the force of her trajectory. When she escaped into the sun-drenched courtyard, she was screaming. Loudly. So loudly that a student, a guy wearing a UCLA shirt, grabbed her and held her tightly, just trying to get her to shut up as Jamie said, "I can't, I can't, I can't."

The UCLA shirt guy lifted Jamie and carried her across the cobblestone, her burned flesh illuminated by an unforgiving sun. Without a word, he placed her beneath an awning next to those already lined up, injured, waiting for attention. And then he was gone. She was alone. Emergency personnel swarmed around her. People lay on the ground bleeding around her as I ate spaghetti, enjoying the afternoon light streaming in through our apartment windows.

As Jamie lay there, alone, someone approached, stood over her, and peered down into her face. Jamie said, "Esther, it's me."

"Who are you? I don't know you."

"It's me. Jamie. From Hillel."

Esther worked for Hillel at Hebrew University. After hearing the blast, she had jumped from her desk and raced across the courtyard toward the sound. Jamie, who years earlier had worked for Hillel at Washington University in St. Louis, knew Esther, a former colleague, a colleague who, scanning bodies, had discovered Jamie lying on the ground just as the paramedics reached her. They began cutting off sections of her charred pants, everything from the calf down badly burned. *Capri pants.* They cut, trying to remove smoldering cloth from her burns, trying to determine how far the burns extended. And as they worked, Jamie felt embarrassed, not wanting to be exposed – felt vulnerable as they roughly calculated that thirty percent of the body had been burned, roughly categorized her as "lightly injured." Then they moved on to the next victim in line.

Esther crouched down and promised to stay with Jamie when she began complaining of a stomach ache, the first sign of internal injuries, a sign that she needed to be upgraded from "lightly" to "moderately." Esther grabbed some rescue workers, said, "She needs help," as Jamie continued to believe in the idea of "lightly." She did not understand the burns. She did not understand the shrapnel. She thought, as I did upon receiving that first call, *Just some cuts, some scrapes.* When the paramedics saw pools of blood coalescing around her abdomen and realized something was wrong internally, Jamie argued with them as they moved her to where the moderately injured were lined up, saying, "No, no. Lightly. I'm lightly injured."

2

I met Jamie immediately after moving to Bloomington, Indiana, for my first job out of college, a fellowship at Indiana University's Hillel Center, the cultural home for Jewish student life on campus. It was the autumn of 1997. I had just completed an undergraduate degree in English literature from the University of Georgia, a degree that, naturally, had prepared me for a career in Jewish community service.

My job was simple: find Jews on campus disengaged from Jewish life and engage them. So I hosted Rastafarian Shabbat dinners, organized indie concerts, and established a "Matzo Ball Soup Hotline" for sick Jewish students – preparing gallons of the stuff for delivery – all in the name of connecting with Jewish students on the periphery.

In essence, my job was to find Jamie. And on a Saturday afternoon in early September, not long after my arrival in Bloomington, I found her.

The air that day was crisp, smelling faintly of barbeque and crushed leaves. Thousands of students were milling around Memorial Stadium, where Indiana was preparing to host Ball State in the football team's home opener. Street vendors lined the sidewalks, grilling bratwurst and hotdogs. Coeds pranced in parking lots holding plastic cups and wearing the school's colors, crimson and cream. Groups of clean-cut men chanted their spirited rites.

I walked past all of them on my way to share a Shabbat meal with the local Chabad rabbi at his home. It was a clumsy attempt to familiarize myself with the competition, for the rabbi was a member of an orthodox outreach organization that proselytized to non-religious Jews, hoping they'd drop the pork, don a yarmulke or long skirt, and preface every sentence with *Baruch HaShem* – blessed is the Lord.

I knocked, standing before Chabad's large, wooden front door. A voice bellowed "*Gut Shabbos*" – Good Sabbath – so I let myself in. When I crossed the threshold, a liminal space that would separate past from future, Jamie was standing before me. She was wearing a summer dress, a cotton shawl draped over her arms and shoulders. Her green eyes flashed a look of expectant curiosity before she tucked her chin into her shoulder, eyes angled down, averted, a suppressed smile on her lips. I felt a sensation rising from the pit of my stomach, as though the house was a roller coaster making a precipitous descent.

An orthodox woman pointed and said, "This is Yosepha – she's a student."

Yosepha is the feminized version of the Hebrew Yoseph, or Joseph. It was like being introduced Davidina or Johnette. I was amused.

After the introduction, Jamie was whisked into the kitchen, where she spent much of the afternoon helping the rabbi's wife prepare and serve food for Shabbat lunch. Once the meal was served and we were all seated, eating, the rabbi began peppering me with a series of questions. While answering them, I stole glances at Jamie. I watched her eat, watched her straight hair shift around her face to the subtle rhythms of her movements, fingers twirling a fork, a napkin touched to mouth, a water glass tilted, emptied.

When the rabbi and his wife made a rare, simultaneous move to the kitchen, leaving the two of us alone, I finally leaned over and spoke my first words to her, asking, "Is Yosepha your real name?"

Jamie flushed and said with an eye-roll, grinning, "Oh, God. No."

In the months following that first lunch of stewed beef and fluffy challah, I periodically spotted Jamie visiting Hillel. Having spent a term abroad in Israel the previous spring, she'd returned to campus in her final year seeking community, unsure where to find it.

One November morning, catching her hovering around Hillel's front door with a friend, I walked over and ventured, "I'm leading a backpacking trip to Brown County State Park this weekend. We're going to explore Judaism's connection to environmentalism. Are you interested?"

"Umm – no."

"Let me know if you change your mind. It should be fun."

"Yeah, I'll let you know," she said.

After that, I began looking for her everywhere. I would poke my head in dining halls and scan the crowded tables, loiter in front of academic buildings, waiting for lectures to conclude and the masses of students to filter out, thinking, *Maybe I'll see her.*

Then, while manning a table outside Memorial Union, peddling my signature matzo ball soup, a friend of Jamie's approached. Smiling, she blurted out, "You *know*, I'm a huge Jamie fan." I grinned and knew. Knew she was looking too.

Our relationship began secretly, since I was in essence an employee of the university. In public, Jamie and I would often exhibit a detachment that bordered on disdain, careful not to tip our hands. It was an outward disinterestedness that belied our growing closeness.

After a full week together – a week in which we spent nearly every waking moment with one another – I rose one morning and froze. Opening my laptop, I composed an erratic email in which I expressed some misgivings. I wasn't ready for something serious, I wrote, wasn't ready for anything intimate, meaningful. Upon hitting "send," I punched the wall lightly, thinking, *You're an idiot.*

After ignoring all of my subsequent messages, Jamie finally agreed to meet me on campus one evening. In front of the cavernous computer science building, she shifted on the balls of her feet and said, "Look. I'm not going to waste any more of my time. Either you want to be with me or you don't. So decide. Right now." Her hair was bending in the breeze, skin taut, face serious. It was an easy decision.

When the academic year concluded, Jamie's undergraduate studies and my Hillel fellowship had run their separate courses. We had also charted separate ways forward. Jamie was headed to St. Louis, Missouri, for a job, and I had plotted a spiritual quest to Israel.

On her final day in Bloomington, Jamie piled boxes into a baby blue Subaru wagon and said, "Time to start a real life, I suppose." I kicked the gravel and fixated on her tires, estimating the pressure. And then the tires were spinning, and she was gone.

I fled to Israel, determined to engage in the earnest study of Hebrew and traditional Jewish texts, thinking the Middle East would be a refuge. The distance would dull our sudden disconnect, I thought, pave over it, make it concrete. But living out of a trailer anchored to a scrubby slope in the Judean Hills, I often found myself rising before dawn not for spiritual purification, but to use an archaic pay phone. In the dark, I would grope for a plastic phone card decorated with a pastoral, desert landscape or some political figure from among the heap that littered my trailer's linoleum floor. Finding one, I would then climb the hill to the yeshiva's main hall, where I'd head to a bank of orange public phones. As my peers shuffled by on their way to chant the morning prayers, I'd lift the receiver to my ear and slide the card into a slot at the phone's base, revealing how many shekels were available for a call to the States. Then, I'd dial.

I did this often, this rising early to catch Jamie staying up late. And the more we talked, the more marriage entered into the discussion until finally, early one morning, tired of the hypothetical, I said, "So, how would you feel if someone were to propose to you over the phone?"

"Umm."

"What would you think?"

"Umm."

"Will you marry me?"

We were married in the summer of 1999, in Jamie's aunt's backyard in Westchester County, outside of New York City. The ceremony was a traditional Jewish affair, choreographed for us rather than our non-religious families. Many were not prepared for the orthodox vestiges which infused our service: the blur of Hebrew chanting; the yarmulke-wearing yeshiva students – our friends – who feverishly danced us toward the chuppah; the long, white *kittel* I wore over my suit, a symbol of purity that matched Jamie's flowing dress.

We weren't orthodox, we were liberals, rooting ourselves in ancient traditions, staking our claim to them in an act of cultural rebellion.

Which is why – after crushing a glass beneath our feet to shouts of "*Mazal tov*!" – we were whisked away to a private room before the festivities commenced. This solitary moment, called *yichud* (seclusion), is when the marriage would have been consummated in Talmudic times. For Jamie and me, it was a moment to eat pizza, embrace, and absorb what had just occurred.

Wiping tomato sauce from my lips, I asked, "Can you believe we're married?"

Jamie nodded, a chocolate chip cookie between her fingers, the crumbs falling upon her billowing gown. "Are you surprised?"

"What?"

"You seem surprised."

"I'm not surprised."

"What are you then?" she asked as we began to feel the vibrating music and the stomping feet of our guests, beckoning us to emerge.

"What am I? I'm happy."

"Good. Me too."

Before our wedding, Jamie and I had decided two things: 1) we would hyphenate our last names, figuring we could alienate our father figures and traumatize any future children in one, swift gesture, and 2) we would travel to Israel after a year of marriage to study ancient Jewish texts. We would throw off the shackles of societal expectations, ignore careers and titles and health club memberships.

We would live.

To do so, however, we needed funds. Jamie was already employed at Washington University's Hillel. And so we decided to settle in University City, an inner-ring suburb just outside the city. As I sought work, we began making a home together in a one-bedroom, shotgun apartment, giddy at the prospect of doing so.

We soon learned that neither of us knew how, exactly, to cook – or, more precisely, how to prepare meals that one might actually want to eat. In a kitchen no larger than a walk-in closet, we spent hours scouring cookbooks, chopping vegetables, and experimenting with dishes. Black bean casserole with cornbread topping. Curried potatoes and cauliflower. Roasted fennel soup. Much of the time, we ridiculed each other for our novice attempts, flicking water from the faucet as we did so.

"You want to put what exactly on top of salmon?" she asked.

"Mustard."

"It's not a hot dog."

"Neither is tofu, but you thought that was a good idea," I countered, unable to help myself.

"I was experimenting."

"Mustard on salmon isn't an experiment?"

"Nope. That's a waste of food."

[Flick.]

These culinary quests were more than clumsy attempts to feed one another: they were community-building ventures. Jamie wanted to throw open the doors to our apartment and host students, friends, whoever might wander by for a Shabbat meal. She wanted to expand our existence, to imbue the newly woven bond we'd created with unpredictable Jewish hues. And because this is what she wanted, I did as well.

We were partially inspired by our close friends, Adam and Lori, who lived across from us on Balson Avenue. Every month, they hosted Friday night services for a patchwork collection of twenty-something Midwestern Jews, the service always followed by the promise of a gourmet feast. In the beginning, the only thing Jamie and I were capable of contributing to the festivities were folding chairs.

In time, though, our apartment also became a Shabbat destination. Jamie would do the inviting, and I would muster the psychic strength to suppress my introverted tendencies. And at the meal, we would harmonize to Hebrew hymns.

We would sing.

Not long after our move to St. Louis, I was able to find work teaching at an elite, private school in the suburbs. My domain was the fourth grade, a group of children mature enough to scratch the surface of complex thought while just young enough not to be inundated by the coming surge of hormones waiting to flood their bodies. Aside from recess, where I was a star on the soccer pitch, lunch was my favorite activity, and our table became famous for riddles.

"Rich people need it. Poor people have it. And if you eat it, you die."

Ben: Poison.
Me: Rich people need poison?
Alicia: Time.
Me: How do you eat time?
John: Nothing.
Me: Exactly.

Once, on spaghetti-with-meatballs day, I was ambushed.

"Mr. H.-G., do you stick your fork in the dirt?" asked Melissa, one of a handful of Jewish students. A giggle punctuated her question.

"Yeah," squeaked Abby, "Do you stick your fork in the dirt?"

Everyone at the table began chanting, "Mr. H.-G. sticks his fork in the dirt." The image itself, devoid of any context or meaning, was enough to elicit sustained laughter. I had absolutely no idea what they were talking about. Smiling warily, I waited for the next round.

"Our Hebrew school teacher said that to make your fork kosher, you stick it in the dirt. You keep kosher, right? So you must stick your fork in the dirt. Do you do it in the backyard?" Melissa continued. Everyone looked at their fork.

In the Jewish legal system, the laws of *kashrut* (keeping kosher) are extremely complex and confusing, particularly when it comes to the status of pots and utensils. A thousand years ago, in an era devoid of chemical cleaning agents, sticking a utensil in the ground was a method of scouring that could, as a last resort, render an item clean and permissible to use under Jewish law. But I didn't know this. Abby and Melissa, two Jewish students who had been exposed in Hebrew school to this archaic tidbit that stuck, certainly did. *Mr. H.-G. sticks his fork in the dirt.*

The bell rang and in an instant the room was empty, leaving me with a littered table and a desire to know about forks and dirt and everything else my tradition had bequeathed to me that had yet to be learned.

Jamie felt the same. We were both hungry, hungry for learning, for texts, wanting to devour them together in the desert air. We wanted to construct upon our foundational love a cultural framework made from Hebrew, from Aramaic, from Talmudic inquiry.

These were the raw materials we sought.

We found them – or the place where they might be acquired – at a pluralistic yeshiva in Jerusalem called Pardes, a place about which Jamie and I had heard much praise. One evening, seated at a dining room table strewn with dirty dishes, we visited the institute's website together. With pop rhythms throbbing from the upstairs apartment, I pointed to the laptop and read aloud, "Pardes faculty do not impose any patterns of observance or belief on students."

Jamie leaned over me, her hand on my shoulder, and continued. "Students are challenged to grow as individuals and as members of our community."

"Rigorous study of ancient texts. Religious diversity. Tolerance," I added.

Jamie nodded, and in that nod, everything that had previously been uncertain about our short-term future was contained. Our destination had been set. We would travel to Israel, intending to indulge in just one year of study before returning to the States, unaware that one year would stretch into three, that we would end up jointly enrolling at Hebrew University to pursue graduate degrees in Jewish Education. When we bought our tickets, we were aware of just this: the start of something mysterious and grand had been set into motion.

Then the time for that motion arrived. So we boarded an El Al flight – Newark to Tel Aviv – and took off, holding hands, thinking, *We are alive.*

3

When the paramedics lifted Jamie onto a stretcher, Esther grabbed her hand and ran alongside as she was wheeled over the cobblestone paths to a row of waiting ambulances. The vibrations shook a metal nut lodged within Jamie's intestines She flinched, squeezed Esther's hand, needed the wheels to find concrete.

When they finally reached an ambulance and loaded Jamie's stretcher, Esther climbed inside and dialed my number. "She's lightly injured," Esther said. "You should come meet Jamie at the hospital" – her casual tone implying that it might be something worth checking out.

The taxi stopped just outside Hebrew University, a few blocks from the hospital. The driver turned and said, "Get out here." He told me to find the back entrance, the emergency room, to push my way in, to push people aside, that it would be the only way. But after stepping from his white Mercedes, there are certain things I don't remember. For instance, did I pay him? I don't remember the feel of money, the stretching of my arm to place bills into his palm as I pulled myself out of the car. It's not that such a detail is something one should remember at a time of panic, a time scrambled by adrenaline-fueled fear. But still, it's unsettling. Did I stiff the guy who risked arrest by driving on the wrong side of streets and running red lights for this American going out of his mind? And when I got out, which I don't remember either, did I run? I don't recall running. You would think, given the situation, that I would have broken into a sprint, streaking across the hospital's drive toward the back entrance, sliding over ambulance hoods blocking my path, hurdling abandoned stretchers, bursting through the hospital's double doors panting, crazed. You would think I might have grabbed people, tossed them aside, against walls, over potted plants, barreling through women and children and the elderly to reach the emergency room where crowds of family members packed the hall and pounded on the locked doors, pushing, surging. It's the type of scene one should remember, acting desperate, heroic.

But all I remember is somehow finding myself standing in front of the emergency room's doors. People were pressing me from behind. Yelling. Demanding to know if their loved ones were within. If their loved ones were alive. A nurse poked her head through the parted doors, looked at me, and demanded a name. "Harris-Gershon," I screamed, watching her check a pad, scanning for mine to match another's. She found it, the match, *You win*, and guided me through a corridor full of drawn curtains. Doctors were buzzing. Machines were wailing.

I arrived at the only curtain drawn back. Someone I didn't know was sitting on a stretcher flanked by two nurses handling wires and blankets. The person was shaking, shaking and looking at me, trying to smile.

I understood before comprehending – my brain pointing out that vision could no longer be trusted: *I don't recognize her*. And then: *That's her. That's Jamie*.

Suddenly, I realized that I must have been led to this spot by the nurse who checked for my name, the nurse who pointed and said, "There she is." Or maybe she didn't leave her post. Maybe I wandered around, confused. Maybe I found Jamie on my own, stopping before the only open curtain and knew when I shouldn't have, knew it was her. But how could I have known? The face charred, bloated, the hair scorched, ends bristling, standing on end like an animated character electrocuted by a live wire, the jolt playful, humorous. *OUCH. Ha, ha! Good one.*

One of the nurses turned to me and said, "*Tihiyeh yaffah*" – She'll be beautiful again.

"She's beautiful right now," I said, the words unleashed while trying to process what the fuck was happening, scanning her burned body, the room, trying to process where I was, what was going on, who this person shaking and bleeding before me might be, what all the lines running from her body carrying pink or green or clear fluids were doing, where they were going, thinking, *She is not beautiful,* thinking, *This is not lightly injured*, thinking, *What the fuck is this?*

A coldness began to emanate from deep within, a shutting down of my senses. I pressed auto-pilot and left the cabin, started drinking in the back of the plane as it hurtled forward.

Jamie looked at me. I don't remember if she spoke. If she did, I wasn't listening, hearing only the din of my racing thoughts, the hospital machines pulsing and pumping and vibrating. But I caught certain words: "metal" and "organs" and "emergency surgery." And I did certain things: moved close; touched her hand; backed away startled when told not to touch her hand; stared at the white gauze covering her shaking arms and legs.

The nurses grabbed her bed without warning. She was moving. I followed. They wheeled her into a makeshift surgery station, beds stacked side-by-side, where a formless doctor approached from the depths of some unseen medical abyss. Jamie told him, "I'm not afraid," told him, "I've lost my Hebrew," told him, "Explain in English." The doctor, now with a shaved head, clean looking, intelligent looking, said, "We have to open you up," said, "We have to see where it is," said, "We may have to keep an organ out of the body for months to let it heal," said, "It's normal."

I nodded, not really hearing anything. Sure. Of course. Normal. An organ outside the body for months. Hanging out, still attached, resting on the nightstand or sleeping on the bed next to her, the doctor's words meaning nothing as Jamie said, "I'm ready."

I stood alongside her in pre-op among those dying and about to be saved, unsure to which category Jamie belonged. When they whisked her into surgery, I stood frozen, staring at those in the beds surrounding me, some of whom were receiving care. Two hospital-assigned social workers materialized, took me by the arms and led me away.

Carrying folders and clicking pens, they moved me into a room and, after sitting, asked in British accents, "Are you okay?" I responded robotically, smiling, leaning back and crossing my legs, assuring them that there was nothing needed – "Thank you for asking. So kind of you. Really." They leaned forward. Elbows dug into their flexed thighs as they shrugged and said, "I guess we're done for now," then pleaded, "Please call when you need us." A folder was pushed into my hand containing documents on trauma, on grief, on those inevitable obstacles waiting to be faced.

They rolled Jamie into emergency surgery and sliced her open, carving a line from her navel to just under her breastbone. Peeling back the skin, doctors probed with thin, cold rods, seeking the shrapnel lodged in her small intestine. A tiny camera was inserted. It tracked the nut's path, documenting the organs hit, the organs missed.

I found the waiting room and sat alone. Teachers called to check on Jamie, and to ask if I knew the whereabouts of Marla or Ben. Neither could be found. There was suspicion, hope that Jamie had been with them – a hope that since Jamie had survived, those missing had as well and were anonymously receiving treatment somewhere, somehow.

And then the Rosh Yeshiva, our head rabbi at Pardes, walked into the waiting room. He sat down and, without a word, placed a Hebrew prayer book in my lap. Looking at its leather, beveled cover, he instructed that I open it and read some Psalms with him, Psalms traditionally read during moments of desperation. Psalms read during moments when people are injured, dying, or dead. Psalms asking God for strength, for help, for faith.

I laughed, not at him, but at myself. At the book. Horrified. Knowing, as others searched for our friends, that they were gone. Knowing that my heart had fled. Knowing I knew nothing of this world.

I took the book, opened it, and flipped to the back, finding the page he had landed upon. And then, while reading, it happened again – a soft, desperate chuckle – when I made a mistake, accidentally read responsively instead of echoing the line back to him. I messed up and grinned as a boxer does just before kissing the canvas, grinning at his opponent after being caught with a vicious right cross, trying to express with a show of teeth while wobbling, *Didn't hurt a bit.*

Me: Didn't hurt a bit.
God: I'm not your opponent.
Me: Prove it.

We finished, and as the rabbi left, friends began arriving to offer support. Only, I don't remember them being present in those first hours of waiting while Jamie's abdomen was sliced open and peeled back. All I remember is laughing. Then the rabbi left. And then the nut.

Four hours after leaving Jamie with the intelligent-looking doctor who spoke of keeping an organ outside the body, they wheeled her out of surgery and into the intensive care unit (ICU). A man in scrubs – the same doctor? – approached holding a closed, clear plastic cylinder. A white label was stretched across the top. Holding it delicately, he reached out and handed it to me, as though I had ordered smoked salmon or hummus.

"Sometimes people want these things," he explained. "It was found in the small intestine."

He talked about the cutting. The re-connecting. The parts they tossed. He talked of those organs the nut had passed on its way, skimming, so close, just missing everything before resting in the soft, expendable tissue that if stretched taut would reach twenty feet. He talked of the burns – second and third degree – covering her legs and hands and back. He talked of a long recovery, talked and talked and then left, pointing to the ICU on his way to cut open someone else, and said, "She's in there."

I stared at the thing. It was so light, the container, the sides of which were streaked with an opaque film. *Is that blood? Pieces of intestines? Bodily fluids?* I held it aloft, to the light, and then shook it, feeling something solid tumble. Feeling dead weight. The lid peeled off easily, revealing a small, contorted piece of metal. An object whose purpose was to secure things. An object which had unfastened more than it knew.

With the doctor gone, I stared at the nut. It was all so absurd – as though a tragicomedy was playing out in which I had somehow secured a supporting role:

Doctor: Here you go.

Me: What's this?

Doctor: Just a little something you might like, you know, to have, something to hold when you look back on these times we shared.

Me: You've got to be kidding.

Doctor: No, really. Sometimes people want these things.

Me: Why on earth would anyone want this?

Doctor: Oh, come on. You know you've wanted this all along, a tragedy, to know whether or not you're strong enough to survive.

Me: Have not.

Doctor: Sure you have. It's something you've wanted, a defining moment, and this nut is my gift to you, a physical reminder of the pain and grief you asked for, felt you always deserved, felt you've had coming to you after a quaint, two-parent upbringing devoid of poverty, sickness or death.

Me: I don't want it, don't want any of this.

Doctor: Whatever. Just take it. You're one of us now. There's no going back.

Me: I can go back.

Doctor: No, you can't. And another thing: you'll never throw it away. It will always be with you. Put it on a keychain or turn it into a necklace. You know, something meaningful, as a reminder.

Me: Fuck you.

Doctor: Bye now.

Holding the container, repulsed, I couldn't imagine why anyone would want such a thing. But I also knew this: he was right. I would never throw it away. And I also knew that there had been times when, walking along busy streets in Jerusalem, I had stopped and thought, *I want to experience it*, wishing for a bomb to explode. I understood this impulse to be an ironic one. A bomb was the last thing for which I'd actually wish, scared by the possibility of sudden violence. But in Jerusalem such a possibility made me feel alive. With the illusion of death seemingly so close, I was alive, perhaps more so than at any point previously. And I thought, *I want to know what it is Israelis feel, what they must deal with, this trauma, this grief,* wondering if a personal experience with destruction was a defining national characteristic. Wondering if, in order to understand what it meant to be fully human, such an experience was essential.

Once, I leaned over to a friend and admitted this, admitted that I constantly felt guilty about secretly pining for a bomb to explode nearby. I felt guilty about turning on the news to see if another attack had occurred, feeling a sense of purpose, a sense of meaning every time a broadcast was interrupted by reporters on the scene, always the same scene, always being simultaneously repulsed and awed by the brokenness, the wailing, the lights flashing. And so I admitted this to him, and he just nodded and said, "Of course," as if such thinking was to be expected amid the bedlam of people spontaneously exploding on public transportation and in cafés.

But standing in the waiting room with the plastic container – with the unknown now known – I flinched as pieces of my core disintegrated. Holding the physical representation of what Jamie had lost, would lose, I understood that this was anything but living, anything but being fully human, wondering if we would ever become whole again.

Following signs in Hebrew that swung from the ceiling on metal chains, I found the blue double doors leading to *Tipul Nimratz* – intensive care. Pushing through, I saw Jamie lying directly before me. She was in the back corner of a shallow, wide room, patients lying in beds along the wall, lined up to my left and her right. Everyone was still.

Jamie's eyes opened. She smiled as I approached and scanned her body. Aside from the bandages, it looked whole. She was whole. Until she said, "I was sitting with Ben and Marla," and it became clear in that moment they were lost, our friends. And as Jamie saw the significance of her words register on my face – I could see reflected in her eyes a recognition of the change in mine – I knew she was lost as well. We both were as she said, moments out of surgery, hours removed from the cafeteria's rubble, "Don't tell me what happened to them. I don't want to know."

"I won't."

"Promise."

"I won't."

Then I left to tell those searching for Ben and Marla what Jamie had said, what she knew, what she couldn't know.

When I returned, the nurses were changing shifts and settling Jamie in for the long night. It had not occurred to me that I wouldn't be permitted to stay with her in the ICU, that I would be asked to leave, to abandon her. And so, not knowing, I kneeled at her side, expecting to remain in that position for the duration of the night, to remain there and watch her breathe.

But the new nurses, the night nurses, began making clear signals that it was time for me to go, noting that she would be in good hands, that I couldn't stand all night – there were no chairs, a hint I'd failed to absorb. I looked at Jamie, unable to touch her, and said, "Goodbye," said, "I'll be back," before exiting the ICU and catching a ride home from one of the teachers who was still in the waiting room.

On the ride home, watching the dust of East Jerusalem fade into the Western city's expanse of stores and apartment buildings, I feigned a sense of ease, a sense of calm, chatting him up about our class, how much I enjoyed it, that I planned on completing upcoming assignments on time – was looking forward to it, actually. When we reached *Ha'moshava Ha'germanit* – the German Colony, a Jerusalem neighborhood teeming with chic cafés, bakeries, and Americans – I thanked him for the ride, said, "I'll see you soon, in class perhaps." He turned his head and stared, smiled weakly, the weakness saying, *You're in deeper than you understand.*

In the ICU, lying in a bed, waiting for whatever one waits for in the middle of the night, attached to tubes, probes, bags, unable to sleep, unsure exactly what happened, knowing exactly what happened, Jamie watched as a Palestinian man approached. Stopping short, he bent down and changed the garbage bag. Then walked away. Agitated, Jamie called for a nurse. "Please check it," she asked, needing assurance that he had not placed a bomb inside, this man, this suspicious man. The nurse understood – knew why Jamie, why everyone else in the ICU for that matter, was there. She checked the garbage and winked. "It's okay, sweet child. It's empty."

She did not sleep.

Nor did I, back at our apartment where every light burned as I lay awake, waiting for dawn to come, for my rightful place back at Jamie's side when visiting hours began the next morning. That I couldn't sleep seemed reasonable given the circumstances. Sleep would have been luxurious, self-indulgent, an easy escape from reality, a reality which, while buried emotionally, had awakened within me a deep sense of responsibility, of honor. Besides, I was a natural insomniac who had difficulty shutting off the brain after even the most mundane of stimuli. But the lights.

After entering the apartment, I traced the floor plan and, pausing at each threshold, slid a palm up and down the walls, searching for a switch. I turned on every light. Living room, kitchen, bedrooms, bathroom, closets, *mirpeset* – the small, concrete deck that jutted away from the building's façade. Then the television, the computer, the oven light. Everything. I feared relinquishing control – a failed sentry wired by the guilt of abdication – and so demanded that the physical structure surrounding me pulse with energy. Demanded that we all remain alert, awake.

Sleep wasn't a question; I knew the night would be long, each second noted by the grandfather clock standing guard in the hallway, keeping its post, a reminder that I had abandoned mine, its swinging arm ticking, saying, *Bomb, bomb, bomb.*

Perhaps it was a genuine fear of darkness which kept the lights burning, a vulnerability reaching back to childhood visions of monsters in the closet and under the bed. Once – when I was around seven or eight years old – I stirred before dawn and peered from under thick covers at the open doorway to my room. A cloaked man stood there holding a compound bow. He raised it and took aim at the bed, firing translucent arrows, the shafts slowly spinning, the feathers swooshing in the air, fixed on my head. Using the comforter as a shield, I retreated underneath. Taking shelter under folds of cotton, I knew the one thing that would end this encounter: light. If I turned them on, he'd disappear. I knew this. But the switch was perched adjacent to the door's frame, inches from his body. A child of television, I remember thinking, *Is this how I die?* Something probably culled from *MacGyver* or *The Greatest American Hero.* Creating a bunker of blankets, forming a hole from which to peek, I formulated a plan: wait for the reload and pounce. It was my only chance. When his hand moved for the quiver, I threw off the covers, sprinted to the wall, and flicked the Mickey Mouse switch with a wet palm. In the subsequent months, I kept a flashlight buried beneath my pillow. Just in case.

Perhaps I subconsciously thought, as I did so often in my childhood, that light would keep those visions crouching in the darkness of my mind at bay. Visions of ripped flesh and gauze soaked red, of a Palestinian wrapped with wires, gripping a button, waiting for me behind the potted palm tree in the living room. *Your turn, Jew.* So the lights stayed on all night that first night as the world slept and I wondered how the world could sleep, how I would ever sleep again.

Through two long, arched windows with sky blue trim, I waited for morning to come, watching the darkness of night slowly swell, the black heavens eventually giving way to lighter tones that matched those pulsing inside the apartment, light rising to meet light. And as the rays mingled together in the dreamlike haze of dawn, I rose and did the only thing I could think of doing: I prayed the morning service. It was something I had done nearly every morning for years: rising early to *daven*, hoping – as a stubborn realist – for elusive slivers of spirituality. However, this time, as dawn approached, there was no religious motivation. Such motivation was dead. Instead, I prayed to pass the time, in the hopes that doing so would shave an hour or so off the wait, turning this holy, religious act into a time-eater, defiling it, an existential *Fuck you* to Whomever.

I wrapped my body with a *talit* – a traditional, four-cornered prayer shawl with tassels called *tzitzit* at each corner, each tassel biblically ordained to remind the wearer that all commandments must be kept. With the *talit* draped over my shoulders, I donned *teffilin*, wrapping the black, leather straps tightly around my left arm, palm, and middle finger. Then, I clamped a black box to my forehead with identical straps, the box containing Hebrew verses from the *Shema*: *Sh'ma Yisrael Adonai Eloheinu Adonai Eḥad* – Hear O Israel, the Lord is God, the Lord is One.

Adorned in the vestments of a religious life once lived, I swayed and mouthed words of praise I couldn't believe, shielding my eyes ritually with a cupped palm as the Muslim call to prayer echoed from a nearby hill. As I prayed, eyes covered, the person I once was fled from my body and departed through an open window. It rose into the Jerusalem night, surrounded by the chanted supplications in Hebrew and Arabic making their way to the dimly lit heavens high above the Old City, circling and weaving to meet the day and the fate of that day as the cityscape winked alive.

4

Jerusalem in Five Acts: Jerusalem is a traumatized land. It is a land that has been held down against its will and forced to witness the plunging of knives and tearing of flesh for thousands of years without pause. It has been the victim of a divine session of waterboarding, the land forced to drink an endless flow of blood. When Cain killed Abel – the first recorded act of biblical violence – God told the murderer, "The voice of the blood of your brother is calling to me from the ground."[4] The land has always borne witness. And witnesses rarely forget.

In the arc of biblical history, what follows may not be the first time a trauma came to Jerusalem. But for me, as a Jew, I cannot begin the story of this land anywhere but the moment God called to Abraham and said, "Take your son, your only son, the son whom you love, Isaac, and go to the land of Moriah, where there you will offer him up as a sacrifice."[5]

Forget that Isaac was the child Sarah carried in her old age after a lifetime of barrenness, after a lifetime of praying for seed to grow in her belly. And forget that Isaac was the child God had promised Abraham, was the long-awaited heir God said would inherit the land of Israel. And forget that Abraham was living in the land of Israel because, when God spoke to him out of the blue at his home in modern-day Iraq and said, "Go to a land I will show you,"[6] Abraham inexplicably went.

Forget all that. What should be noticed is the way God commands Abraham to commit filicide. "Take your son, your only son, the son whom you love, Isaac." See anything unusual? The medieval rabbis – who viewed every biblical word as essential – sure did. Their question: Why did God identify Isaac in four different ways when commanding Abraham to sacrifice him? Why not just say "Take Isaac" and get it over with?

Many answers have been given, but one from Nachmanides, a thirteenth-century Spanish commentator, sends chills: "[God is repetitive] to make the commandment greater." In other words, God's intention is to make the task so fucking hard by hammering Abraham over the head with reminders of how painful it will be to kill his son that going through with it won't just merit normal commandment-abiding points, but super-metaphysical bonus points as well.[7]

But the land. Jerusalem.

Abraham takes his son to a place called Moriah, drags him up a mountain of God's choosing, and there builds an altar of stone upon which he binds Isaac with twine. This place, this land of Moriah, is a mystery. Where is it? With few clues, the medieval commentators artfully concluded that it must be Jerusalem. And the mountain? It's the Temple Mount, the heart of Jerusalem's Old City, where the Western Wall and the Dome of the Rock now dominate a political/religious space that has been the geographic fulcrum of the Israeli–Palestinian conflict for as long as memory serves.

And it is this space where Abraham raised the knife, prepared to plunge it into Isaac's flesh, before an angel stopped the bloodshed mid-stroke. It is this space, in the heart of Jerusalem, where Isaac is traumatized by his father's attempted murder. The Bible says nothing of this trauma, of course. But it doesn't need to. Isaac disappears from the text for several chapters, is never seen with his father again, and only surfaces to attend Abraham's funeral, unable to step forward until his father is dead and gone.

When thinking about Israel as a traumatized place, I begin with the Binding of Isaac because of its incomprehensibility – that such a trauma was orchestrated by God. The story makes little sense, the commandment going beyond any recognizable reflection of the good, humane world in which we hope to live. And His preferred place in that world for such an incomprehensible test of brutality? Jerusalem.

It's been this way ever since.

Act I – Thursday, July 18, 2002: For several months during the spring and summer of 2002, high-level talks between Palestinian and Israeli officials had gone dormant, the negotiations for peace having been obliterated by unchecked violence. But by early July, after a time of relative calm, Israeli Foreign Minister Shimon Peres had quietly begun meeting with several Palestinian cabinet ministers.[8] An attempt at a new beginning. Again.

Then, on July 16, predictably, the violence came, violence meant to railroad such talks. It worked.

Activists from Fatah's Tanzim – the Palestinian Authority's new-guard armed wing – ambushed an Israeli bus in the West Bank. Then, a double suicide bombing in Tel Aviv, leaving scores of civilians dead over a two-day span. So familiar.

In response, Prime Minister Ariel Sharon banned Peres from talking further with the Palestinians. Then, he ordered the borders immediately closed, borders which were virtually closed already, sealed since June.[9] The Prime Minister, it appeared, wanted retribution after the attacks – as so often is the case, each side reacting reflexively. He was waiting for the right moment, the moment that would come, days later, the moment I refuse to accept.

But first, July 18, the day Peres was forced to abandon talks with the Palestinians, talks that would have focused on easing those travel restrictions keeping Palestinian workers home – travel restrictions meant to keep the terrorists out.[10]

July 18, when Israeli families held funerals for the innocent – for the mothers, fathers, and infants murdered by masked gunmen running and firing and screaming in Allah's name.

July 18, when Jamie took me to breakfast at our favorite café, where we enjoyed an Israeli breakfast of eggs, cucumber-tomato salad, and toasted pita.

July 18, thirteen days before Jamie would bend down beneath a cafeteria table, reaching for a workbook, just wanting to study for an exam.

Act II – Saturday morning, July 20, 2002: On Saturday morning, something happened. And depending upon one's frame of reference, it was either meaningless or extraordinary.

Sharon and Israeli military officials would reveal that, to them, what happened was meaningless. Much of the world would see it as extraordinary. In less than three days, it wouldn't matter, for the event and the momentum it produced would be buried under rubble and the wailing of sirens in Gaza. Arguably an unprecedented moment in the Middle East. A moment that happened. A moment which disappeared in the desert sand.

Here is what happened: on Saturday, July 20, Palestinian Authority officials from Fatah – the Palestinian Authority's largest political wing – met with high-ranking members of the Islamic groups responsible for the majority of terrorist attacks against Israeli civilians. They met with Hamas. They met with Islamic Jihad. The goal? Convince them to discontinue the use of suicide bombings against Israeli civilians as a legitimate form of resistance.

Convince them to stop killing innocent people. Convince them that terror wasn't working. Never would.

Extraordinary. Or meaningless.

The meetings were the result of a European-led diplomatic effort supported by Jordanian and Saudi delegations, an effort described by journalists and Palestinian officials as unprecedented. Saudi Foreign Minister Prince Saud al-Faisal, one of several observers to the talks, indicated the groups had been productive during initial meetings and had quickly begun working jointly on a ceasefire document – a document stating that it was time for the Palestinians to make a strategic shift in their struggle for independence.[11]

According to a key, unnamed Palestinian figure close to the talks, the shift was not only strategic, but social in scope, precipitated by the unease among prominent Palestinians about the destructive forces that suicide bombings were unleashing within Palestinian society:

> *In the past two months there has been a sea change in the way that Palestinians have looked on this strategy. They are really worried that their children are growing up with posters of guys wearing suicide belts. It's not just a tactical point, many have begun to accept it was a moral mistake.*[12]

Now, questioning the morality of suicide bombings against civilians, on the surface, shouldn't impress. Nobody obtains morality points for questioning whether blowing up innocent people is a mistake. However, what does impress is this: those evil enough to have championed suicide bombings as a legitimate form of resistance were reportedly being pressured by Palestinian society – by political, economic, and social forces – to consider abandoning terror against civilians. Not solely out of a concern for Israeli civilians, it should be noted. But because such tactics were damaging the fabric of Palestinian society, were doing more harm than good.

And thus Hamas and Islamic Jihad, invited to sit at a negotiating table set by the Palestinian Authority, not only accepted, but engaged in productive dialogue. The talks generated a fair amount of optimism from observers not accustomed to seeing these groups meet, much less agree on anything. However, an anonymous official qualified this optimism by stating, "It [will] be hard for the Palestinian Authority to reach a deal to stop bombing attacks as long as Israel keeps carrying out military operations against the Palestinian people."[13]

Propaganda. Political posturing. Prophesy.

Act III – Saturday night, July 20, 2002: Those in the Knesset, Israel's seat of government, knew of the meetings being held on Saturday between the various Palestinian factions. They also knew of their significance, their theoretical potential. And it was this knowledge, perhaps, which inspired Sharon to send Peres – banned from speaking with Palestinian officials only two days earlier – back to the negotiating table. For on Saturday night, Peres met with the Palestinians' chief negotiator, Saeb Erekat, and Ahmed Razak Yehiyeh, the Palestinian Authority minister responsible for security forces and the lead negotiator for the ongoing ceasefire talks amongst Hamas, Islamic Jihad, and the Palestinian Authority.[14]

In their three-hour meeting, Peres, Erekat, and Yehiyeh discussed many issues related to Israel's role in improving life for the Palestinians. They talked about easing curfews in the West Bank and about opening borders so that Palestinian workers could reach their jobs within Israel. They talked about scaling back Israel's military occupation of major cities and towns. They talked about life's quality and how to improve it. For the Palestinians, anyway. A one-sided conversation. A start.[15]

Few things were said publicly after the meeting concluded, though Israeli minister Danny Naveh, who also took part in the talks, indicated that Israel had a "clear interest" in improving its own security by improving the economic situation amongst the Palestinian people.[16]

The words weren't empty.

Immediately, funds Israel owed the Palestinian Authority, funds which Israel had frozen since the Intifada ignited in the summer of 2000, were transferred to Yasser Arafat's government. Not all of it, but a significant amount: $200 million. It was meant as a gesture, a show of good faith, something that had not been done in over two years, a time during which Israel refused to hand over customs and tax revenue to the Palestinian Authority for fear such money would be funneled directly to organizations of terror, would be used to support the violent uprising.

Now, after one of the first reported meetings between top Israeli and Palestinian officials in over three months, Israel was willing to hand over the funds, and Peres, on Sunday morning, indicated that if the money transferred was not misused, Israel would be willing to hand over all $420 million it owed.[17] Just like that.

Just like that. The about-face was stunning. Perplexing. What was said in that meeting, at an undisclosed location, late that Saturday night? What did Erekat tell Peres? Did he implore the senior Israeli official to consider that, this time, things were different, that things were happening between Palestinian leaders that had never happened before? Did he reveal that Fatah officials had, for the previous three months, been flying secretly to Tehran to meet with Hamas's senior spiritual leaders? And that these leaders had, for the first time, agreed to give "silent support" to a ceasefire calling upon the cessation of civilian terror? Did Erekat continue by revealing to Peres that Fatah's jailed leader, Marwan Barghouti – whose popularity among the young, armed members of the Tanzim was unparalleled – had given his support to such a ceasefire?

Much of this must have been revealed to Peres, for in their meeting Erekat handed him a report revealing the significance of the ceasefire declaration – then a work-in-progress – that Fatah officials were hammering out with Hamas and Islamic Jihad, a report that implored Israel to cease its targeted assassinations in order for such a ceasefire to succeed.[18]

I wonder if Erekat slid the actual declaration across the table, allowing Peres to see its text, to understand intimately the significance of the words being agreed upon by rival, militant factions. Is that what created more momentum toward peace in a twenty-four-hour period than had been achieved in the previous two years?

After finding an archived copy of the ceasefire declaration – along with a letter to Israel that would have accompanied it – I can only conclude one thing: Peres was handed some papers. And after scanning them, he blinked and thought, *Please let this be the moment history demands of us.*

Intermission – The Declaration: What follows is the text of two documents – one the ceasefire declaration, and the other an accompanying letter – that would have been delivered to Israel on Tuesday, July 23. They were obtained by *The Times* of London.

Text of the ceasefire declaration:

> *We, the representatives of the Tanzim and Fatah, in the names of our members and the political organizations that we represent in all of the cities, towns and villages of the West Bank and Gaza, declare that we will end attacks on innocent, non-combatant men, women and children in Israel and in the West Bank and Gaza.*

We call on all Palestinian political organizations, factions and movements to end all such attacks immediately, and to do so without hesitation or precondition.

We will immediately cease all such operations, we will work with other Palestinian political organizations to gain their support for this principle, we will police our own memberships to make certain that no such operations are planned or carried forward and we will engage in a national dialogue to convince our people of the wisdom of this program.

Our efforts will be relentless, our actions tireless, our commitment permanent. Our revolution goes forward under a new principle. We will continue our struggle. We will defend our people. Aggression against our cities and our families, the confiscation of our lands, the destruction of our orchards, our businesses, our homes, the closings of our schools, the detention of our young men in squalid camps, the curfews and closures, the demonization of our leaders and their assassination, the deportations of our people, the slow, purposeful, seemingly inexorable destruction of our society and our dreams – the continued Israeli military occupation of the West Bank and Gaza – will be resisted.

Excerpts from an accompanying letter:

We understand … how you feel about us. We are a gang, and a bunch of murderers … We can't be trusted.

But maybe, just this once, you should drop these prejudices and listen … We, the leaders of the most influential political movements among the Palestinian people; we, who represent those who, like you, have been orphaned and widowed; we who desire the comfort and security of not just a state but a home – we choose the future.

We will do everything in our power to end attacks on Israeli civilians, on innocent men, women and children, in both Israel and in the occupied lands of the West Bank and Gaza. We make this declaration without seeking or demanding any prior conditions.

Why now? The bombings of the last few months have transformed your society. Those bombings horrified and angered your people, and sent your nation into despair. It did that to us. It sparked a rethinking of who we are as a people. It marked a shift in our perceptions – not of you, but of ourselves.

For a time we were able to put this horror out of our minds ... Our eyes look out to see what you are doing to us in our towns and villages every day, but the same eyes look in at the hardened hearts of our children. It may take a generation for us to teach our children a new way, to soothe their bitterness, to erase their hatred, to teach them that there is hope for the future. But we must begin. It is for them, for their future, that we have made this historic decision. The rivers of blood that have so embittered our people will be staunched. The suicide bombings will be brought to an end. By us. Now.

We will not stop fighting for our land, we will not renounce our dream or betray our birthright ... This is not a surrender, this is not a retreat. We will continue to fight every moment of every day for our rights and for our state. We are certain that we will achieve this, that we will be victorious.

Act IV – Late Monday night, July 22, 2002: Ninety minutes after the ceasefire's text was finalized, Israel attacked. It was an American-made F-16 that dropped the one-ton bomb in the crowded Gaza neighborhood. The blast killed Sheik Salah Shahada, a senior Hamas leader, and demolished the apartment building in which he was sleeping. It also partially destroyed two adjacent apartment buildings, killing along with its mark children, the elderly, entire families.[19]

Here is what is now known: by Monday night, every major Israeli player knew about the Palestinian ceasefire declaration. Sharon was getting regular updates on its progress from European diplomats working alongside the Jordanian and Saudi officials in a small room in Jenin. And ninety minutes after word came that the document had been finished, that Fatah officials had settled on a workable version ready for international release at daybreak – declaring a unilateral cessation of suicide attacks – Israel's Prime Minister approved the targeted bombing.[20]

Why. Not a question, a statement. An exhalation.

After the dust had cleared, after all fifteen bodies had finally been recovered from the rubble in Gaza, a July 25 *New York Times* article would confirm what most assumed: Israel didn't believe in the ceasefire effort, and wasn't bothered by having undermined it. The article revealed the attitudes and postures that allowed the bombing to take place, a bombing that came minutes after *perhaps* – this being the operative word – the most important step Palestinian leaders had collectively taken toward ending terror as a strategic option in years.

Israel felt differently:

> *Israeli officials acknowledged that they had known of a possible Palestinian ceasefire proposal before the bomb was dropped, but they dismissed it as a futile attempt by Palestinians without influence over terrorist groups.*
>
> *Raanan Gissin, a spokesman for Ariel Sharon, Israel's prime minister, acknowledged that there had been talk of a ceasefire, but he said it was being exaggerated ... that*

> *several ceasefires had already been negotiated and ignored during the 22-month [intifada]. "They had so many opportunities to really issue a ceasefire," Mr. Gissin said. "Not in one case did we learn about orders issued down to the [Palestinian] field commanders to say, 'You've got to stop.'"*
>
> *A senior Israeli military official said, "There was no chance it was going to happen. It was only thoughts or dreams or desires of some people who have no influence on terrorist activities."*[21]

Thoughts or dreams or desires. They're all that remain. Dreams. Desires. The thoughts of what might have been prevented.

Nine days later, on July 31, a Hamas terror cell blew up the cafeteria at Hebrew University. It was a Hamas cell taking orders from a Hamas organization that, according to media reports, had finally hinted, during ceasefire negotiations with Fatah, a willingness to shift away from terror attacks and their all-or-nothing stance: the destruction of the State of Israel by any means. Not a change in ideology. That never changed. But strategically, Hamas seemed on the unprecedented verge of scaling back its violent strategy – even if temporarily. It was aware of the punishment Palestinians were enduring because of its suicide bombings,[22] aware that the Israel Defense Force's brutal and incessant presence in West Bank towns, the choking checkpoints and curfews, were partly a response to men strapping their bodies with explosives and walking into fruit markets, restaurants, shoe stores. Hamas, it appeared, was beginning to shoot for less lofty goals, if the destruction of a democratic state can be viewed as lofty. It wanted the Israeli military out of the West Bank, wanted Israelis out of the West Bank, wanted a chance to achieve lasting religious and social improvements within Palestinian society. Most importantly, though, it wanted a chance to win big at the polls when the next election came. The decision was almost purely political, the organization beginning to realize that terror, and the military wrath it brought upon Palestinians, was now doing more political harm than good, was making it more difficult to win popular support among secular and moderate Palestinians. So a partial ceasefire, a movement away from killing civilians while still maintaining its militaristic voice, was showing itself to be a savvy, practical move.

But that was before late Monday night, July 22. The night Sheikh Salah Shahada was killed by a one-ton bomb. After that, revenge was reclaimed.

A revenge which tore open my wife's scorched body and killed our two friends.

Act V – Sheikh Salah Shahada: Sheikh Salah Shahada deserved to die, and Israel wanted him dead. Shahada had been placed atop Israel's "most wanted" list soon after the Intifada began in 2000.[23]

To understand why he was target number one for the Israeli military, why Sharon could have cared less about some theoretical ceasefire when Israeli intelligence officials barged into the Prime Minister's office on the night of July 22, claiming they had pinpointed Shahada's whereabouts, it's necessary to understand Shahada the terrorist.

Having founded Hamas's military wing, he *was* terror. And he was still serving as the leader of Hamas when the one-ton bomb fell upon him from the night sky. In the early days of Hamas's violent ascension, Shahada wrote the book on suicide bombings, and had been teaching its message to militant ideologues for over ten years,[24] a span during which he planned hundreds of attacks.[25] He murdered and created murderers. He was good at his job.

After escaping one in a series of failed Israeli assassination attempts in early July of 2002 – just weeks before the one that would finally get him – Shahada had brazenly revealed on an Islamic website the rudimentary tactics Hamas used to ensure the success of its terror operations. They were tactics he invented and saved for posterity. Among them: "We take advantage of any security breakthrough [reported by network intelligence], define the target, and take some camera shots to decide whether the operation will be conducted or not."[26]

A camera shot of Shahada shows an image the Western world has come to associate with Islamic extremist leaders: the long, black beard; the white layers of flowing cloth covering wrinkled, olive skin wrapped around eyes that appear singularly focused. The association in this case was accurate: he had become not only one of the most influential Islamic leaders fighting Israel's existence, but one of the most extreme as well. In the years before his death, he had grown close to Hamas's ailing spiritual leader, Sheikh Ahmad Yassin. So close, in fact, that many within the movement were looking toward Shahada as Yassin's successor, as next in line.[27] As divine.

Shahada's death sent supporters into hysterics – hundreds of thousands poured into the streets of Gaza for his funeral (and those of the other victims).[28] Internally, Hamas operatives were set aflame, as revealed by the following statement released after Shahada's death:

> *Retaliation is coming and everything is considered a target. [There] won't be only just one [attack] ... After this crime, even Israelis in their homes will be the target of our operations.*[29]

But it wasn't just his death that so enraged the masses; it was also the attack's unintended brutality: 145 injured and fifteen dead, including nine children. And the scenes. The scenes which played over and over on Palestinian television. Scenes identical to this one, recounted by a visiting Dubliner, captured hours after the bomb fell:

> *I ran here and just saw pieces of flesh everywhere, one man running away holding a lump of flesh on a metal tray and another pulling out a baby boy with half his face blown away, obviously dead.*
>
> *Everyone was screaming, shouting, crying and shouting, "Revenge to the Israel child-killers." I have never seen anything like it. I just kept thinking: "If the British Army wanted to take out Gerry Adams (President of Sinn Féin, Northern Ireland's largest nationalist party), would they use a bomb that size in a residential area like this?"*[30]

After the attack and the images that relentlessly played on Palestinian television, there would be no chance for a ceasefire. Everyone knew this, and the international community took out its frustrations on Israel with harsh statements of condemnation, as per usual. But this time, it wasn't the typical scenario: the Western world (Europe) bullying Israel with one-sided expectations of restraint, leaving the United States to step in and defend its democratic baby brother. This time was different, for the White House, remarkably, joined a deafening chorus of disapproval for Israel's actions, something the Bush administration – itself still reeling from the terror of September 11, 2001 – very rarely did. White House Spokesman Ari Fleischer summed up the President's view thus:

> *[President Bush is often] the first to defend Israel, but in this case he sees it differently ... The President has said before Israel has to be mindful of the consequences of its actions to preserve the path to peace and the President*

> *believes this heavy-handed action does not contribute to peace.*[31]

This statement from the White House – severe by its own standards – merely underscored the powerful reverberations that rippled out from Sharon's decision to attack, with some critics cynically going so far as to accuse Sharon of intentionally sabotaging the historic ceasefire talks.[32] Diplomats intimately involved in the negotiations, having witnessed a senior Fatah official meet with Hamas leaders to hammer out a workable draft just two hours before the F-16 strike, certainly felt this was the case, as evidenced by an assessment from an international mediator, who wished to remain anonymous:

> *Those directly involved in drafting the [cease-fire] statement believe that this was a purposeful initiative on the part of the Israeli leadership to undermine what the Palestinians believed was the chance to stop the suicide bombs. This was a very ham-fisted operation on the part of the Israelis. They were apparently desperate to short-circuit whatever they wanted to short-circuit and obviously in the short term the chance of any such declaration is now gone.*[33]

Even though Sharon remained defiant in the face of such criticism, calling Israel's targeted assassination "one of the biggest successes,"[34] there were immediate calls from within Israel's government to investigate what happened, to find out how the military's intelligence – which claimed the attack would have minimal collateral damage – could have been so woefully misguided. Nobody was happy. It had been a disaster. A horrible mistake.

All this history, or the appearance of history, compressed, the contemporary Middle East squeezed into a four-day span, a snapshot, a week-in-the-life-of.

The above events, stitched together using journalistic reports, reports that almost unilaterally point the implicit finger of blame upon Israel, make up only part of the story. For there are partial-truths, details left out, details found buried just beneath the surface. It's a matter of narrative construction – a matter of history cut and pasted by those in the business of disseminating information. Which story to tell?

The following detail comes not from a journalist's pen, but from counter-terrorism experts at the International Policy Institute for Counter-Terrorism in Israel (ICT), which proclaims itself as "the leading academic institute for counter-terrorism in the world."[35] See, what wasn't reported in any newspaper after the Hebrew University bombing was the fact that after September 11, 2001, the U.S. State Department had updated its list of terrorist organizations, placing Hamas on it. It was a move that reverberated loudly in Gaza. Hamas's literature became obsessed with the influence and presence of the United States in Israel, calling it, among other things, "the patron and participant in the Zionist project in the region." It was an early sign that Hamas operatives were beginning to consider the United States as another enemy at home, and its citizens as fair and desirable targets.[36] And in the winter of 2001, Hamas's intentions were made clear in a statement intended for world consumption: "Americans are the enemies of the Palestinian people" and will now be considered "a target for future attacks."[37]

This detail was absent from newspaper accounts after the bombing of Hebrew University's cafeteria, in which five Americans were among the nine killed. Also absent was mention that Hamas operatives had likely targeted the location because of the number of American students who frequented the area, had targeted it because Americans had explicitly become legitimate strategic targets of terror for Hamas. The organization had been planning to strike Americans for months, well before Shahada was killed. And the preparations for the Hebrew University bombing were made before ceasefire negotiations between the Palestinian Authority and Hamas reached their apex. It was meant to happen all along, though a ceasefire could theoretically have delayed or canceled the operation.

When Israeli officials were quoted after Shahada's death, were asked to justify the bombing in the midst of a Palestinian ceasefire effort, no media outlet chose to substantiate their claims by going to counter-terrorism experts for a word. If they had, those Israeli officials who were made to appear as insensitive, as callous – calling the ceasefire between Hamas and the Palestinian Authority "futile" and "pointless" – would have been supported by much of the intelligence community. For ICT seemed to affirm, in a series of articles written between 1998 and 2002, Israel's justifications for killing Shahada. It described Hamas as highly decentralized, as an impossibly chaotic organization incapable of controlling its terrorist wing, a wing composed of individual ideologues independently congregating under Hamas's Islamic umbrella. It would have been highly unlikely for any ceasefire declarations to have actually found across-the-board adherence, much less recognition. Leadership on the ground simply didn't exist in a traditional sense. Nobody had control over the actions of a fractured terrorist wing at a time when Hamas had no official political might.

Meaning: Israel may have been justified in assassinating Shahada; meaning: the journalists may have gotten their stories partially wrong; meaning: Israel as the bad guy worked better, sold more papers, made good copy. Blame the Jews. A common theme throughout history, no?

And absent from all media reports, after Shahada was killed, was the following excerpt contained in an article filed in late 2001 by Dr. Ely Karmon, a senior ICT researcher:

> *[Israel] should give priority first and foremost to the destruction of Hamas' ... operational and strategic leadership ... through precise targeted operations, including the use of elite units in the heart of PA [Palestinian Authority] territory. This should significantly reduce the threat of suicide and other attacks in Israel's heartland, and also prevent the transformation of Hamas as the leading political force in the territories.*[38]

So Israel was following the best intelligence available at the time, however flawed such intelligence may have been.[39]

But questions remained. If Sharon's government truly believed the ceasefire was futile, then why did Israel release funds to the Palestinian Authority? Why allow Peres to renew high-level talks when days before he had been banned from speaking with the Palestinians? These don't seem like the actions of a government taking things lightly. They don't square with the post-mortem justifications rattled off by Israeli officials after Shahada was killed. Things simply don't add up. Never will.

And the fuzzy mathematical equation that led to Israel's assassination of Shahada – and Hamas's subsequent bombing of Hebrew University – reaches farther back into the shadowy recesses of state politics than most realize. It reaches back to calculations Israel made decades previously, which unintentionally assisted Hamas's birth in the 1980s.[40]

In the 1960s and 1970s, the Muslim Brotherhood movement (from which Hamas would eventually emerge) migrated from Egypt and established itself in the Israeli-occupied territories. The movement's overarching mission was to lead an Islamic revolution in Palestine – a social and religious awakening within a Palestinian society dominated by the PLO's secular, nationalist stance. The Brotherhood was not explicitly political in its structure or solely nationalist in its vision. Instead, it was intent on influencing Palestinian society, and thus the nation, by grabbing the hearts and minds of citizens rather than the state levers of power. It thus focused its efforts on Islamic education and social construction, building mosques and educational centers in conjunction with a focus on *da`wah* – the communal development of broad-based social welfare services.[41]

The Brotherhood's desire was ultimately the formation of an Islamic state, but its efforts were focused on "internal jihad" – a cultural and religious initiative within Palestinian society – rather than "external jihad" against Israel and the West. And this reformist approach adopted by the Brotherhood, this building of social and Islamic institutions from the ground up, was seen by Israel as desirable. It was seen as a potential way to weaken the PLO by mitigating its nationalist reach with a competing, cultural Islamic revolution. The Brotherhood's war was internal. To Israel, it was innocuous. And so Israel gave "tacit consent"[42] to its actions by ignoring its initiatives and, sometimes, even encouraging them[43] by allowing the Brotherhood's institutions, unencumbered by Israeli suppression, to thrive.

During this time, the Brotherhood had no violent arm, and was not engaged institutionally in terrorism or violence directed against Israel. The organization was viewed in practice, if not in principle, as pacifist.

But things would change.

In the mid-1980s, Islamic Jihad was formed by breakaway Brotherhood activists, who created an organization that embraced a political, violent struggle against Israel. The ideological foundations of this struggle were Islamic, thus melding nationalist aspirations with religious ideology. And after several, high-profile attacks against Israel, the organization enjoyed growing popularity on the street – a popularity that did not go unnoticed by the Brotherhood.[44]

Then in 1987 the Intifada erupted – an uprising that swept through Palestinian society in the form of nationalist demonstrations and nonviolent protests, giving the PLO a shot of adrenaline. The Brotherhood, which bristled at the PLO's "claim for exclusive national authority," saw Palestinians taking to the streets and knew it needed to make an institutional shift or risk losing its influence. The Brotherhood looked to the right and saw Islamic Jihad's popularity. It looked to the left and saw massive crowds waving PLO banners and chanting nationalist slogans. And when it looked straight ahead, a hybrid path appeared. And Hamas was formed.

In the Intifada's infancy, Hamas immediately became a nationalist, political movement focused on gaining power and influence, with the social and educational foci moving to the side, but not out of the picture. Sure, the Brotherhood's original purpose remained: the Islamization of Palestine. Its methodologies, however, changed. Hamas created an Islamic Charter delineating in party terms its core principles. Among these principles was the reclamation of every inch of Palestinian land. Palestine was defined by Hamas as "an Islamic endowment" (*waqf*), and fighting anyone defiling a Muslim land was charged as a religious duty (*fad'ayn*). War with Israel thus became a core Hamas principle, a meld of its newly formed nationalism with right-wing interpretations of Islamic law.[45]

The internal jihad had become external.

Killing Israelis became a national *and* a religious duty for an organization of growing influence. Pacifism was dead. Terror was about to be embraced as Islamic militarism became, for Hamas, both an expression of nationalism and a principal recruitment tool.

Israel hadn't seen it coming.

All of this historical excavating is meant to uncover one thing: how Hebrew University came to be bombed. But more than that, it's an attempt to ride history backwards in order to point a finger and say, *It's your fault.* The only problem is this: I don't have enough fingers. Because one could point to America's flawed Middle East policy, which helped propel radical Islamists in various countries (including Osama bin Laden before the transformation of al-Qaeda). One could point to Muslim extremists' doctrines of hate. Or to Israel's penchant for disproportionately violent solutions to a violent problem. Or to suicide bombings and targeted assassinations. To military checkpoints and Qassam rockets. To a Palestinian rage generated by intense suffering. To Israeli machismo driven by a post-Holocaust fear of extinction. Or one could point toward a God continuing to use the Middle East as a poker table. All impersonal. All theoretical. All illusory.

Haunting is the face in the mirror, the image of Mohammad Odeh's face.

Haunting are the statements made by Hamas after the Sheik's death, the statements I remembered reading in the *Jerusalem Post* on July 27, as Jamie and I lounged in Marla's living room in Jerusalem on a Shabbat afternoon, enjoying the breeze and the company. I even, ridiculously, had read aloud the article about Shahada's death, reciting the statements of revenge that had been put out by Hamas's leaders. They were statements we talked about, naive, happy, unaware they would apply to us, that these statements would kill Marla and Ben, wound Jamie, and shatter everything:

> *We promise ... that our eyes will have no rest until the Zionists see human remains in every restaurant and bus, at bus stops and on every street.*[46]

Days later, Mohammad Odeh would set his bag down in the Frank Sinatra Cafeteria at Hebrew University – a place considered by many as off-limits, out-of-bounds. He would rest a folded newspaper upon it and walk away. The phone in his pocket. The call to be made. A call made because of calls that were made by others.

Part II

Disconnection

5

Jamie spent the night in the ICU with a dozen other victims needing constant monitoring. When I arrived the next morning, I was greeted outside the unit by a small gathering of friends. They had nowhere else to go, they said. There was nobody else to see, they said. Ben and Marla's bodies had been identified. They were gone.

I rang a buzzer and gained entry to the ICU. Jamie smiled when she caught sight of me. Her face was covered with a transparent cream, her body being soothed by the rhythms of oxygen flowing, liquids dripping, electronic beeps monitoring her, keeping time. It was a syncopated show of survival.

The nurses had brought chairs into the room, so I sat.

"How are you?"

"I'm okay."

There wasn't much else to say, much else that could be said. And so I sat with her, both of us mostly silent. When she asked, I would dip a small sponge attached to a plastic handle in a cup of water and raise it to her lips, letting her suck, giving her mouth some moisture. It was something I could do, something to show that I was there, that I would care for her. After a time, she asked that I leave, being wholly focused on healing, on resting. *Please don't let anyone in,* she said.

I nodded and returned to the waiting room to find friends and teachers with food, board games, and silent support. I was thankful for them. I was thankful for their presence as I absently munched on Doritos, waiting for a nurse to step forward and let me know when Jamie had awoken. The weight of my own limbs was barely perceptible as I watched the door, a pervasive numbness having worked its way up my spine, a numbness that gave me license to behave in ways I'd never before dared. At one point, a pack of twenty American Jewish leaders who happened to be touring Israel on a fundraising mission gathered unannounced around the ICU's double doors, expecting entry. They wanted to touch the American terror victim who had survived, who had made it out alive, demanding to express their sorrow, their regret, their anger. I was unsure how they had found her, but I was certain they were looking for Jamie. The numbness made me hard-nosed and pushy. I rose and blocked the door. "Get away, now."

A bearded man approached as though attempting to sidestep me. He looked past my shoulder and said, "We'd just like to share our sympathies."

"This is a freaking ICU. She doesn't want to see anyone."

"But we – "

"Leave now. All of you."

As they shuffled off, I thought, *Assholes.* All strangers, even Jewish tourists, were now potential perpetrators, potential harbingers of harm.

It would be the first in a series of confrontations I had with people trying to get close to Jamie in those first forty-eight hours after her admittance into the hospital. I turned away: Israeli politicians looking for a photo-op; American emissaries searching for ways to be useful; journalists looking for some blood to suck out of the trauma. After Jamie had whispered that she didn't want to see anyone, had said, "Don't let anyone in," I obeyed. I'd failed her once. I was not about to do so again.

So when the press secretary for Jerusalem's mayor, Ehud Olmert, called, expressing the mayor's desire to visit Jamie, I scoffed and hung up. When reporters rang from the *New York Post* or *USA Today*, sounding officious while pretending to care, I hung up. When a U.S. congressman traveling in Israel on a diplomatic mission wanted to speak with Jamie, I hung up. It wasn't anger, merely duty. Cold, detached duty. Something to do. Something upon which to focus. *Take care of her.* This was my lone responsibility, my only thought, echoing, repeating, a mantra.

There was only one person I allowed entry: Jamie's father. While I was rejecting journalists and politicians, he called, wanting to hear her voice, wanting to know that, yes, *She is alive*. I held the phone to Jamie's ear. Then took it away. Then learned what she had heard.

"David, he's flying here."

We had tried to conceal from family members the extent of Jamie's injuries. She didn't want anyone to worry, thought maybe it would all just go away, that if nobody would bear witness, there was nothing to see. It was a fantasy we shared, motivated not by a desire to protect others, but instead by a desire to protect ourselves. I needed to protect myself. I had been shamed by what had happened, by that which I had caused. The wife I failed to protect, the daughter I failed to protect. So together, we deliberately downplayed what had happened when on the phone with family in America. But once Jamie's father said he was coming to Israel, once we knew the jig was up, we shifted our tactics from deception to damage control.

Right after the bombing, after doctors wheeled Jamie into emergency surgery, I called home to my parents, to a mother who obsessively watched CNN and who would have seen the words "Hebrew University" crawl under the report. When I got her on the phone, I lied. "I'm here visiting a friend who was injured."

She asked pointedly, "Is Jamie hurt?"

"No."

She didn't believe me. I could sense by her hesitation, her unwillingness to stop asking questions. But it didn't matter. There wasn't any information to give her, only images. Snapshots of Jamie's damaged body. Nothing more, nothing concrete – no medical diagnoses or reports from the operating room. So I withheld what little I knew as long as possible, withheld that Jamie had been caught in the blast, that her intestines were being held together by sutures, her body prone, her mouth dry. I would have withheld this for a lifetime had the doctors not said, after Jamie emerged from surgery, "Months. It will take months for her to heal." Then I understood that I would have to reveal what had happened, that it would have to be known, this thing.

Even after it was revealed, with Jamie's father on a plane, making his way to Jerusalem, we were still in damage control mode. We wanted to show that things were not so bad. Really. Which is why, on Jamie's third day in the ICU, with her father en route, we played around with a miniature mirror, trying to find Jamie's good side. Her face had been lightly burned in the blast – first degree burns. It was red and slightly swollen. She didn't look like herself. And so I held the mirror, flexed and turned it as Jamie gingerly moved from side to side and determined, "The right side, take him to my right when he comes in. That's the good side."

I agreed. Though when Jamie's father entered, when I ushered him in, trying to explain that things were not as bad as they seemed, that she would make a full recovery, his face clearly told us, *There is no good side.* And there wasn't.

6

In the summer of 2000, Jamie and I arrived in Israel to study. Doves were circling Camp David when our plane banked high above a chalk-lined surf off the Tel Aviv coast as we arrived after a year of marriage to study our bequeathed culture and internalize biblical Hebrew and Talmudic texts with wizened teachers and progressive peers at our chosen yeshiva, Pardes. Bill Clinton was confident about a final peace that never came. We were confident as well. But just after arriving, talks between Ehud Barak and Yasser Arafat collapsed in Maryland, and the Intifada took root. Not long after settling into our fourth-floor apartment on a picturesque street lined with limestone homes, the bombs began.

Palestinian terrorists started wearing heavy coats in the heat of September, wires tangled within the insulation. Israeli artillery responded by shelling eastern villages just over the Judean Hills. From our flower-filled balcony, the echoes were unmistakable. "So this is what war sounds like," we whispered. Yet we decided to stay. We would not be scared away. Instead, we made concessions: avoid buses, cafés that lacked armed security guards, open-air markets, large grocery stores, crowds. We were careful.

I learned Hebrew that first year by reading newspapers designed for new immigrants. Despite being rather elementary, with simple sentence structures and cartoon images designed to soften the shock of ancient characters and guttural sounds, I learned how to speak about suicide bombings – of the injured and the dead – before learning how to ask for a menu. Once, on my way to pick up the latest issue at the local *makolet* – a phone-booth-sized store selling newspapers, children's toys, and cigarettes – I encountered mayhem. At our favorite café, a tattooed waiter had tackled someone. The man, a Palestinian, had approached the waiter to ask for a glass of water, his voice timid, his skin sweating intensely. He was immediately clothes-lined like a wide receiver coming free over the middle, the detonation device ripped from his grip. An angry crowd formed, collectively holding him down until the police swarmed, a sneering smile stuck on the bomber's lips.

Still, we stayed. Even with the regular calls from our worried parents, asking that we come back – *please, come home* – we stayed, enrolling in a two-year graduate program at Hebrew University to pursue degrees in Jewish education. Our plan: graduate and return to America for teaching careers in Jewish community day schools.

At Hebrew University, our lives were serene. We congregated in sunny atriums, lounged on grassy knolls, and ate in large, swank cafeterias without the slightest hesitation. This despite the cautious way we lived near our home, less than five miles away. For a meal of falafel and chips, gun-toting security guards were demanded; for a trip to the mall, metal detectors were required; for a rare movie, only matinees in empty, cavernous halls were allowed. This is how we lived, making routine decisions based upon the likelihood of not being killed. We constructed invisible walls and lived within them, closed to the illusion of danger – the danger of illusion.

But on the Hebrew University campus, we were artists impersonating the impressionists, painting the campus quiet, brushing ponds and lily pads under the school's limestone arches. Everyone did. Israelis. Palestinians. Exchange students. We all pretended the university was off-limits. An oasis of integrated study outside of the greater conflict. An agreed-upon no-fire zone.

And though I chose to drop our rules for survival at the university's gates, I never relinquished my fears, never checked my suspicions at the security booths leading into campus. Walking around, I'd quietly watch Palestinian workers, worried. When alone, I sat in remote corners of eating establishments to avoid being hit by a spray of shrapnel should something go off. I knew the dangers. But I never mentioned these things to Jamie, not wanting to ruin our dream with my neurotic nightmares, neuroses that were irrational, overblown. I didn't want to scare her, a woman already close to the edge, close to calling it quits, close to heading home. I didn't want to see us pack our bags. Which is why I didn't mention that, months before Mohammad struck, Hebrew University's student newspaper had exposed the pathetically lax security on campus. The paper even imagined a hypothetical scenario in which a suicide bomber detonated himself within a busy cafeteria in an article that was largely dismissed by students and ignored by the administration – an article that substantiated my fears.

I chose not to mention it.

7

While Jamie was confined to the ICU – and I to the closed circuit running from her bed to our apartment and back – things were happening. Our community at Pardes was grieving. Impromptu ceremonies were convened, where people wept and shuddered together, without Jamie. Without me. Without Ben and Marla. One evening, they gathered on the tarmac of Ben Gurion Airport and sent off Ben and Marla's caskets, listening to teachers choke through remembrances and politicians paperclip their deaths to Israel's struggle before loading their bodies into the bellies of El Al Boeing 777s. Then, they said goodbye.

It was another world, a world focused on grieving, not healing, the wheels moving slowly, grinding painfully outside our antiseptic-swiped cocoon of survival. And in the midst of this, Michael called.

The Shabbat afternoon before the bombing, Marla had invited us over for lunch with her and Michael, the man we all knew she would marry. We had grown close to Marla during our two years in the Pardes Educators Program, Jamie particularly so. For these last two years they had studied together in a *chevruta* – a partnership traditional in Talmudic study, the text serving as a fulcrum between two arguing learners. Most mornings they sat across from one another in the *Beit Midrash*, teasing out legal decisions more than a thousand years old with a bubbly enthusiasm that would have alarmed the rabbis whose judgments they were studying.

When Jamie and I walked into Marla's apartment, the smells of a Shabbat afternoon, of already-cooked food slowly warming on a hotplate and flowers settling into their new liquid life, were noticeably strong. The meal was casual. Sunlight streamed through the open windows as we sat around a coffee table in the living room, our plates perched on scrunched laps, munching and chatting.

What remains from that lunch is more sensational than imagistic. My dominant memory is a feeling of warmth. But a single, vivid scene does stand out distinctly, in three dimensions: Michael, sitting across from me in a recliner, looked over and said, "This is nice. This is what life might be like if we moved to the same city, hanging out on Shabbat."

"It is nice," I replied, picking up the weekend *Jerusalem Post.* I scanned the lead story on a deadly Israeli missile strike in Gaza, a strike that killed a notorious Hamas leader named Sheikh Salah Shahada as well as scores of civilians in a residential area. The article struck me both for its horror and for what it seemed to portend – there were reported calls from Hamas militants to launch revenge attacks. I showed it to Michael, who nodded. That summer had been a relatively quiet time, and the attack seemed brutal, ominous. It stuck out.

So we nodded – unaware of what was to come – then returned to reading, to the lives we wanted to live.

When Michael called, I picked up.

"David."

"Michael," I said, not knowing what else to say, struck by the guilt of being the lucky one – the secondary survivor.

"I need to do something, and I want you to come with me, if you can. I don't want to do it alone."

"Okay."

"Here it is: I need to go to Marla's apartment and begin gathering her belongings. I've been asked to send her things home by her parents."

"Okay."

"Will you come with me?"

"Of course," I replied. The request seemed natural, as though I had been waiting for it to be made this whole time, being the friend capable of understanding the rawness, the ridiculousness, the unspeakable reality of it all. And so, early in the morning on Jamie's third day in the ICU, I went with Michael to Marla's apartment.

When we reached the building, Michael placed a key in her door, jiggled it, and pushed open into the stillness we knew was coming. It was the moment I realized that Marla, who had been sitting opposite Jamie in the cafeteria, was really gone.

I watched Michael sort through Marla's effects. I watched him breathe in her clothes, then riffle through hundreds of *TV Guide* crossword puzzles stacked neatly in the corner of a bureau – perplexed and amused as to why she would have collected them. Scanning the apartment, I noticed black, dusty fingerprint marks caked on the sides of cups, countertops, and door handles. The FBI had needed fingerprints to identify the body, to make it official.

As Michael worked and I watched, the landlord walked in, an elderly woman, slightly hunched. She caught a glimpse of some purple flowers still resting in the window and said, "Look at these flowers. She was such an angel." The woman began rambling in Hebrew. She wouldn't shut up, this poor, elderly woman clutching at a corner of the grieving that belonged to Michael. She wanted to hold it, to own it too.

I looked directly at her and said, "*Maspeek*" – Enough. I asked her to leave, to give us time, to give Michael time. And then it was time for me to return to the hospital, to Jamie. When I approached her bed, it was late morning.

"Where were you?"

"I needed to do something."

"You didn't tell me you wouldn't be here."

"I did."

"I don't remember."

"I'm sorry. I told the nurses not to let anybody in to see you."

"Where were you?"

"Just had to help Michael with something."

"Can you not do anything else?"

"I won't."

And I didn't, staying by Jamie's side as she struggled through an excruciating recovery, being treated for second- and third-degree burns over 30 percent of her body. I stayed by Jamie's side when, after being moved from the ICU to a private room, the medical staff began torturing her. Twice a day the nurses would take Jamie into the shower, unwind her bandages, and scrub the burns to remove the layers of dead skin. Then, they doused those areas with an alcohol-based antiseptic solution to help prevent any infection from setting in. While the nurses scrubbed, I would stand guard outside Jamie's room and listen to her wail, waiting for the nod from a nurse that signaled it was over, that it was time to enter the room and comfort my wife. Each time, I would open the door to find Jamie on the bed, her body convulsing as an automatic response to the shock of prolonged pain. Leaning down, I'd place my hands upon her chest – as I had been taught by the lead nurse – and apply pressure to help Jamie breathe deeply, to help her calm down.

I never saw the burns. But I saw the effects of the burns. On the eve of her transfer to Hadassah Ein Kerem, the hospital that housed Israel's preeminent burn center, I saw her plead with the lead doctor, who had popped in for a visit with his thick Russian accent and his flushed cheeks. I saw her beg, "Please, please don't do this anymore. Do you have to? Please don't have to. It's enough."

He agreed and said, "Okay. We can stop." And they did.

The next morning, Jamie was placed on a stretcher and wheeled toward an ambulance waiting to transport her and several other patients to Hadassah Ein Kerem. She was nervous. It was a winding, forty-minute drive through the Judean Hills. A long ride. A bumpy ride. As we exited the hospital's front doors, Jamie gazed up at the open sky – a sky she had not seen since lying outside the Frank Sinatra Cafeteria thinking, *I'm lightly injured.* She left the hospital in exactly the same way as she had entered it, on a stretcher pulled from the hull of an ambulance. Workers flanked each side and pushed her into the vehicle, the collapsible legs automatically buckling and folding underneath. She reached for my hand as I said, "It will be fine."

Jamie looked at the driver smoking outside on a bench as I crawled in. "Tell him to drive slow," she said.

"I'm sure he'll drive slow," I replied, knowing he would not.

"Will you tell him if he doesn't?"

I nodded, grabbing a seat on one of the benches running along each side of the ambulance. A Palestinian woman and her daughter sat opposite me. The engine started. Jamie braced for movement.

"I need help."

"What?"

"I can't calm down."

The ambulance began rattling over the city's streets, the driver braking hard and honking through the traffic.

"*Efshar L'ha'ayt, b'vakashah*?" – Would it be possible to slow down, please? The driver glanced in the rearview mirror and nodded as I looked down at Jamie, her eyes clenched. Fishing through my backpack, I pulled out a portable CD player and popped in an acoustic mix of Neil Young recordings.

"Would this help?" I asked, holding up the player.

She shrugged as I fitted the speakers over her ears. "What is it?"

"Neil Young."

"Is it relaxing?"

"I think so – do you want something else?"

"No, it's okay. Just not too loud."

Her left eardrum had shattered in the blast. The internal damage was permanent, and she was particularly sensitive to noise despite the lost hearing. I turned the volume down and "A Heart of Gold" softly pulsed in Jamie's ears as she meditated on the music, on Young's gravelly voice, on the harmonica humming discordantly as the van descended into the hills, the words "I want to live" echoing within her.

After arriving at Ein Kerem and admitting Jamie to the burn unit, I tried to stay the night with her that first night. I tried to stay with my wife now afraid to be alone, afraid of the dark, of the monsters lurking. I tried. But it did not go well. For a week, while she recovered in the ICU at Hebrew University, I had held up miraculously, had been the hero, revealing unimaginable strength under the stress of everything. My emotionally deadened existence was my superpower. The swallowed anger, sadness, and grief – I had buried all of it. But that night, after the transfer, after the long, bumpy ambulance ride, I started cracking. I couldn't handle her wakefulness, her pain, her dependence. Sitting next to the bed, placing my head on arms draped over the metal rails, I dozed for minutes at a time, sighing heavily whenever something was needed – a pillow shift, a sheet positioning, a call to the nurse for more painkillers. "You want OxyContin? Oh, morphine? Yes, I can do it. I'm fine. I'm going."

When morning came, Jamie said, "I don't want you staying the night again." It was the first time I hadn't been able to cut it. The adrenaline was gone, and exhaustion had set in. Everyone noticed. Everyone saw the lines on my face, including one of the Anglo directors of the hospital, who worked some bureaucratic magic and gave me a room at the bunker across from the hospital – a makeshift town full of temporary housing for medical students. It was a collection of ill-conceived concrete squares built along a winding, dirt road that hugged a severe precipice from which one could look out for miles. It was a place to take naps, to recharge during those afternoons when I couldn't remain standing, when I needed to shut down.

My room was a cricket-infested, eight-by-eight square of peeling linoleum with a bed in the middle and a rusty sink near the door.

It was perfect.

In the evening, I would relinquish my watch to one of many friends and acquaintances who came to spend the night with Jamie during her month-long recovery at the burn center. Back at our apartment, I would often lie awake, unable to sleep, waiting for visiting hours to begin again. But at the bunker, I slept. At the bunker, I walked in, set an alarm, fell upon the moldy mattress, and slept as a soldier should.

After a week of this – sharing bathrooms with Hebrew-speaking medical students, cat-napping in the bunker after a shift spent supervising Jamie's care – I began imagining myself as a resident, a medical professional. I was on call. It was a game played coyly, the hospital becoming an academic hoop through which I had to jump. *You're a damn good intern*, I thought, learning the medical lingo in Hebrew and grilling the nurses about dressings, doses, side effects, and alternative courses of treatment. I shadowed doctors, stamping out their discarded cigarettes, and read their charts. I fell asleep against walls in between drug-runs. Fraternized with technicians taking blood. Twirled my bunker key while scanning the halls, watching the movement, becoming a part of the movement, a part of the machine responsible for aiding those unable to move freely.

My patient was making progress. Jamie was starting, a week after the attack, to leave the bed for brief stretches, sitting propped up in a high-backed chair, her blood slowly circulating. And then she began walking, leaning on my arm for a minute on the way to the water fountain here, two minutes on a walk down the hall there. Re-configuring her muscles, the skin around her muscles. When she slept, I'd stroll to the Chagall windows in the medical campus's synagogue, allowing the tinted light streaming through each of Jacob's twelve sons to rest on my face – the yellow of Joseph, the blue of Dan, the red of Judah. I walked the grounds and considered the buildings carved into the hills, with wildflowers and rocks clinging to the slopes. And I thought, *This is a beautiful place*; thought, *This is a good place*; thought, *You're lucky to be working here.*

Soon after arriving at Ein Kerem, a nurse walked in and said to Jamie, "We're placing you on a high-calorie diet – you're going to need three thousand a day." She nodded silently as I looked to her, curious how the words "high-calorie diet" could be reconciled with the fact that Jamie's small intestine had recently been spliced and re-attached to itself. But then I learned the menu: cans of a nutritional drink called Ensure, a sludgy, milkshake-like concoction packed with potent levels of nutrients, calories, and protein.

The nurse, after imparting the news, beckoned me with a curled index finger and walked away. I followed her to a miniature fridge that resembled the one I rented as a freshman in college. Only, instead of finding a few beers and peanut butter within, row after row of Ensure stared back. Like a secret drug cache. Chocolate. Vanilla. Strawberry. Medical grade. Take your pick.

I was instructed to coax Jamie into pounding a case daily, to turn her into a nutritional-drink lush, a binge drinker. Her body was working furiously, was under construction, replacing skin layer by layer, and she required large amounts of raw material.

Six a day, that was our goal – approximately five hundred calories and twenty grams of protein a piece. Things started out benign enough, with me wearing out a familiar path to the fridge, retrieving cans, and gently coaxing Jamie to chug. "Come on, finish it already." But after a dare – "taste it yourself, jerk" – I began to lean on them, first as an occasional snack, then for breakfast, and finally for my entire diet. I double-dipped when nobody was looking, grabbing a chocolate for myself and a strawberry for the patient. I started gaining back the weight I'd lost since "the accident," and guarded the fridge jealously, worrying whenever the stash began to thin. I wondered if I should stop as patients everywhere sat up stiffly, drinking at all hours.

At times I imagined being Mick, Rocky's hardened trainer, holding a can to Jamie's lips and saying things like "Just one more sip" and "There you go, champ," while Jamie breathed heavily. This is how we spent much of each day, with me serving up a non-stop regimen of geriatric shakes and her loving me unconditionally, feeling grateful. "If you put that to my lips one more time, I swear I'm going to puke all over you."

So I'd finish the can. And then I finished my own, calorie highs that became an obsession, or at least a distraction, one in a series that occupied my existence as I searched for things to digest, to keep the blood flowing to my stomach and away from my brain. *Don't think, act.* It's how I survived. These addictions saved me.

There were others.

For example, the flower watering. At our apartment each morning, before heading to the hospital, I watered the flowers on our back porch, each species requiring a delicate balance of liquid and fertilizer for survival. I had never cared for them before with any diligence, never approached the task with any sense of duty. But now, I worked tirelessly to avoid wilting petals or browning leaves. I pruned. Groomed. Watered with measuring cups. Monitored the soil. Talked to them. "What's this we have here, hmm? Do you need me to remove that yellow leaf? Do you? Let me get it. There you go."

Fifteen minutes a morning, minimum, I coddled them. Trying to keep them alive. They had to live. I wouldn't let them die, so fragile, so needy, many of them out of their element – chrysanthemums and impatiens – not meant for this place, this desert full of dust and heat. Each morning, before leaving to visit Jamie, I'd think, *Thrive.* Thinking I meant the flowers. Thinking I was actually worried about the flowers, about a few opening blossoms, which were actually quite ugly, in my opinion.

But I had to save something.

One morning, while walking toward the hospital, I encountered a Palestinian man lying on the sidewalk, face up. He was clearly in distress, and had either passed out or succumbed to something greater than he could bear. His eyes were closed, his breathing slow. A small crowd of Israelis had gathered around him, encircling the fallen at a comfortable distance. I stopped. Looked at him. Then looked at the towering hospital structure one hundred yards away. Curiously, nobody moved to help – we just watched, mute, as if stumbling upon a wild animal in the wilderness.

I scanned the body, looking for wires, for something bulging from underneath the shirt, for a sign of danger. I was not alone in this. Fear had paralyzed us, a group of onlookers afraid to recognize this poor man's humanity as we clutched at our own.

Moments before, I had been caring for flowers with unnecessary diligence. But standing there, I felt nothing. At some point, just as I was preparing to leave without doing a thing, inexplicably thinking, *Tough shit, you fuck*, medics from the hospital arrived, squatted next to the body, and prodded cautiously as the silent audience backed away.

I turned and continued on toward the hospital, refusing to watch the care being given, to see the scene become intimate, personal, just as I had refused to face the reality of what had occurred at the cafeteria. An attack had taken place, this I knew. But in my mind it remained passive and impersonal, as though the bombing had materialized on its own, was simply the inevitable consequence of living in Israel. It was just the result of some larger political struggle, mechanical, faceless. It was safer that way. Nobody tried to kill her. It just happened.

It just happened – this is what I clung to, a month into Jamie's recovery, when news spread that a Hamas cell had been captured by Israeli police. It was a cell responsible for multiple attacks across Israel, responsible for bombing cafes, petrol stations, pool halls, and a university cafeteria. The front pages of Israeli newspapers projected four faces, Mohammad's among them, of the men who choreographed their bloody shows of resistance. I looked away. Friends brought me copies, pointed to the pictures, and said, "At least they caught them. At least there will be justice." I looked away, frightened to recognize in the faces of those who wanted us dead an image of myself, of humanity hopelessly flawed. *In the image of God He created them.*

8

Three years. For three years I woke in Jerusalem, inhaling sand and the scent of baking *barrekas*, and walked to the industrial section of Talpiot. I would pass flocks of Israeli children skipping to school, Chasidim rushing to minyan, and Palestinian workers grouped on street corners, waiting for rides to various job sites. My destination was Pardes, where I regularly prayed the morning service at sunrise with a small group of egalitarian Jews forcing gender-equality into the traditional script, the act revolutionary, evolutionary. The routine was steady, and the praying for me was more an exercise in discipline than the fulfillment of any spiritual need. I could just as easily have been running or working out with free weights. It was practice, a daily rhythm. Though admittedly there were moments when I would breathe deeply, close my eyes, and try speaking with the Divine, pretending She existed.

There is a section in the Hebrew weekday prayers, recited three times daily, called the *Amidah* – literally the Standing – in which the community rises and silently cycles through nineteen prayers that move from praising God to humble requests. Among these requests is a catch-all entreaty:

> *Hear our voice, Lord our God – have compassion and take pity on us, and compassionately and favorably accept our*

> *prayer, because You are a God who hears our prayers and supplications. From before you, our King, please don't turn us away empty, because you compassionately hear the prayer of your people Israel. Blessed are You, Lord, who hears prayer.*

Most mornings, upon reaching *You are a God who hears our prayers and supplications*, I would insert a personal appeal, asking God to protect Jamie from harm, from the dangers of this place. During the hour-long session, it was perhaps the only moment each morning I consistently dropped my cynicism and blathered from the heart, hoping that Something on the other end was cupping a palm and receiving the words. Hoping there was a receptacle.

I come from a long line of God-haters. My maternal grandparents were Holocaust survivors, the grandfather I never met having lost his first wife and family to the ovens while himself escaping, then finding a new wife, my grandmother, who had also escaped. Together they fled Europe to Jacksonville, Florida, where the Holocaust and the camps were never mentioned around my mother. The one exception being at the Passover Seder, when my grandfather, full of wine, would sometimes begin to talk.

My mother hates God, has always been existentially angry, her parents dead long before their time, the stress of life having stolen decades from them. Her uncles, aunts, and cousins all murdered a lifetime ago. She's never exactly said, "I hate God," and the word "hate" may be too harsh, but the silent anger she's carried all these years is unmistakable. It's an anger I'd always understood and sympathized with, but hadn't necessarily felt.

Growing up – forced to attend Hebrew school by parents who didn't seem enthusiastic to embrace the religious observances being taught by ruler-wielding Israelis in suburban Atlanta – I had to blame someone for the hours of boredom and dogma. God seemed appropriate enough. And so after my bar-mitzvah, I walked out of Congregation Etz Chaim on Roswell Road and washed my hands of the Divine. I had escaped, and turned to roaming the city's basketball courts during my free afternoons. Hardwood floors and vaulted ceilings became my sacred spaces where, for hours a day, I would practice jump shots and crossover dribbles, honing physical skills that filled the void. I was focused on making Pope High School's basketball team, focused on joining a new congregation full of kids who spat, swore, and slapped each other on the ass. Standing five-foot-three, full of hustle and grit, I made the team, and traded the pew for the bench.

It wasn't until college, as I suffered through journalism school and mild depression at the University of Georgia, that I realized my subconscious desire for a spiritual existence. It happened by chance one Friday afternoon while heading home on a campus bus, thinking about how to pass the lonely weekend, when a bearded, dreadlocked fellow I vaguely recognized sat down in a nearby seat. Spotting me, he leaned over, grinned, and asked, "Dave, right?"

"Yep. I'm sorry," I said, tentatively extending a hand, "Remind me your – "

"Bartholomaus."

"Cool."

"What are you doing this weekend?" he asked.

There must have been a desperation in my eyes at the prospect of answering, for he said without a word, "We're going hiking in North Carolina. You should come."

After listening to my protestations of not wanting to impose on a group of people I did not know, he insisted, and two days later, I found myself sitting on an outcropping on the summit of Standing Indian in the heart of the Blue Ridge Mountains. A group of intellectual hippies flanked me on adjacent rocks as I watched a thick morning fog move through us, obscuring our vision and creating the illusion of flight. For an hour, we stared blindly into a fog that slowly dissipated, revealing in stages the most spectacular view, a view that, moments before, had been an aspiration. The silhouettes of distant mountains appeared, gently sloping statesmen standing in the early light, followed by muted reds and greens that played hide-and-seek as the haze broke. Then, as if the god of mountain vistas had decided to whisk away what remained, a southern autumn appeared, full of rustic red and earthy orange bouquets shimmering in the slanting light.

It was a spark, perhaps the first, and it kindled a desire in me to be consumed by the power of wilderness.

For the next three years, trekking through the mountains became a steady weekend routine, and my poetic sense, my Wordsworthian consciousness, was awakened by eastern bluebirds and mountain streams. Enfolded by the embrace of Appalachia, I sensed there was more, wanted more, a longing which propelled me to seek a semester abroad in Israel.

Only a few months after landing in Israel, I found myself praying in limestone caves with Hasidic masters, touching the stone walls of Tzfat's narrow alleys, and thinking, *God is in this place.* I dove in head first and was taken by the undertow of irrational faith, giddy as Hebrew filled my lungs. But I also recognized how fast it was happening – this awakening – and the speed scared me, made me skeptical, a skepticism that over time led to the development of an off-and-on-again relationship with the Divine. I'd get close, fall in love, and then reflexively push God away, always believing just enough to be both hopeful and bitter, seeing images of Palestinian children being beaten at checkpoints or reading of terror attacks in Tel Aviv and thinking, *What the fuck, Dude?*

It continued like this for years – the breaking up, the getting back together. But after the prayers I mouthed daily in Jerusalem – *Please protect Jamie from harm* – and God's answer when the bomb went off – *Nope* – I quietly began to hate God as a lover might a former flame. As my emotions ran dry, as I became numb in the hospital, seeing Jamie shaking, I grabbed my stuff from God's apartment and walked out. Slammed the door. Wanted nothing more to do with Her.

9

When it became clear that some of Jamie's third-degree burns were not regenerating, and never would, large squares of skin were sliced from her left thigh and stapled to her hands, legs, and back – the body forced to take one for the team. *The Lord giveth. The Lord taketh away.*[1] After the procedure, when the anesthesia had worn off, she lifted up the layers of gauze to show me the flayed areas – perfectly measured patches of crimson – as though her thighs had been stenciled with an airbrush and set to dry.

But she wouldn't show me the hands, the staples. Nor had she shown me, at any point, the burns blistering under bandages that covered thirty percent of her body. She refused to let me see her exposed. "It's disgusting," she'd say. "I look like a monster," she'd say. "You don't want to see," she'd say. I never asked to see underneath the bandages after she'd said, "You don't want to see." I believed her.

But curiously, she had chosen to lift up some gauze to show me her flayed skin, the patches on her thighs that had been peeled away, perhaps overtaken by the bizarre symmetry, the cannibalistic holism of the procedure. It would be one of only two parts of her injured body Jamie would share during her recovery, the other being the hole that had been created just below her left hip by the nut that entered in the flash of the blast, traveled up her side and into her small intestine. The nut I still have.

In the autumn and early winter, after being released from the hospital, Jamie received ongoing care at home. During those months, we watched the hole slowly close.

This is how it worked: a nurse would clean out the smooth, concave opening, then gently stuff it with gauze – ostensibly to absorb miscreant fluids and give the skin something against which to heal. Each day, the nurse arrived with her bag of supplies. She unwound the bandages, smoothed ointment over the burns, and rewound new ones over the still-healing skin. In the beginning, the hole was easily a half-inch in diameter and an inch deep, and during this phase the nurse would simply remove the used gauze and insert clean strips with her pinched, gloved fingers. But as the hole began to shut around the soft, foreign inserts, it became necessary to use tweezers, each morning's event becoming the childhood game of Operation, trying not to touch metal to the opening's edge, trying not to – *buzz.*

And then, the hole was gone. And so was the nurse. And we were alone, forced suddenly to figure out what to do with the rest of our lives.

A week before the bombing, Jamie and I had decided to start trying for a family, understanding that life was tenuous, thinking, *Better start now. You never know.* It was a decision preceded by months of debate, a decision I had been lobbying for against great resistance as Jamie tried to make sure I understood the stakes:

"David, it's not going to be like a pet."

"I know."

"It's going to be full-time. Non-stop. It won't be a toy."

"I know."

"They don't come with off buttons."

"I know."

She had reason to resist. While in Israel, I had become obsessive about learning both spoken Hebrew and Talmudic Aramaic – spending nearly every waking moment in pursuit of proficiency in each – and Jamie had a hard time envisioning me being able to slow down, to ease off the accelerator and care for a child. There was plenty of evidence to back up such suspicions. Once, during our first year in Israel, I came home and made a pronouncement:

"I think we should stop speaking in English."

"What?"

"I really want to learn to speak Hebrew, and with all the Americans we're around, it's virtually impossible."

"But our vocabulary isn't good enough to just speak in Hebrew."

"It would get better."

"By just speaking in Hebrew?"

"Yeah."

"I don't think so. I kind of like having a relationship."

"It would be fun."

"Speaking to each other like toddlers? Look, I'm tired at the end of the day. I don't want to struggle through Hebrew with you when I just want to relax and spend time together."

"Okay. But what if I chose to speak just in Hebrew? You could use English if you want."

"You can't do it."

"I can try."

"Fine. Whatever."

Later that evening, while I was washing our blue, plastic dishes after a dinner of grilled cheese with tomato and avocado, Jamie asked from the living room where she might be able to buy some gloves.

I didn't answer.

"David?"

No answer.

"David, can you hear me?"

I turned around and nodded, shutting off the water.

"Why won't you answer me?"

I paused, considering my options. "I don't know how to answer in Hebrew."

"Are you kidding me?"

I shrugged.

"You chose not to answer me because you didn't know the right Hebrew words rather than answering me in English? Please tell me that's not what you did."

"I guess maybe I shouldn't do that when I can't find the words, huh?"

"You guess?"

"Yeah, I'm sorry."

"Maybe you need an Israeli girlfriend. You could speak all you want."

"Hey, that's a great idea."

"Ha-ha. Very funny."

The episode was emblematic of a determined focus on my part, which, the summer of the bombing, had peaked. As a non-citizen barely able to hold a conversation with Israelis, despite having graduated from *ulpan*, a Hebrew language training course of study, I searched for ways to be immersed in the language. I set up a chess board at cafés with a sign that read *Rotzeh L'sachek*? – Want to play? I schmoozed with supermarket clerks. I talked with children clinging to their mothers in line at the bank. Finally, I found the opportunity for sustained Hebrew immersion by volunteering for the municipality, and was placed in Jerusalem's summer camps division. When I first showed up at the run-down building in the heart of the city, there was mild confusion.

Rega, lama rotzeh la'avod cahn?	Wait, why do you want to work here?
Lilmod Eevreet.	To learn Hebrew.
Eevreet? Americaye, nachon?	Hebrew? You're American, right?
Cain.	Yes.
Ma iym ulpan?	What about *ulpan*?
K'var avarty.	I already graduated.
Lo m'shalmim,	Nobody's going to pay you, you know.
Ani yodeah.	I know.
Muzar.	Weird.
Ma?	What?
Ashir?	Are you rich?
Lo.	No.
Lama b'aretz.	Why are you in Israel?
Lomed b'universita v'yeshiva.	I'm studying at university and a yeshiva.
Dati?	Are you religious?
Lo bidiyuk.	Not exactly.
Ma'anyen. Okay – baruch habah.	Interesting. Okay, well – welcome.

During the days, I filed paperwork, answered phones, and ran errands for an army of women trying to run the city's slate of summer camps out of a disheveled, musty office across from city hall, rambling to me in Hebrew with reckless abandon, pointing and smoking and cursing.

That summer the World Cup was held in South Korea, and during lunch breaks I would descend to the local coffee shop and join those who were continuously gathered around the big screen, pumping their fists and shouting, despite Israel's absence from the pitch. The United States was doing unusually well, having upset Portugal, and Israelis, hearing my accent, would pound me on the back and ask for my opinion on Claudio Reyna, the U.S.A.'s stoic mid-fielder, or launch into an analysis of America's strategy. And so during the days, I learned how to talk about corner kicks and summer camp scholarships. At night, after returning home, I posted myself before the computer and learned Talmud online, reading pages of Aramaic while listening to MP3s of a rabbi explaining the myriad legal mazes. I felt compelled to keep up with the *Daf Yomi* schedule, the daily page of Talmud learned by Jews around the world.

It was an existence consumed by language, a self-directed schedule of linguistic immersion in the present and the past. And it was within this existence that Jamie and I decided to begin building our future together. "I think we should start trying," I said one night in July.

"I do too," she answered, surprising me.

And then, a week later, the bomb went off.

Months later, Jamie's medical care ended – the hole closed, and the nurse left our apartment saying, "You're done." We said goodbye, closed the door, looked upon each other and tried to resume our lives, tried to pick up where we had left off, Jamie seeking out a doctor and asking, "Is it safe to get pregnant?" The concern was her internal injuries, whether or not pregnancy was a risk given the surgery on her small intestine. The doctor, an Israeli, a woman who understood the fragility of opportunity, and seeing nothing physically holding Jamie back, encouraged her, said, "You should do it."

Jamie came home and reported, "It's okay."

"Really?"

"Yes."

"What should we do?"

Jamie looked at me and said, "What we can."

Here's what we couldn't do: remain in Israel. Jamie's sense of vulnerability, after Jerusalem had failed her, was too much to bear. Quick trips in the neighborhood were bringing moments of panic. While strolling on the sidewalk, Jamie would angle away from an approaching bus, anticipating the sudden shattering of glass. In the local grocery, she'd scan the produce section's floor while picking through the broccoli, looking for abandoned bags ready to go off. Things were no longer sustainable. She had to leave. And though we needed to flee the Middle East – unable to find sanctuary amidst the bombs and artillery shells – we found shelter in each other again, reclaiming not only an intimacy that the bombing had stolen, but an intentionality that had existed as well. The first moment Jamie was physically ready, despite the anxiety geography was inducing, we began trying again for a child. We wondered if the months of pain-killers had been washed away, her body cleansed, wanting to take advantage of the blood pumping hot and fast, wanting a child before one of us – forgetting to duck – disappeared suddenly. Still reeling, dizzy, disoriented, we wanted wholeness, normalcy. We wanted stability. We were desperate to reclaim the lives that had been lost forever.

In December, Mohammad Odeh's trial was held in Jerusalem – a high-profile affair pasted on the front pages of newspapers and analyzed on newscasts. Murder charges were brought against him and the three other members of the Hamas cell responsible for numerous attacks across Israel. Some of our friends attended the trial and stared him down as he entered the courtroom among the bereaved, among those flailing, trying to pry past courtroom security, fists clenched, wanting to feel the crack of bone on bone, shouting, "Murderers, bloodsuckers, you should all be executed;" shouting, "My girl. You murdered her in cold blood two months before her wedding;" shouting, "I can only visit my son in the grave."

But we didn't go. We didn't want to go.

"Jamie, do you want to go to the trial?"

"What trial?"

"The trial of the guy who they caught – "

"Absolutely not."

"Okay."

"Do you?"

"No."

"Then why'd you ask?"

"I don't know. Thought maybe you'd want to."

"I don't want to."

"Okay."

"But you can go," she said, raising an eyebrow.

"I can't imagine wanting to go."

"Then we're not going."

"Okay."

It was the last thing I could envision doing, for the seed of desire to meet Odeh had not yet been planted. It lay dormant. I felt nothing. The possibility of a trial provoked nothing. There was no anger, no rage, merely paralysis – a desire for things to remain distant and faceless. *It just happened.*

So did this: one afternoon, walking back from the supermarket, Jamie stopped, pulled on my arm, and said, "I think that's the guy."

"What guy?" I asked, seizing up.

"The guy who helped me. The one wearing a UCLA shirt."

I looked and saw a twenty-something man walking toward us, the one who Jamie told me had grabbed her as she ran from the cafeteria screaming.

"I think I should say something to him."

"Okay."

"Think he'll remember?"

"Yeah, I think he'll remember, Jamie."

She walked up to him and said, "Hi."

"Um, hey," he said, not recognizing her, Jamie's face smooth, polished, beautiful.

"Oh, sorry. I'm Jamie. You helped me at Hebrew University." His face darkened as Jamie introduced me, gave him our number, and invited him over to our place. I could tell he didn't want to come, that he was scared, but a week later he showed up anyway, showed up timid, quiet, forced to relive the moment when he had grabbed Jamie and held her. He showed up to help us again by reliving that moment so I could understand what he had seen, how he had helped her. And I remember the awkwardness. The talk of getting together again as though the experience, him soothing Jamie as she screamed from the shock and the horror and the pain, might create a natural bond, a friendship, when in reality, neither he nor we wanted to see each other again.

We never did. When he left, we said goodbye, said we'd get in touch – Jamie and I already preparing to leave, preparing to say goodbye to everything here. Nothing was the same. Nothing could be the same. We didn't want to see him again.

When we returned to Pardes, a sculpture hung before the doorway, shards of broken glass protruding from layers of black paint. It was an artistic expression of torment crafted by a friend, the piece rotating idly, spinning on a string. Fragments of glass cut through the air. We looked at it and then looked through the familiar glass door now coated with a bulletproof laminate. I did not want to enter. It was over. We were the survivors, the ones still alive, but our previous lives had ended, and it was uncertain how they could begin again. In the *Beit Midrash*, we stared through texts, the Hebrew script moving right-to-left as our eyes moved from the foreground to the background, blurring and widening, absorbed by the periphery. I glanced to where Ben and Marla's empty chairs stood, unable to concentrate. With a voluminous *Masechet Sanhedrin* open before me, I learned about the laws of lost property, thinking about loss, about losing, about all that had been stolen.

After weeks of staring through books – through the miniature screens of our eyelids upon which the past was continuously projected – we packed our bags and left.

At Ben Gurion Airport, waiting in line to check in, our passports at the ready, Jamie was stopped by a young female security agent and interrogated.

"Where are you flying?"

"Home."

"And where is home?"

"America."

She plucked the passport from Jamie's hand and began flipping pages before asking, "And what was the purpose of your visit?"

"To study at Hebrew University."

"And what did you study?"

"Jewish education."

She raised an eyebrow and looked at Jamie. "What month is it?"

"December."

"What is the Hebrew month?"

Jamie furrowed her brow and glanced at me. "It's *Kislev*, right?"

I shrugged.

"*Kislev?*"

The security agent shook her head. *No.* Holding the passport, she stopped abruptly and fixated on Jamie's gloved hand. Jamie was wearing pressure garments on certain areas of her body, tightly fitting nylon which pressed the skin flat to prevent hypertrophic scars – raised, nodular formations that restricted movement and flexibility. I wanted to step in and explain to the security agent that the scar tissue was still forming, that the glove was applying pressure to the epidermal layer, forcing the scars to form smooth and flat. I wanted to explain that Jamie had to wear them at all hours for a year. That it wasn't our choice. That she should just let us go, please, let us go and check in and leave.

"I was injured in a terrorist attack," Jamie said, watching the agent.

"Which one?"

"Hebrew University."

"*Ayzoh mizkeinah*," she said, pulling up the rope, letting us through, victimhood giving us license to leave, justification to want to leave. It was enough.

As we walked to the gate, Jamie turned around. "What did she say?"

"*Ayzoh mizkeinah*. It means poor thing."

"I know what it means. I just didn't hear her."

"Oh."

"I don't like people looking at my hand."

"I know."

"I'm not sure I can come back."

I nodded, looking at the *Channukiot* left over from Hanukah in the window at Duty Free, the lights gone.

"Want some Scotch?" I asked.

She grabbed my hand. We walked onto the plane, silent, feeling abandoned, feeling as though we were abandoning a life we once loved, a life taken away. *The terrorists won*, I thought. *They fucking won.*

Part III

Recovery

10

After Jamie's physical recovery, we left Israel and settled in Washington, D.C. – a new city, a new place in which to start over, to begin this new beginning we'd been granted by chance.

We grabbed a one-bedroom apartment in the neighborhood of Mount Pleasant, where Salvadorian fruit sellers and Mexican CD pushers mixed with not-for-profit ideologues and lawyers at the Justice Department, where the smells of fish and coffee and smoking tortillas mingled with turbulent currents of hip-hop and reggaeton.

We'd chosen to live in the city despite landing teaching jobs at a Jewish high school in suburban Rockville, Maryland. We'd chosen the corner bakery, the walk-in hardware store, and the neighborhood bank over manicured lawns and strip malls disguised as small towns. We'd chosen bustle and distraction over sterility and calm. And despite fleeing Israel with our first child growing in Jamie's belly – this new life only months away from choking out her first breath – we'd chosen risk along with the rewards. Two months after settling in to our urban apartment, the pop-pop of gunfire echoed one night in the dark, followed by an ambulance siren's wail. Looking out from our fifth-floor window, we watched the police and television crews gather on Park Avenue at the corner of Mount Pleasant Street. And then the ambulance, lights turned off, left our building's front stoop with its cargo, rolling away slowly, silently.

Jamie looked over. "Does that mean someone just died?"

"I think so."

We looked at each other, neither of us capable of speaking, understanding nothing more could be said without saying everything, without asking whether we had made the right decision, without asking whether we could handle the slightest hint of danger given the things we'd fled to arrive at this place. Our new home.

"We should go to bed. I need to go to bed," she said.

"I know."

She took the first shift in our one-bedroom apartment's sole bathroom. As she got ready, I absently launched an online chess game, seeking to bury my head in an abstract haze of strategic calculations and precise movements. While the screen told me that my opponent was an intermediate player from Ireland, I knew better – knew that the adversary I was about to face resided in my mind. I shut my eyes and tried to channel Bobby Fischer, who before the greatest match of his life, said, "I don't believe in psychology. I believe in good moves." I nodded. *You don't believe in psychology. You believe in distractions*, I thought before escaping into the pixelated board where light and dark pieces were pitted opposite each other. I played black – on the defensive from the start – as my opponent probed for vulnerabilities easy to find. I touched the mouse to various pieces, illuminating squares where movement was possible, revealing a pawn blocked, a bishop on the move. I found solace in the knight, in jumping over everything.

"Come to bed," Jamie said, fatigued and flossing her teeth. She had come out of the bathroom and was standing over my shoulder. "Just close it."

"But I'll lose."

She looked at me sadly and tilted her said as if to say, *Please don't be a fool*, before trailing off into the bedroom. I shut down the computer and angled toward the window for one last look into the dark. The television vans with their retractable antennas had left. The gaggle of police cars honking and flashing had left. In their place was something new – a police trailer, long and white with blue lights ignited on its roof, still, unmoving. It was an anti-gang unit.

For the next week, that trailer idled on our block at all hours, the officers always inside, unseen, watching.

Work had brought us to the capital. We'd both been hired by the Charles E. Smith Jewish Day School (JDS), the city's eminent non-denominational Jewish high school, after an unconventional joint interview. Expecting separate chit-chats, we were surprised when the principal and administrators shepherded us into the conference room together, motioned for us to sit around a circular oak table, and commenced with the interview as though we were a tag team. When a question was lobbed before us – "How would you describe your teaching philosophy?" – it was nearly impossible to discern whether it had been directed at anyone in particular or simply thrown up for grabs. Each time I felt the desire to tag Jamie's hand and exit the ring.

Whether they knew Jamie had been in the Hebrew University bombing was unclear, and we hoped somehow they did not. We had braced ourselves for it to sneak in offhandedly during a traditional interview, but in this chaotic, debate-style approach, I could feel it lurking in the opposing team's playbook, ready for it to be hurled at us while Jamie delivered brutal clotheslines and I took a series of elbows to the face. When the interview was over, Jamie had clearly won on points – they smiled every time she opened her mouth.

Fortunately, I was offered a teaching position as well, most likely to sweeten the deal, my offer little more than her signing bonus.

But Jamie decided to decline JDS's offer, choosing instead to stay at home for the year, waiting for our infant to arrive, waiting to be a mother, to be the caregiver, finally. And so I found myself navigating D.C.'s public transportation system alone on the first day of school.

Standing at the corner of Park and Mount Pleasant, surrounded by historic row houses and bundled against a crisp, early autumn morning, I waited for the H4 bus to Cleveland Park, where I could catch the Metro to Rockville. It was before dawn. Around me were construction workers, mothers holding infants and high school kids wearing baggy pants, bobbing to their MP3 players. Scanning the group, noticing the dented lunch boxes, the aluminum Thermoses and stylized backpacks, a surprising thought bubbled to the surface: *I'm not looking for a bomb.* As the H4 approached, I stumbled forward to the door, shoved by the realization that it had been years since I'd boarded a bus without wondering if my flesh would be torn open by a spray of metal. And as we vibrated downhill, crossing through Rock Creek National Park, I looked around me – at the mothers holding their children and the students awkwardly flirting – and was overcome by amazement, thinking, *These people aren't afraid of dying. They aren't suspicious.* For a moment, I remembered what normal life, life removed from a war zone, felt like.

At Cleveland Park, I followed the crowd to the Metro station and caught the Red Line north to Rockville. As we rocketed underground, I realized I had misjudged the commute. I was late. When the train finally reached the suburbs, I hustled to JDS, splitting hedges and hopping guard rails to make up time. When the school finally came into sight, my first class was due to start in only fifteen minutes, and I had to make a choice: cut down a steep hill behind the school, or take the long, winding sidewalk around the sprawling campus to the main entrance: thirty seconds versus three minutes.

I took the hill, failing to notice the smooth, slick sheets of moss, wet from the morning, blanketing the slope. I tried to compensate by alternating my steps, digging my heels in as though I were ice climbing, feeling my soles slide and then, suddenly, lose contact with the ground. I stabbed my hands backwards and slid down the hill as though wheels were attached to my palms and feet. When I reached the bottom and stood up, amazed that I had somehow managed to keep the seat of my slacks from hitting the mud, I saw the blood spurting from my right palm.

Cutting through a back door to the school, I found a restroom and grabbed a handful of paper towels, then slid into class as the bell sounded. Everyone looked up. I wrote a name on the board and introduced myself to my first class – an eleventh-grade survey on biblical texts – while squeezing paper towels above my head to staunch the bleeding.

"What happened?" a giggling, Abercrombie-clad girl asked.

"Yeah, you okay?" asked a few others.

"I'm fine. Just a first-day wound."

"How'd it happen?"

"Oh, just some newfangled hazing ritual rookie teachers must undergo. I'm fortunate Rabbi Sandler called off the pit bull so quickly. You should see the English teachers."

The teenagers, many of them Ivy-League bound, gazed back at me, eyebrows cocked. They were not impressed.

Despite the inauspicious start, I was complimented early in the year by the school's administrators for my innovative and effective teaching. I was making things look easy. Take, for example, my toughest assignment: seventh-grade Bible studies. The curriculum entailed a thematic run through the Torah, from God breathing life into Adam's nostrils in Genesis to Moses' death upon Mount Nebo in Deuteronomy. Now, most middle-school students are so flummoxed by hormones that they can devolve, without warning, into banana-throwing chimpanzees during even the most engaging of classes. My little chimpanzees were an entirely different sub-species, coming from some of the most prominent Jewish families in the nation's capital – families who produced exceedingly intelligent and witty children. Among my students were the children of prominent journalists, high-ranking politicians, and ambassadors. These students were capable not only of throwing objects with their hands but with their minds as well. Particularly when they were bored.

My solution was to transform the class into a simulated FBI operation, grouping students by fours and fives into field offices – Philadelphia, Chicago, Los Angeles, Boston – with me as the chief stationed in Washington. The text was our playground, and when the monotony of learning became too much to bear, or when the curriculum demanded that I put them through the rigor of learning an interpretive skill, I'd reach into a drawer, don a police cap and pronounce, *Get into your FBI agencies* as a bunch of twelve-year-olds scurried to their 'field office.' Then, sitting quietly, ready for their instructions, they'd eye me intently, ready for the textual mystery that needed to be solved.

Things were going well on the surface, a surface that appeared to most everyone as smooth and placid. But that's the problem with still bodies of water – you can glance down and, suddenly, see your reflection.

Deep within, things were off. It began with suffocation. During one of my first classes, while my eleventh-graders were busy generating philosophical questions about the Garden of Eden, an internal drawstring was suddenly pulled, and in a beat my lungs constricted. Hands on my chest, I tried to catch myself and started gasping, unable to take in much more than a shallow breath.

Silently standing and retreating to a bathroom, I locked the door and gripped the sink, light-headed, leaning into the mirror. In subsequent months, this would become the norm, suffocating while checking my email or walking to class, unable to expand my lungs, unable to breathe deeply enough to feel sustained, to feel safe. Then one evening, while I was at home grading papers, it happened. I heard Jamie say, "You're not okay."

"I'm fine," I responded, mouth open, trying to force the air in, frustrated and amazed by my inability to perform such a routine, automatic function – to take a breath.

"You don't look it."

"I just can't breathe, is all."

"Is all?"

"Yeah, is all." I tried forcing a yawn, opening wide and attempting an intake into the back of my throat. After five seconds frozen in that position, a yawn came, and the sensation of oxygen enriching cells tingled my chest. I was ecstatic.

"Just had to yawn. See?"

"Mm-hmm."

Jamie had been in therapy for over a year, and had made significant steps toward mitigating much of the raw anxiety that she felt after the trauma. This success compelled her to drop subtle hints about my own refusal to seek help – "You're an idiot, just go." But I refused, believing that I was fine, thinking, *I just can't breathe, is all.* And anyway, I was adjusting to a new city, navigating a new job, and expecting our first child. Symptoms of stress didn't seem worrisome. These were just jitters. Nothing that wouldn't dissipate over time.

Such rationalizations were quickly flooded by reality when Jamie started contractions just as Tropical Storm Isabel was forming off the coast. We drove to the hospital, through Isabel's outer bands of rain and wind, on September 17, a six-foot storm surge building up in the Atlantic and making its way to Chesapeake Bay. It took nearly twenty-four hours for the waves to course through the varicose waterways leading into Washington, and as the waters began to pour into the Potomac River,[1] its banks beginning to crest, Jamie began pushing. I held on to her leg as something emerged. The midwife leaned in and pressed a blue bulb syringe into an indistinguishable mass that immediately popped out in response. It was as though a crumpled, rubber mask had been flipped inside out and formed into a face. "That's my daughter," I whispered at the moment of recognition, the moment they placed her on Jamie's chest, the infant's mouth instinctively suckling as Jamie's milk flowed and the rain pounded outside. The world had shifted irreversibly; I was a father. A permanent caregiver. And while love came at first sight, so too did its consequences. Jamie was right. I was not okay.

The stress of parenting quickly became intolerable. Caretaking, caring for another – another who needed me for survival, for comfort, for sleep – I couldn't do it, at least not well, having already done more than I could bear in Israel.

I never yelled. Never hit. Never expressed anything but a gentleness that belied what was actually going on inside me, my lungs tightening even more, my stomach eating itself. But I shook off such symptoms daily, hourly, minute-by-minute, thinking, *Calm down. She's beautiful. You're in love. Just be okay.* But I wasn't, and so I became obsessed with making things right for my daughter, Noa, with making her okay instead.

And Noa did have a serious problem that needed fixing: sleep. At three months, she wouldn't do it, wouldn't stay down for more than thirty minutes at a time, this tiny mess having absorbed everything in the womb, having felt the umbilical cord's constriction. A PTSD baby, born neurotic, always alert and sensing a coming threat. Noa seemed unable to handle the dark, just like her father, who took it upon himself to "cure" her infant insomnia, to make her relax, as if such a strategy has ever worked: I'll *make* her relax.

Jamie should have known that I was the problem. She should have said, "This will pass." However, suffering herself from a mind-numbing fatigue induced by Noa's all-night escapades, Jamie agreed that we had to do something.

We first considered sleep consultants, then tranquilizers, before settling on a fascist regimen outlined in a book recommended by mothers online, *The No-Cry Sleep Solution.* The title appealed. I didn't like the crying; I liked sleep; and most of all, I liked solutions. The book promised results: a baby who would sleep through the night, a serene baby for the ages. Photographs of sleeping babies punctuated the pages to prove the soundness of its methodologies. And not just any babies, mind you, but the author's own children, slumped in high chairs at the dinner table or drooling on pillows, eyes closed, page after page. *Amazing.* We bought it, and I bought into its ninety-five-step plan, tracking sleep patterns on spreadsheets and plotting trends. I kept a pad next to the bed and marked every night-waking precisely, seven, eight times a night. Up at 3:30. Down at 3:48.

I was stubborn, committed, and utterly useless. Things were not good.

I wasn't sleeping. Noa wasn't sleeping. Jamie was growing impatient. My yawns were increasingly becoming both a genuine physiological response to sleep deprivation as well as desperate attempts to take in enough oxygen when normal breathing failed me. But instead of relenting, I upped the ante and went all in with a measure the book called "Pantley's Gentle Removal Plan," named after the author, a pox on her name.

According to the book, the problem with our pacifier-using baby was something it called the "sucking-to-sleep association." In short, Noa was a full-blown sucking addict, only able to settle down once a nipple, or a nipple-substitute, was between her lips. The problem came when her pacifier, having dutifully fulfilled its mission, slipped from her parted, sleeping lips, at which point she would startle. My job, according to Pantley's Gentle Removal Plan, was to wean her from this rubber dependence using trickery. I was to launch a smoke-and-mirrors strategy after pulling the pacifier from her lips as she slept:

> *Often, especially at first, your baby … will startle and root for the nipple. Try to very gently hold his mouth closed with your finger under his chin, or apply pressure to his chin, just under his lips, at the same time rocking or swaying with him. (Use your key words if you have developed them.) If he struggles against this … go ahead and replace the nipple or pacifier, but repeat the removal process as often as necessary until he falls asleep.*[2]

Use your key words if you have developed them. The only key words I'd developed were fuck, shit, and fucking shit. Still, I was diligent about the technique, memorizing the steps and practicing the chin hold – thumb under the chin and index finger on the nose – which was supposed to mimic the pressure of a pacifier lodged in Noa's little mouth. Whenever she drifted to sleep, I'd pounce, wiggle the pacifier away, and squeeze her mouth closed. This often resulted in flailing, not the promise of continued slumber. After the first episode – watching me wake Noa by ripping the pacifier from her resting lips – Jamie threw in the towel. "This is absurd." But I remained diligent, becoming the sole practitioner of Pantley's Gentle Removal Plan. I was dedicated to its methodology, to its misguided system for imposing calm and order where none could possibly exist.

"How long do you plan to do this?" Jamie asked, completely spent after a night in which I intentionally tortured the three of us.

"The book says that we can break her, if I'm vigilant and consistent, in around ten days."

"Ten days? You plan to take the pacifier out every time she falls asleep for ten days?"

"I guess."

"I don't think so."

"But the book says we should see a major reduction in night wakings if I do this."

"Here's an idea: we'll see a major reduction in night wakings if you don't *wake her* by taking the pacifier out of her mouth when she's sleeping."

"But that's not the plan."

"I can't take this for ten days."

"But what if it's the only way?"

Jamie looked at me, holding our daughter, who had fallen asleep in her arms while feeding, and shook her head.

For months, Jamie had been undergoing a therapy called EMDR, for Eye Movement Desensitization and Reprocessing, which aided psychotherapeutic recovery through a strange blend of bi-lateral stimulations, such as alternating beeps fed into stereo headphones. The technique was a bit of a mystery, and sounded suspiciously New Age. But the woman who created EMDR, Francine Shapiro, had tested it on trauma victims, people who had gone through terrible experiences – Vietnam, sexual assault and molestation, emotional abuse[3] – and claimed magical results. Jamie was also claiming magical results.

One night, after getting home from a therapy session and putting Noa to bed, Jamie sat me down on the living room couch and, with the sort of energy I usually reserved for recapping fourth-quarter comebacks or walk-off home runs, began giving a play-by-play of the day's therapy session:

"Today was really interesting. Want to hear?"

"Sure," I said, fidgeting.

"Okay, first thing Suzy did, after giving me the headphones and vibrating things to hold – the ones that alternate right–left in sync with the beeps – was to get me to envision a younger version of myself, not exactly my inner child, but along those lines."

"Uh-uh."

"So I thought about 'her' in my old room – you know the one in Pittsburgh that my Dad's turned into a workout room?"

I nodded.

"So anyway, I envisioned myself in my old room, an adolescent me, and then was told to envision myself now, my present-day self, walking into the room and engaging the girl in conversation."

"Why?"

"To help with some anxiety I'm having now."

"From the bombing?"

"Yeah."

"Wait, so why the imaginary girl talk?"

"Who I am relates to how I'm responding to things now."

"Oh. Okay." I didn't understand.

"So anyway, I did what Suzy asked, the whole conversation thing, and it was really strange."

I stared out the window, trying to figure out if the pulsing light atop the Washington Monument was blinking at a rate slower or faster than a true second.

"Hey, are you even listening to me?"

"Yeah, of course."

"What did I just say?"

"You said you were in your old room talking to yourself."

"Basically. Ask me what my conversation was about."

"What?"

"Ask me."

I tried to sound curious. "What was your conversation about?"

Jamie mapped it out for me, after which she said, "The really amazing thing is that after this imaginary talk, I suddenly felt amazing relief."

"That's great," I said, deciding the blinking light was pulsing slightly slower than the pacing of a second hand.

"And then Suzy described what was happening in my brain. This is a simplification, but basically some of my memories are stored separate from my emotions, and the back and forth stimulations, the vibrations and stuff, make connections between each side of the brain. So it kind of helps extract emotions from one side to go along with the memories on the other. Helps reunite them so they can be processed. Kind of amazing, huh?"

"Sure," I said, trying to sound sincere.

"You should do it."

I laughed. "I don't think so."

"You should think about it. There's another person in the practice who uses EMDR who I got a recommendation for."

"Naw, but thanks."

Just then Noa let out a whimper. I hopped off the sofa, crept to the doorway and peered in, hoping everything was fine, hoping she'd settle on her own – that things would just resolve themselves without the need for any intervention.

We abandoned the sleep book and Pantley's Gentle Removal Plan, at which point I had to confront the fact that my insomnia rivaled my daughter's. Unable to settle down most nights, I would pacify myself with the Internet, playing chess with some stranger in Singapore or finding an amateurish distraction at www.addicting games.com. My favorite there was Kitty Cannon, a game I first encountered at JDS after hearing the giggles of middle-school boys coming from the corner of a computer lab. I snuck up on them to find students huddled around a single screen, shooting an animated cat from a silver adjustable cannon. The group's spokesman, Ben, turned around and began a sales pitch.

"Hey Mr. H.-G., have you ever seen this?"

"Nope."

"It's so funny. Watch this." He then shot a kitten, the screen scrolling in tune with its velocity across a green field riddled with explosives, razors, trampolines, and Venus Fly Traps. After bouncing off a trampoline into the air, then hitting some dynamite held by a floating balloon, which further propelled it forward, the kitten finally bounced to a bloody stop. Six hundred and seventy-five feet.

"Aw, that's weak," squeaked one of Ben's sidekicks.

"Yeah, that was a bad one. I got over one thousand feet once," Ben gloated. He pointed to the screen and explained. "See the red number? That's the angle. You can adjust it to set the cannon any way you like. And the power bar you just have to hit at the right time, when the line is full. Want to play?"

"This is the dumbest thing I've ever seen," I said, properly assuming my role, despite salivating internally.

"It's not dumb, just silly."

"Fine, but shouldn't you guys be doing research?"

The bell rang, and everyone scattered, a smattering of Shabbat Shaloms echoing around the lab. My students had forgotten to log out, and Kitty Cannon sat idly on the screen, waiting for some action. *Just once*, I thought, and started playing.

Kitty Cannon began taking its toll. I fell into a pattern of consistently dozing on the Metro during my morning commute, occasionally missing my stop. At school, the complicated block schedule confounded me such that I'd realize, as my students waited for me in a classroom, that I was supposed to be teaching. And at home, simple acts, such as remembering to turn off the stove, proved challenging. At one point, I put a dirty diaper in the microwave and a burrito in the garbage, my mouth open, trying to intentionally yawn.

It got to the point that Jamie didn't have to convince me to seek help – it was clear that I needed fixing, that I needed an intervention. Deciding to give therapy a try, I sheepishly asked Jamie for a recommendation.

"I don't know how to do this," I said.

"I'll help you," she promised, deciding upon a therapist and scheduling an appointment for me.

A week later, I found myself on the twelfth floor of a Dupont Circle office building, attempting to appear relaxed while reclining on a suede couch. Sitting across from me was Kathy[4] – a tall, attractive blonde with a gentle manner that masked a professional ferocity.

In our first few sessions, Kathy allowed me to dance, to bob and weave, around the topic of the terrorist attack. I offered detached shrugs and averted eyes, keeping my elbows tucked close to my body, the gloves under my chin, a defensive posture. Eventually, tired of the show and the footwork, she swung. "David, let's just lay everything on the table so we can see what's what. It's the first step, getting the whole story out. Which is why I'm going to ask that you please recount, in painful detail, the entire narrative of your traumatic experience, from beginning to end."

After forty minutes of going through the chronology for the first time – plucking images of Israel from constricted layers of grey matter and placing them before us both – I walked out of her office and felt absolutely nothing. No paroxysmal convulsions brought on by recalling all the muck. No clichéd breakdowns, on my knees supplicating with fists clenched. Just disembodiment.

On the way home, I felt relief – not because any psychic healing had occurred, but rather because I'd achieved a great escape. I had managed to talk about the attack, finally, with no emotional fallout.

I was a brick wall. I was impenetrable. I was one tough fucker.

In our next session, I showed up prepared to analyze my narrative, assuming we'd spin our wheels around the story. I knew enough about psychoanalysis to suspect an impending Freudian dive into the past in order to claim it, or understand it. But I was taken aback when Kathy sat down and, after cycling through some pleasantries, said, "I think we need to talk about your guilt."

"My guilt?"

"Yes."

"Guilt about what?"

Kathy smiled faintly and explained that she wanted to seize upon something I'd recalled during the narrative construction of the attack. Something that I had let slip tangentially, she said. Something that stood out, she said. She always looked for the tangents, she said.

The tangent to which she referred was something I had apparently mentioned offhand, as a bit of back story, about how we had all created a magical world of make-believe in Israel in order to remain sane. We had pretended that Hebrew University was a collegial oasis of integrated study outside the greater conflict, a universally agreed-upon no-fire zone. Kathy mentioned how I had recalled for her, unprompted, my walking around the campus before the attack, quietly inspecting Palestinian workers, about the newspaper article, the one which dreamed up a hypothetical attack, about how I knew the dangers all along.

Kathy: Do you not remember telling me about all that?

Me: I mean, I remember it. I remember the article. And I guess I said all that stuff last time, since you clearly know it. But I honestly don't remember talking about it.

Kathy: You were on auto-pilot.

Me: Yeah.

Kathy: What we're going to do is try to take you out of auto-pilot.

Me: But what if I like being on auto-pilot?

Kathy: Exactly.

Sitting before her on the sofa, picking at the parallel lines of suede running down the square cushions, I listened as she discussed the power of guilt, the overriding control it can have in obfuscating everything, in tamping down everything, in shutting off our emotional centers. That guilt was responsible for my numbness, for my ability to tell the story of Jamie being bombed without a hint of sadness or anger, without any emotional fallout. Where was the sadness? Where was the anger? Where were any of the normal stages one passes through when processing and moving beyond a trauma? I wanted Kathy to be wrong, but intuitively I knew she was right. And that was when she decided to hit hard:

Kathy: You need to grieve.

Me: Umm –

Kathy: See, it's your story. You can sit here. You can tell it – but it means nothing to you. It's just floating, disconnected from anything real, disconnected from who you were before the attack. Because if you truly felt how the story of what happened relates to you now, you'd have grieved, or felt grief. Or sadness. Or anger.

Me: Okay. So – what now?

Kathy: Do you have anything tangible, anything physical that could help you?

Me: Help me?

Kathy: Help you access what happened. Something that you can look at or hold that recalls what happened.

Me: Umm – I don't know. I mean, even if I did, and I'm not saying I do, there's nothing that it could connect with. I was caring for Jamie in the hospital, isolated, knew only that world. I never flew back for the funerals, never went to the memorial services for Ben or Marla, never really processed any of it. They're just gone.

Kathy: You don't understand – forget your friends. Have you ever cried for Jamie?

Me: What?

Kathy: For what she experienced: the physical pain, the horror of it all, the guilt of surviving, the long recovery. In all that time you were caring for her, did you cry?

Me: I don't think so.

Kathy: Forget your friends for the moment; you haven't grieved yet for your wife. For all she lost. For all she endured. That's your narrative before this, David, your life with Jamie. Didn't you say she might have been pregnant?

Me: Maybe. I don't know.

Kathy: Have you grieved for the fact that your first child may have been killed in the blast?

Me: Why are you doing this?

Kathy: I'm trying to help. You're paralyzed. No anger. No sadness. At least not expressed as such.

And yet you feel tense, can't breathe, always feeling overwhelmed, wondering why.

Me: I'm sad. Really, I am.

Kathy: When was the last time you cried?

Me: I got choked up a bit when watching the movie *Magnolia* recently. I get like that sometimes when watching emotionally-layered dramas, particularly those involving people struggling to overcome situations or past events. I seek them out, actually.

Kathy: So when you've attained a distance, a disconnection, you're able to feel some emotion, particularly when characters might be struggling like you have in the past. You seek out movies to feel that emotion, don't you? To see how others, struggling like you, express their darkest, most painful emotions.

Me: I'm not struggling.

Kathy: You're in therapy for a terrorist attack that's rendered you semi-functional.

Me: You said therapy is normal, that I shouldn't feel like a freak when I told you I felt uncomfortable paying to talk with someone, that I felt like it was some strange form of urban prostitution.

Kathy: That was nervous wit, not honesty.

Me: Fine.

Kathy: You want permission to grieve, permission to feel all those things you should be feeling, all those things characters in the movies you watch feel. But instead you feel guilty about not having prevented all this, and now feel guilty about feeling guilty. You feel guilty about not crying, about not feeling any emotion. So much guilt.

Me: I'm Jewish.

Kathy: Not funny.

Me: That's just because you're not Jewish.

Kathy: Here's my suggestion. Find articles online, or pictures even, relating to the attack. Look at them, look at them and think, "I didn't do this." Say it over and over again until you believe it. It may take minutes, may take hours, may not work at all, but it's worth a try.

Me: Why do I want to do this?

Kathy: For anger. The anger you feel toward yourself, which we'll call guilt, needs to be re-directed toward those who actually did this. It's an opening, a cognitive trick which I hope will release you from the burden of responsibility and help you realize emotionally the stakes of your story. I know it may sound strange, but it's worth a try. The self-blame has paralyzed you – your belief in it has paralyzed you and continues to generate anxiety responses, the manifestations of which you complain of – shortness of breath, insomnia. You believe you are responsible for the attack. You believe you did it by failing to mention the dangers. And every time you think it, even if you don't realize you're thinking it, it's causing debilitating symptoms. Our goal is to change your thought from "I did this," which is not even a conscious thought but is nonetheless wreaking psychological havoc, to "I didn't do this." If we can change your thinking, we might change how you relate to your story. That's the theory I'm going with, anyway.

Me: But I blame God, too. I'd rather play that guy.

Kathy: Let's stick with blaming yourself for now.

Me: Okay.

That night, I went home and, for some reason, heeded the doctor's advice after Jamie fell asleep, turning on the computer and rolling a chair to the screen, where I searched for articles, wanting information, data – impersonal bits of dry, formulaic exposition. And I found them: archived pieces chronicling the attack, the destruction, the numbers maimed, killed, missing. Remembering the phrase – I didn't do this – I began uttering it repetitively while monitoring myself: *Do I feel anything yet?* Reading sentences, repeating the phrase, I took internal readings: *Nope, nothing yet.* The thought arose that perhaps I was trying too hard, that such emotions couldn't be forced. It had to be a natural, organic process. So I tried scanning the articles free of motivation, free of expectations, and became obsessed with my approach, couldn't stop thinking about it, wondering if I was doing the exercise naturally, correctly: *Am I doing this right?* Flummoxed, I moved from words to pictures, unsure what I was looking for or how to go about absorbing whatever it was that lay in wait for me to find. Most newspapers had archived photos of the attack, the majority of which depicted the physical wreckage – the beams bent, the ceiling collapsed. Occasionally, there was a photo of random people sitting, blood running down a forehead or streaked across a face, people looking dazed. None of them did anything for me, despite my mumbling, "I didn't do this," to which I sniped back occasionally, "No fucking shit, genius," the sarcasm skipping a needle working hard to detect something deep in the grooves, circling back on itself, going nowhere.

Then, a disturbing thought came to me. *Maybe I should look for Jamie. Maybe if I see her, saying* "I didn't do this" *will work.* But I couldn't find an image of her, and her absence elicited a perverse new distress as I scanned countless pictures, hoping to find her face, hoping to find an archived, imagistic record of history. Something capable of proving that all of this had happened. That it was real.

The psychological experiment was failing badly.

Me: Is that anger? No, just frustration. You're frustrated about not finding a photograph of your injured wife so you can say, "I didn't do this," because your therapist told you to do so, because you don't already know it.

Me: You realize you're looking for photos of your wife, injured. And you're mumbling.

Me: I know. You think I've lost it, don't you, that all this is crazy.

Me: Actually, I think it's comical, all of it. You should see it from where I'm sitting, over here. All this manic activity. And the irony piled on, that thing you keep saying, having the opposite effect.

Me: This isn't funny, you fuck.

Me: Was that anger? That's anger. Well done.

Me: I'm talking with myself. I'm mad at you. Meaning me. Meaning it doesn't count.

Me: Now that's funny.

Me: Go away.

I should have stepped away from the computer, the experiment ruined by my hyper self-awareness, by my biased attempt to skew the outcome, the failure proving that the experimenter should never double as the subject. Superimposing a mantra on my psyche was clearly not going to work, but I refused to give up, just as I had refused with Noa's pacifier. So I moved to Google's image search, which brought me to an Israeli site housed by the Foreign Ministry that, unbeknownst to me at the time, collects photographs taken by Israeli investigators from every terrorist attack ever perpetrated against civilians. Evidence of war, of injustice, of the Garden not yet attained. For posterity.

Realizing what I had stumbled upon, I swallowed, then clicked, and clicked again. I typed in the words Hebrew University, and froze. I wasn't prepared. Wasn't prepared for the image that appeared. An image of bodies covered partially by black bags and scattered in close proximity. Some faces were exposed. Others shielded. The picture had been taken from above at some distance, most likely from the cafeteria's roof. One of the bodies, sprawled on its back, only had the face covered. *That's Ben,* I thought. His body was large, distinctive. I knew. The mouse in my hand gripped tightly. Looking at him, lying on the ground, dead. *Why is this online? Why is his head covered? This shouldn't be here.*

I am still uncomfortable with what happened next. For an hour, I looked at these images from the attack that had been archived by the State of Israel, scrolling, copying, and pasting pictures into a graphics program, zooming in, trying to identify my friends, to know for sure that, yes, *That's her, That's him,* that they hadn't simply disappeared.

Maybe it was an unhealthy dedication to the task at hand, a deranged, focused attempt at trying to evoke something, to open an emotional well and produce some cognitive surge within. Looking at the bodies, knowing my wife could have easily been among them, I thought, *I didn't do this.* Copied. *I didn't do this.* Pasted. *I didn't do this.* Enhanced, zoomed in on hair, on the legs, on the shape of things. *I didn't do this.*

By the time I had closed the graphics program, deleted the pictures, and shut down the computer, it was nearing dawn, a pinkish haze beginning to illuminate the Washington Monument's tip miles to the south. The refrain, *I didn't do this*, was etched in my mind, the idea of self-blame branded there alongside those images of partially covered bodies sprawled on the campus cobblestones.

Rising, I reflexively searched for the nut pulled from Jamie's intestine, which had been placed in a backpack not long after her surgery and forgotten. I found the black bag, made by Swiss Army, stuffed in the closet. After pulling it out, I reached in and felt around for the nut. It was still there, wrapped in a plastic sandwich bag.

I thought about its trajectory: made somewhere in Israel, bought in Jerusalem, taken to Ramallah, placed in a bomb which was placed in a backpack which was placed in a cafeteria at Hebrew University on July 31, 2002, then thrown into my wife's body by the force of a remotely-detonated blast, removed by surgeons and dropped in a plastic container, handed to me, taken out in a hospital bathroom, scrubbed with shaking hands, placed in a plastic bag, then transported to Washington, and forgotten. Until now.

The nut had once been hexagonal, but now one side was caved in, giving it the shape of a half moon, except that the concave side bent by the blast was jagged, with two of the hexagonal sides forming teeth, a wicked smile. A jack-o'-lantern's mouth. All Hallows' Eve. The nut's original purpose – tightening – was still apparent in the threads winding within it, while two sides on the unbent portion, the portion that must have been facing outward, away from the explosives, were smooth and angled perfectly at 60°. But the smile was scored, rough, the bent edges sharp, capable of drawing blood. And despite its size, the metal had an impressive heaviness to it, a denseness exposed by gravity's jilted pull when lifted, when rolled around between the thumb and pointer finger.

Taking it out of the plastic bag, placing the nut between my fingers, I tried to squeeze it, to bend the steel back, to change the shape of things, make it round, whole, wondering how something so solid could be rendered malleable in the flash of an instant, nauseated by an explosion that could achieve such power.

But then I thought that, perhaps, I was overestimating things, giving the blast too much credit. Maybe the nut, rather than bending from the combustion-induced torque, bounced off of something hard before finding Jamie. Maybe it first hit the floor, a wall, the table's synthetic surface. Maybe it wasn't bent by the mere force of heat and release when the bomb exploded, as I'd always assumed, as though how it bent mattered, as though it changed anything. Regardless, it felt like a revelation, this thought – *maybe the nut hit something first.*

A few days after Jamie's surgery, I had finally opened the lid of the plastic container in a hospital bathroom and pulled out the nut. There was a fine, transparent film covering the crooked hole, a dried, plastic-like layer of organic material – some hardened fluid from Jamie's body. I swallowed. Then, I ran the nut under hot water, scrubbing it vigorously, hoping to remove everything stuck between the threads, wedged in the smile's teeth.

After cleaning the nut, I put it in a pocket, held on to it, despite the memories it elicited, because it was the first thing I could wrap my fingers around and think, *This is something.* Everything else was ozone, air disappearing.

11

During our next session, Kathy was eager to receive word on how things had gone regarding my *in vivo* "I didn't do this" experiment.

Kathy: So, how are things?
Me: Your homework assignment sucked.
Kathy: Excuse me?

I explained how it hadn't worked – explained the copying and pasting and deranged zooming in on bodies sprawled along the ground, the manipulation of images. She pivoted in her office chair and reached into a drawer, dragging out cords and electronic dials. After she'd finally untangled everything, she tossed over two plastic knobs attached by wires to what looked like an antiquated game controller resting on her desk.

Kathy: Have you ever heard of EMDR?
Me: Unfortunately. Jamie's told me a little about it.
Kathy: Well, we're going to try something different.
Me: So you're not preparing to shock me with all those electronics, right?
Kathy: No, nothing like that. We're just going to use some physical stimulation alongside our cognitive work, since it appears you had a bit of

trouble correcting how you think about your trauma narrative when you were on your own.

Me: So no zaps or shocks?

Kathy: No, this won't be painful. It's bi-lateral stimulation. Just vibrations and sounds that might help "massage" your synapses as we talk.

She handed me pair of headphones, put two plastic knobs in my hands – a tiny L and R printed on each one – and ignited the machine. High-frequency beeps softly alternated between my ears while the plastic knobs buzzed in synchronicity. L: beep-buzz. R: beep-buzz. It felt as though I was being given a hearing test while holding a couple of agitated hornets. I was immediately incredulous. This commotion was supposed to correct my trauma narrative? This is what had granted Jamie magical results?

Me: What in the world?

Kathy: You can adjust the level of vibration with the dial there. You see it?

Me: Yeah.

Kathy: How's the volume? The beeps should be faint, but audible.

Me: Yeah, they're good. But –

Kathy: Great. So let's start by quickly outlining your trauma narrative again.

Me: Again? I'm kind of tired of telling it –

Kathy: Yes, again.

Jamie was eager to see EMDR work its therapeutic magic on me. But her hopeful expectations only complicated matters, for while I was afraid to disappoint her, I also knew that significant results would not be forthcoming.

"I just don't believe in it," I confessed one evening, returning home after yet another lukewarm session.

"You just have to give it a chance. Can't you pretend to believe?"

"I'm too self-conscious. It's obvious what's going on while it's happening, and I can't take it seriously. Today, I was supposed to convince myself that there aren't any terrorists lurking around in our lives, and that I don't have to protect you from anything anymore, as if I didn't already know this. That's what I kept thinking: *You already know this.*"

"Maybe you don't know it."

"Maybe I don't. Maybe I do. The point is it's just too obvious, the whole approach."

"It's as though you don't want it to work," she said.

"You know, they say the more intelligent you are, the more difficult it is for this type of stuff to work. That's probably the problem."

Jamie sighed heavily – the sarcasm failing to distract this woman too sharp to be sidetracked by such nonsense. "Don't you think it's helped some?" she asked.

In truth, it had, to a degree. The physical symptoms – the suffocating and insomnia – had dissipated somewhat, though not entirely. And fatherhood had improved substantially. Despite this, it was clear that my most persistent, deeply seated anxieties had not been rooted out by therapy, as evidenced by some transparently absurd displays of hyper-vigilance. One moment, everything would be fine; the next, I'd be driving to Wal-Mart at midnight for mouse traps or a smoke detector – whatever item that moment called for in order to keep everyone I loved from dying.

Yes, there was more work to be done. But I was done with therapy, and informed Kathy that the time had come to say goodbye, using finances as an excuse, unable to justify the money we were spending given the modest salary I earned as a high school teacher in one of America's most expensive cities.

And while I kept telling myself that hyper-vigilance was part of becoming a father, was an evolutionary imperative, the evidence continued to stack up against me.

Exhibit A: The Toilet Lock: When our daughter morphed from a cute, stationary blob into an agile crawler, our small, one-bedroom apartment revealed itself to be a hazardous minefield. Everything was dangerous: the coffee table corners capable of knocking a teetering baby unconscious; the shelves, which were poised to topple over with one good yank; the cords running from our lamps and other electrical devices waiting to wrap themselves around an unsuspecting neck.

Determined to defend my child from the persistent dangers the world now presented, I found myself open-mouthed, purposefully yawning, in the safety section of Babies "R" Us. There were outlet guards, cabinet latches, table-corner pads, window-blind-cord wind-ups, floor electrical-cord concealers, shelf and armoire tension-cable mounts, baby gates, and toilet locks. Everything displayed was manufactured by Safety 1st, the market seemingly cornered by this outfit branded with a phrase routinely intoned by firefighters and cops visiting classes of fidgeting but impressionable kindergarteners.

Safety first, I thought, nodding obediently, buying one of each.

At home, Jamie seemed genuinely grateful as I crawled around our living room floor, lining the walls with plastic tubes (cord concealers), adhering transparent buffers to the coffee table (corner pads), and unscrewing the outlet covers to be replaced with bulky, box-like structures that opened with a latch and hid electrical plugs from wandering hands (outlet guards). Then, I pulled it out.

"What's that?" Jamie asked.

"A toilet lock."

"A what?"

"A toilet lock. It's to lock the toilet."

"Why are we locking our toilet?"

"It's a drowning hazard."

Jamie looked at me incredulously. "You think Noa is going to drown in our toilet?"

"I don't know. I mean, she could crawl in there. It's possible. Otherwise they wouldn't make this locking thing."

"Why don't we just close the door when we're not in the bathroom?"

"Yeah, but what if we forget?"

"You're seriously going to lock our toilet."

"Yeah."

"How does it work?"

"I have no idea," I said, pulling it from the package and reading the instructions. "There's this swinging arm, which is designed to spring over the closed toilet." I held up a plastic rod.

"How do you attach it?"

"It looks like I have to take off the toilet seat and screw it between the seat and the cover."

Jamie rolled her eyes and left the room as I disassembled the toilet and installed the lock. When I'd finished, I product-tested it, closing and opening the toilet, watching the arm magically lock over the lid when it was closed. I invited Jamie in to admire my handiwork.

"See if you can figure out how to get it open."

She inspected and declined. "Could you just show me how to unlock our toilet?"

"Yeah, just press the red button – hold it down – and swing the arm away from the lid while opening it up."

Jamie tried unsuccessfully. "You need three hands for this. How do you press the button, move the arm, and open the lid at the same time?"

I stepped in and demonstrated the technique. "Press the button with your left hand and swing the arm with your right. Then, when the plastic arm has moved all the way off the lid, release the button real quick with your left hand and grab the arm before it swings back. Then you can open the lid with this one," I said, waving my right hand.

"I'm supposed to perform these gymnastics at 3 a.m., when I have to pee?"

I nodded.

"Why are we doing this?"

"So Noa doesn't drown in the toilet."

Often, friends visiting would excuse themselves and reappear a few minutes later with a sheepish grin: "How do you open your toilet?" At which point Jamie would look at me, embarrassed, knowing that it wasn't just a toilet seat lock that was the issue. I'd skip over to the bathroom for the demonstration, saying, "It's to protect the little one;" saying, "You never know what can happen."

Exhibit B: Mattress Wrapping: After Noa was born, Jamie and I shared one common fear: Sudden Infant Death Syndrome (SIDS). We had read the pamphlets – tucked in clear, plastic shelves on the walls of Jamie's doctors' office – about how, for no perceptible reason, babies everywhere were silently dying during the night, parents finding them motionless in their cribs, cold to the touch. Researchers, confounded and grasping at straws, said that infants sleeping on their stomachs had a higher propensity for dying during the night.

Doctor: Put her to sleep on her back. The prevalence of SIDS is greatly reduced.

Us: Why?

Doctor: We have no idea.

And so we placed Noa on her back when we put her to bed for the night.

We also rejected the crib-down-the-hall approach, instead embracing co-sleeping, refusing to allow our infant to cry herself back to sleep, alone, in a darkened room. The three of us slept in one bed together, where we tossed and woke each other up nightly. Friends and family were worried that Jamie or I would roll over and smother Noa in our sleep, but I knew such horror stories were rare, an awful plight primarily restricted to heavy drinkers and the morbidly obese. That wasn't my concern. Instead, I couldn't stop thinking about SIDS. During the night, after we'd abandoned the sleep book, I'd wake, lick a finger, and place it before Noa's lips to make sure she was breathing. I felt wholly out of control, having no way of knowing when or where it might strike as I pressed my ear to the sheets, staring at her abdomen, looking for the rise and fall of her chest in a darkened room where nothing could be seen.

I decided to research the subject, to wrest control away from this mysterious plight, and came across a bit of obscure literature about Dr. Jim Sprott, a chemist and forensic scientist in New Zealand who claimed to have uncovered the cause of SIDS. His theory was that the fire-retardant chemicals found in bedding, when consumed and processed by the fungi that commonly and quite naturally accumulate in mattresses, are converted into nerve gases that interfere with an infant brain's ability to transmit signals to the lungs and heart. Which is why, according to Dr. Sprott, infants sleeping on their stomachs expired more often – their faces were buried right in the source of these noxious gases.

Dr. Sprott's defense against the SIDS epidemic was simple: wrap mattresses with a plastic barrier to eliminate the effects of potentially toxic off-gassing. His data were so compelling that in 1994 New Zealand's government adopted and promoted his advice, encouraging parents to place baby mattresses in a specially designed plastic bag. I found Dr. Sprott online and read on his mattress-wrapping product's website – www.cotlife200.com – statistics which seemed unimpeachable. No babies had died in New Zealand on wrapped mattresses.[5] Or so his numbers told.

Convinced, I decided to encase our king-sized bed with plastic sheeting, an initiative which was quite daunting. When Jamie walked in to see me maneuvering our bed and asked what I was doing, she vetoed the idea of out of hand.

"You're not wrapping our mattress."

"I know. I'm just seeing if it's possible."

"Well, you can stop. It's comfortable, and I don't want it turned all crinkly."

"But Dr. Sprott – "

"David, stop. I read that co-sleeping babies do much better. But maybe you can wrap the crib. For the naps."

"Good thinking."

So I rushed out to Home Depot and grabbed a roll of ten foot by one hundred foot construction sheeting.

On returning to the apartment, I placed the plastic on the living room floor and wrestled with the mattress. The trick was to cover it tightly such that one side remained a perfectly flat, comfortable surface upon which a baby might sleep, an objective that proved nearly impossible. Each time a side was lifted, folded over, then taped, the material would buckle, forming crisp, raised ranges of creased plastic. The harder I pulled, the firmer the creases became. Jamie, watching me grunt and tug with frustration, suggested treating the plastic as though it were wrapping paper, slitting the material so as to form four parallelograms, one on each side that could easily be folded over.

"This isn't a present that has to be wrapped. It's more like toxic waste that has to be hermetically sealed," I explained.

Picking up a roll of duct tape, I kneeled over the mattress, flexing my fingers and forearms. There was only one way to go about things. I had to impose my will. Grasping handfuls of plastic with spear-tipped strikes, I fought until a section was successfully taped to the exposed underbelly. I made my way around the mattress systematically, progressing until all of the exposed cloth was secured. When I flipped the mattress over, the surface of Noa's bed looked like disorganized bubble wrap. I worked my fingers into the pockets of trapped air, massaging each one to the open edge of the plastic, pulling the plastic tighter to be secured with more silver strips of industrial-strength tape.

After two hours, I sat on the ground, soaked and disheveled, fingertips rubbed raw and peeling. Jamie walked in.

"You're done."

"Yeah."

"That took a long time. You used the whole roll of duct tape?"

I nodded.

"That's a lot of tape."

"I know."

Jamie walked to the bathroom and returned with a large bath towel, a soft layer to be placed between the crinkling plastic and Noa's bedding. She sat down on the ground opposite me, and silently we smoothed the towel flat against the mattress and pulled the fitted sheet over, smoothing down the edges, while Noa lay face up on the floor of the hallway, a domed mobile entertaining her, her legs kicking absently.

Exhibit C: The Xylophone Incident: Once, we took a trip, left our apartment for a week, and gave the neighbor, a nice guy, a gentle guy, our mail and door keys, asking him if he would be kind enough to collect the bills and junk catalogues for us while we were away. Which he did. But after returning, on our first night back, lying in bed, I started to think, *What if he made a copy of our key? What if he's not so innocent? Isn't that what people always say on the news when something tragic happens? "He seemed nice enough," or "He was so quiet, I never would have suspected."*

I rose and started thinking tactically. *Okay, it's midnight. Too late to get the locks changed, and barricading the door would be ridiculous. That would wake everyone up.* Finally, I saw it and grinned: Noa's toy xylophone, out of which I constructed a makeshift alarm. With the xylophone propped against the doorframe, metal keys facing out toward the ceramic floor, it was certain to produce a racket if disturbed. Satisfied, I returned to bed with a hammer and placed it under the pillow. *Just in case.*

I spent that night awake, acutely aware that the source of this improvised security system reached back to Jerusalem: reached back to the Israeli security apparatus that had failed us, to bi-national strategies of violence that had failed us, to the unstable and unsustainable Israeli–Palestinian conflict that had failed everyone. I had enough experience with Kathy to diagnose myself: using a child's xylophone for home security was a post-traumatic response to a post-traumatic life. I knew my brain was yelling, *Someone tried to murder her*, was yelling, *You didn't protect her then.* Everything connected back to the source, back to burned flesh and skin grafts and shrapnel covered with blood. And I knew, *You're not healed. You're not where you want to be.*

My head on a hammer and a xylophone against the door, I wondered if I'd ever move beyond the trauma, if I'd ever overcome all that continued to press tightly around me. The thought of stasis brought on a quiet, cold panic, which rose solidly from my diaphragm and swirled around the back of my throat, a frozen steel rod being washed in the esophagus. *I can't continue this way,*

I thought, drifting fitfully into a recurring vision of some ethereal exodus, wandering the sand-swept wilderness of the Negev, beyond Mitzpe Ramon, descending into a steep crater where I let the bone-crushing silence press everything noxious out of my eardrums. I lay down in a cracked wadi, blood dripping from my earlobes, listening to the ibex scrabble down the crater's red walls, looking for a drink. Glancing sideways, I locked eyes with a bronze sand fox, creeping close, and said, *It's fine. Drink. You can have this.*

He didn't believe me, crouching, wondering which part of me would be the first to flinch. I wondered the same, draining slowly into the yellow earth.

12

A few weeks before Mother's Day in 2004, with the cherry blossoms exploding, marking spring's arrival, Jamie looked at me one afternoon and said, "Write me a poem."

I don't know why she said it, having never before asked for a poem or seen me write one. But the request ignited an impulse that had lain dormant within me for years. As an undergraduate at the University of Georgia, a newly minted English major who had never considered writing as a pursuit, never desired writing as a pursuit, never needed it, I was introduced to James Wright's *The Branch Will Not Break* by one of my teachers, Coleman Barks, a romantic Santa Claus renowned for his translations of Rumi, the thirteenth-century Persian mystic. By the time I devoured Wright's work, the thought *I too must write* consumed me. I hunted poems in back-alleys, half-packed bongs, and in the Blue Ridge Mountains. I sought meetings with wizened professors, elderly townies, and stumbling-drunk homeless men, hazing myself with experiences befitting a burgeoning writer, shoving the funnel down my throat and pouring in everything that would slide down, excited to find what would come back up to find life on the page.

During my senior year, I found Edward, an eighty-four-year-old vagabond who approached leading his green, antique bicycle as if it were a lover. Whenever he sat down to chat, as he so often did on summer afternoons in downtown Athens, Georgia, it was impossible not to stare at his intensely wrinkled hands, splotched and flecked by the years, or the strange blue and red formations that mapped his bald head. He liked me, I could tell, and intentionally played the part of storyteller, detecting ears eager to digest his stories. Once, after interrupting me while I was writing at Blue Sky, a hip coffee shop in the center of town, he sat down and, in a blended European accent, asked, "Did I ever tell you about my apartment in Paris? My bedroom was on the second floor, and the women, David. The women. So much sex. So much love. We'd make the floor shake, keeping my landlord up at night. Paris, David. Paris."

So this is being a writer, I thought, listening closely as the world opened to me, revealing its beauty without begging or even asking. I wrote voraciously. But the writer in me was killed by my warped perfectionism, realizing – as I read the literary masters – that my scribbling would never reach their heights. *What's the fucking point?* I scrawled one afternoon, recognizing my writing was nothing when compared with that of William Faulkner. The pain of failure overwhelmed those first pangs of need, and so I put the pen down.

But after writing Jamie's poem, a half-decent number full of awkward metaphors and enjambments, I was stricken with a sharp sense of loss. Then, one night, sitting down for a quick game of Kitty Cannon, I opened up Microsoft Word instead. Without thinking, I began to type some verse and noticed my body expand, a metal frame made malleable by the heat of creativity. And I thought, *How did I let this go so easily*? as I typed through the night and then through the next year – publishing several pieces in small literary magazines across the country. *Colorado Review. Burnside Review. Stickman Review.* Pieces about my grandfather and trips to the doctor with Noa and pissing in the bushes as a child. But nothing about the terrorist attack. Not a word.[6]

On Mother's Day the next year – May 8, 2005, a Sunday – we hired a babysitter for the first time and walked to Lauriol Plaza, a famed Mexican restaurant nearby. Over a brunch of *huevos rancheros* and *salmon à la parrilla*, while talking about this sudden freedom from diaper-changing and drool-wiping, Jamie brought up the subject of my writing.

"You've been writing a lot."

"I know."

"I think it's great."

"Yeah, I wish I had more time for it."

"Do you think you'll ever write about it?" she asked cautiously, fiddling with her fork.

I shrugged – a shrug that concealed an answer I had already realized: I needed to write about it, felt compelled to write about it. I'd moved beyond therapy, having reclaimed small pieces of myself during the process, and was now reclaiming the artist within, an artist beginning to feel an out-of-body compulsion to construct this story, our story, on the page. I wanted to wrestle with it in the hopes of choking out something transformative: choking out a blessing. Not as therapy, but as art, as a redemptive expression. I had to try. This was all I had left – a sense that only through storytelling, I could reclaim myself.

But I couldn't tell Jamie. Not yet, not as she sat opposite me sipping fresh-squeezed orange juice. I shrugged, embarrassed by the cliché – the writer with a book that needed to be written – wondering if wholeness might reside in the pages I'd not yet composed. And then Jamie said, "I think you should write about it. Maybe it would help."

"I don't know," I shrugged again.

"You haven't thought about it?"

I had thought about it at length – had thought about how, between changing diapers, doing the dishes, and grading papers, between full-time employment and full-time parenthood, I didn't have the space within which to even consider beginning such a tortuous process. I already felt overwhelmed by daily life, barely able to breathe, much less breathe life into a past which had taken the breath of our friends, and which had nearly taken Jamie's last breath.

I longed for stretches of time that looked like a coastline upon which I could pour out the Israeli desert sands that were rubbing coarsely under my skin. I was afraid to admit this to Jamie, apprehensive about her possible response. After all, she'd already given too much time to this narrative. She'd lived it. And I feared making her live it again. But I needed to tell her.

"I've been thinking about graduate school, about an MFA in creative writing," I said.

"Really?"

"Yeah. I just feel like I need time if I'm going to actually write about everything. It's not about the degree or anything like that. I've just been thinking about ways I could get the time I need to write, and it's the thing I keep coming back to."

"So you have thought about writing about what happened, then."

"Yeah."

"And graduate school?"

"Yeah."

"I don't think we can afford something like that, David."

"I know. I know we can't. I've just been thinking."

"Well, I'm glad you told me – I didn't know you were thinking about this."

"I know."

"Have you looked at schools?"

"Kind of."

"Really?"

"Just a bit."

"Interesting."

"Is it?"

"Well, a little. I don't think we can do anything like that, with Noa and everything. But – you should at least look into it."

"Look into it how?"

"I don't know. Just find out information," she said, giving permission, herself intrigued by the permission she was giving.

Several months later, I sent in applications to several writing programs along with requests for teaching assistantships, knowing that, financially, it wasn't feasible under the rosiest of circumstances. A twelve-thousand-dollar-a-year assistantship was worlds away from sustainable for our family. And Jamie was pregnant again. Applying to graduate school was plain foolery, I thought.

Jamie disagreed.

The following spring, a professor from the University of North Carolina, Wilmington called to inform me that I had been accepted into their program and was being offered an assistantship. By then, memory of my applications had been erased by the birth of our second daughter, Tamar, an event so disorienting it warped time, making it appear as though everything that preceded it existed on a separate plane.

Jamie strolled into our living room one evening late into her pregnancy and announced plainly, "I think my water just broke." The casual beginning seemed appropriate, since Noa's delivery had lasted for twenty-four hours. We assumed we had plenty of time. There was no reason to hurry. So I waited while she got her things together and arranged care for Noa. Then Jamie dropped a bag, leaned against a wall, and said, "We need to leave right now." I jumped off the couch. Her contractions were coming every thirty seconds, overwhelming her, overwhelming me as I tried to get her to the car.

"Shit. How are you already contracting like this?"

"I – don't – know," she said, teeth clenched. I finally eased her into the car and took off, running red lights and skirting the wrong way down one-way streets, Jamie grabbing the handle above the passenger-side window, flexing her body toward the door, attempting to push herself through the glass and onto the asphalt, seeking relief. As we neared the birth center, I was forced to stop at a major intersection, where I cracked the windows for fresh air, trying to relieve her convulsions by doing something, anything. The baby was close.

Jamie groaned, "Hurry." Then, closing her eyes, focused completely internally, she let out a primordial scream. I looked past her and into the eyes of a teenage boy in the car waiting next to ours, his face stricken. There was no doubt in my mind: *She's going to have this right now*. The light turned green and I skidded the car into the birth center's parking lot. It was dark, and the doors were locked.

"Press the button."

I pressed the buzzer. Nothing. Pressed it again. Then a voice came over: "Can I help you?"

"I'm having a baby!" Jamie yelled, the word *baby* trailing up, forming a sarcastic question where no question existed. The door buzzed open as a nurse greeted us from the top of a steep flight of stairs. "Just have her come on up and we'll – " she said as Jamie bent over and wailed. "Oh my, she's having it right now. Do you think you can get her up here?"

"I hope so."

"Then do it now." She disappeared. I grabbed Jamie's arm and guided her up the stairs to a room with a bed. Jamie got on it and immediately started pushing as the nurse reported that the midwife wasn't going to make it, that there was no time, that we were going to have to do it on our own. I wasn't prepared. Noa's delivery had been an exercise in procrastination. But Tamar was suckling on Jamie's belly before I'd processed what was transpiring. We were a family of four, just like that. And just like that my thoughts of confronting the terrorist attack within the cozy confines of graduate school dissipated entirely from my mind.

Jamie and I began adjusting to life as a family of four, our house transformed into a wrestling ring with three others always on the mat with me, all of us stomping and ricocheting off the ropes, a flurry of activity that was blinding and exhilarating. It was in the midst of this brawl that the UNCW professor called, inviting us to live along the coast, speaking warmly, calmly, saying, "The Department of Creative Writing really wants you," saying, "The writers here are really excited about your work," saying, "You'll love the ocean, how time stretches flat and long and open along the coast from Wrightsville Beach to Fort Fisher," saying, "You can roam here, be free, like the terns and sandpipers."

We talked for weeks about the impossibility of such a move, looking at our finances, the numbers never adding up. Noa and Tamar bounced off the ropes, reminding us that they needed to be included in our calculations. My students at JDS bounced off the walls, reminding me that I'd be abandoning them as their FBI chief. The city hummed, reminding us of the bustling community we'd be leaving behind. Then one day, Jamie said, "Let's just do it. The ocean sounds nice. And we'll make the numbers work. We'll find a way, somehow."

In truth, we were both ready to escape the traffic and the sirens and the political chatter, which seemed to push time, a bit quicker than it should. We delighted in the words *small* town, *beach* town, *southern* town. By mid-July, nearly four years after the attack, we were ready to abandon Washington for Wilmington.

We woke up at 4:30 on a summer's morning, our apartment emptied of everything save an inflatable mattress from our last night's sleep. We had decided to rise bombastically early to avoid rush-hour traffic, to escape under the cover of perpetual movement and our children's slumbers, giddy to reach North Carolina. But seven hours later, as we approached Wilmington on I-40, driving through the drab, flat landscape punctuated by clumps of browning pines, the decision to move south no longer seemed sound.

"I wonder what this is going to be like," Jamie said. She looked concerned.

"Maybe we should have visited first?"

"I'm sure it will get better."

"It has to," I said, wondering how many Jews per square mile lived in the towns we passed – Watha, Burgaw, Rocky Point – suddenly feeling foreign and vulnerable. Finally, our exit arrived. We were funneled off the interstate and onto Third Street, toward downtown Wilmington, where we were greeted by austere colonial homes and moss-draped oaks whose branches formed a canopy over the road. We sighed at the beauty, at the tranquility, at the coffee shop we found with pastel rocking chairs planted on the sidewalk. We stopped, got out, sat down and exhaled.

"We're here," I said to Noa.

She looked around, taking in the storefronts. "This is our house?"

"No," I chuckled. "This is Wilmington. The place we're going to live."

"Oh. Where's our house?"

"We have to find one," Jamie explained.

Noa's brow crinkled quizzically until her eyes focused on the cinnamon roll I was holding. Reaching for it, she said, "I know what. Let's go find a home."

We found a rental in one of the town's oldest neighborhoods, where the houses hugged each other closely and the front stoops pressed against the curb, providing a cozy, residential main-street feel that harkened back to the turn of the twentieth century. Our house was from the 1930s, painted light green and buttressed by a spacious porch. When we opened the door to get our first look, Noa was immediately enamored, skipping into the living room and yelling, "We live in a castle," bouncing around each of the three bedrooms in turn, echoing off the hardwood floors, while Jamie, smiling, cradled Tamar on the threshold of our new life.

Still, it wasn't until I was sitting on Wrightsville Beach, watching Noa build sand castles and Tamar waddle unsteadily with a diaper weighed down by sea water, that I understood the seismic shift. Barefoot, I walked down to the water's edge, and what once seemed foreign, vulnerable – writing about Israel in a sleepy southern town – suddenly felt natural. I dipped a toe in the ocean, envisioning a line leading directly from it across the Atlantic to the Mediterranean and Tel Aviv, then overland via Highway 1 inland to Jerusalem, thinking of these two coastlines and these two states as my topographic bookends.

On my first visit to the writing department, I thought of bookends, of UNCW and Hebrew University as intellectual peaks, the valley of my narrative running between them. In contrast to Hebrew University's limestone structures, UNCW's campus appeared modern – bricks and angles and manicured swaths of grass occasionally interrupted by a sandy pocket, a miniature dune rejecting the landscaped sod. But it wasn't the sand that most stood out as a sign, a signifier, that I was standing on coastal land. It was the laxity. The unfettered freedom of movement. The leisure. No gates. No security stations. No metal detectors or wand-wielding guards. No soldiers carrying M-16s or professors sporting gun holsters instead of pocket protectors.

Finding a café tucked inside the university's library, I watched groups of students mingle and felt at ease. It seemed an appropriate place in which to begin the process of committing everything that had happened to us to the page, and once classes began, I allowed myself to inhale, deeply, as though I was a long-distance runner at the starters' block, pressing the balls of my feet into the floor and my fingertips into a keyboard, thinking, *It's time to start digging*.

I did not know then that my digging would take me back to Israel, back to Jerusalem, where I would desperately seek a meeting with the terrorist who tried to kill Jamie.

13

Research. It began with research on a campus computer. It began by sifting through archived newspaper articles, this time seeking information rather than an emotional conversion, as I had with Kathy. It began by zeroing in on the man I had been avoiding, whose existence I had been unable to face, afraid of what such an encounter might bring.

I learned his name – Mohammad Odeh. Learned he was the one who placed the explosives-filled backpack in the cafeteria where Jamie sat, eating.

The one who worked for Hebrew University as a painter.

The one disguised as a student, waiting in line with perfumed hands.

The one who ignited a cell phone, calling the bag next to Marla and Ben, a folded paper balancing on top of it, a paper Jamie ducked beneath when his thumb opposed "send."

The one who murdered.

The one who tried to murder.

The one who shoved hammers under my pillow and xylophones against our door.

The one who fashioned bereaved parents and siblings and lovers from nails and bolts and scrap metal.

The one with a young son, an infant girl.

The one nobody would understand. Ever.

The one I would eventually decide to confront.

I learned his name. And it became personal, this ability to point and say "Mohammad," the primordial act of naming, of identifying with syllables, with established grunts and pauses, feeling as powerful as creation itself. He was named. He existed. But further details provided by the *Jerusalem Post* and *The Times* of London encouraged me to remain dispassionate: he was part of a Hamas terror cell, just one of many who had perpetrated, with the push of a button, numerous mass killings in restaurants and on buses across Israel. He was presented as another generic representation of evil, a representation that was comforting, that coaxed me into believing there were no fingers to point, no what-ifs to consider – it had just happened, because evil happens, and that was all.

Newspapers: Forget Mohammad. He is just an archetype.

Me: Sure thing.[7]

At first, I was prepared to accept this – to accept things the way I had for years. I focused on piecing together the logistics of how the bombing had happened, keeping a healthy dose of emotional restraint on hand, moving from A to B to C with the cold clarity of a statistician. But then I found something strange, something wrong. A misquote. Or a typo. It was embedded within an Associated Press article covering Mohammad's 2002 capture:

> *After his arrest, Odeh told investigators he was sorry for what he had done since so many people died in the university attack, [Israeli] officials said.*

Odeh told investigators he was sorry. It had to be a mistake – ideologically crazed terrorists don't apologize. They don't express remorse.

They praise the struggle, hold up the jihadist's banner and proclaim, in the name of Allah, for continued acts against the infidels. They are programmed, robotic, repeating the same predictable refrains while marching, faces disguised, guns raised toward the sky. *Death to all Jews. Praised be the martyrs. Allahu Akbar. God is great.*

It wasn't supposed to be this way. Mohammad was not human. He did not reflect any recognizable sliver of the world I recognized as sane, rational, acceptable. He was not sorry. He could not possibly be sorry.

Me: I thought you said he was an archetype.
Newspapers: Oops.

I was on unstable ground, unable to discern where to step given this unanticipated, unmapped terrain. Not only was Mohammad named, not only did he exist, but his existence was abruptly made impossible. How could a person capable of orchestrating and executing the mass murder of innocent college students have the capacity for genuine contrition? How could a member of Hamas let slip such a statement? *Odeh told investigators he was sorry.* It was incomprehensible. I wanted to pass it off as editorial malpractice, or at the very least an inauthentic response to days of interrogation, and possibly torture, hoping the word sorry had been squeezed out of him as Israeli police poured water into Mohammad's mouth. But two items from the article forced me to think otherwise. First, he was the only one of fifteen terrorists captured to have made such an expression. Second, Odeh's family in East Jerusalem responded with disbelief:

> *"My brother just goes from home to work ... and has nothing to do with any other thing," Samr Odeh told the Associated Press outside his East Jerusalem home as Mohammad's six-year-old son Hamza stood crying nearby*

> *at the mention of his father. "I deny the charges that the Israelis are trying to put on him."*[8]

It was clear that Mohammad's family did not consider it possible that he could have bombed a cafeteria, did not want to consider it possible. This was not an ideologically extreme clan, a clan eager to embrace a son's and brother's martyrdom and proclaim his glory. Instead, they denied the veracity of the accusation. Samr's words indicated a family horrified by Israel's claim.

Mohammad had come from what appeared on the surface to be a moderate family, a family unwilling to accept his involvement with Hamas, with terrorism. But Mohammad had done it. He had admitted to doing it. And according to anonymous officials quoted in this reputable media outlet, he had expressed remorse. I couldn't digest any of it, couldn't stomach the digestive process. The experience felt akin to when, after years of vegetarianism, I broke down and ate two hotdogs laced with sauerkraut during a University of Georgia football game. The lining of my stomach had not been prepared to process a pound of hormone-filled beef then, and today it wasn't prepared to process the incongruity of learning that the terrorist who had tried to kill Jamie might be sorry for what he'd done.

I had spent years giving little thought to the fact that an actual person had been responsible for the bombing. Now, I was consumed by thoughts of the perpetrator as a fellow human, a remorseful criminal, a man with a crying son and a traumatized family. It was all I could consider, and such considering induced digestive distress. I was ill.

One evening soon afterward, Jamie and I went out to eat at Indochine, a Thai establishment whose interior glittered with emerald green and polished gold, its self-contained fountains trickling steadily, soothing streams in the background. In the foreground, a costumed waiter took our order. For Jamie, vegetable drunken delight, a rich serving of bamboo shoots, lotus roots, and broccoli drenched in a mild wine sauce. For me, green curry aubergines, a dish full of coconut and eggplant, a dish I couldn't pronounce. After we made our choices, the waiter gave us further options. Mild. Medium. Spicy. Jamie chose mild.

"How spicy is spicy?" I asked.

"It's spicy. Do you like spicy food?"

"Sure, I can handle spicy food," I said, needing to make up for mangling "aubergines," for not knowing what the word meant by pretending to be a veteran of all things curried.

"Then you should be fine."

"Wait, David, he's not asking if you can handle it. He's asking if you want it," Jamie interrupted.

"I know." I looked at the waiter confidently. "Spicy."

"Very well," he said, taking the menus and departing with our order.

Jamie looked at me. "I didn't know you like really spicy stuff."

"Of course I do."

"Really?"

"I'm sure it will be good."

As we nibbled on a salad with peanuts and caramelized shallots, I wanted to tell Jamie, "This guy who tried to kill you might have expressed remorse," wanted to say, "This fuck might have said he's sorry," wanted to say, "Can you believe such bullshit?" But I couldn't. I couldn't mention it. This was my process. This was my game, a game to be played solo, because Jamie had already moved beyond the attack, had shaken it off in ways I couldn't seem to replicate. So I kept quiet as our meals were delivered to us.

Lifting a piece of tofu between pinched chopsticks, I slid it into my mouth and began choking, the curry burning the back of my throat.

"Are you okay?"

I nodded, fist pressed to my mouth, head bent over the plate. The food was too hot. It was more than I could bear.

But I ate anyway, choking through dinner with my eyes tearing and my lips burning, sporadically giving myself over to convulsive fits between bites. I was determined to finish. Jamie glanced up sympathetically as she ate. All I could think was, *Just finish the meal. Just finish it.*

14

It mattered. Mohammad's sincerity, the veracity of his statement, mattered. Why, I could not articulate.

Me: Why does it matter?
Me: I don't know.
Me: So he might have expressed remorse? So what?
Me: It's important.
Me: But it changes nothing.
Me: I know.
Me: He's still a monster.
Me: I know.
Me: What, then?
Me: I don't know how to answer.
Me: You're pathetic.
Me: Thanks.

Unsure from where this impulse had arisen, but sure that the impulse existed, I tried to dig up the truth.

My first thought was to contact the Associated Press journalist who had recorded Mohammad's "words" from four years earlier. *He was sorry* – was it true? Maybe she still had her notes, maybe she would remember her source. I wanted her source. After finding her email on a site for professional newspaper reporters, I requested the information. But no reply came.

The only way you'll know is to ask him, I thought. A nod came from deep within me, without any rational understanding of the mechanics involved. A decision had been made: I would try to secure a meeting with Mohammad, the idea feeling shaky. Seeking a confrontation with the perpetrator of the bombing had never been placed upon the buffet of potential treatments by those attempting to assist in my healing and recovery. Nobody had set this in a metal bin and identified it as an option. *Here, psychotherapy au gratin. And next to it, sautéed compartmentalization. And just in this morning, a freshly caught terrorist who talks, answers questions, and is reportedly remorseful.*

I had heard of victims intent on confronting their perpetrators. I knew about restorative justice. But such initiatives had always seemed bizarre. Self-flagellating. However, after learning that Mohammad may have felt remorse, the word began to resonate with possibility: restoration. I sensed that the only way I might understand what happened was to understand Mohammad, an understanding which could somehow give me back my lungs, my life.

As I began the convoluted process of attaining a meeting with Mohammad, I couldn't stop asking, *Why are you doing this?* It's a question I repeated after calling the Ministry of Public Security in Israel, trying to discern how one would go about the process of requesting a meeting with an imprisoned terrorist. It's a question I repeated when representatives called me from the Israel Prison Service, suspicious, asking about my motives. It's a question I repeated after tracking down an official fax number from a diplomatic aide stationed at the Israeli Embassy in Washington, D.C., and composed an official request in Hebrew to the Israeli government for the chance to speak with Mohammad. A question I repeated as I pressed send, faxing the request to Lieutenant Colonel Orit Stelzer at the Ministry of Public Security.

In the comment section of my request I wrote:

> *What follows is an unusual request. The Prison Service's liaison to the Embassy in Washington, D.C., has indicated you are the address for such unusual requests to be made. And while I understand the sensitive nature of what I'm seeking, I hope that my position will be favorably reviewed. For it must be.*

As the paper slid through the machine, I asked myself again, *Why are you doing this?* There was no answer.

In the beginning, after the attack at Hebrew University, there had been darkness, there had been blindness – not knowing who had perpetrated the attack or how it had happened – and that blindness was good. It was good not knowing the details, not having Mohammad's name and face attached to the pictures of punctured bodies and fractured beams, to images of Jamie shuddering from unyielding pain. As time went on, I clung to that blindness, pretending that darkness had not yet been separated from light.

But those words – *he was sorry* – backlit everything, threw shadows upon the walls which the darkness had concealed. I saw myself. I saw Mohammad. I saw the destruction. And for the first time, I felt an intense need to speak with Mohammad, to understand him. To understand how he could say such a thing when he was the face of evil.

As my campaign to gain an audience with Mohammad became entangled in webs of bureaucratic paperwork, I was forced to consider this need to meet with him, my need for self-flagellation. *Why are you doing this?*

For the answer, I went elsewhere, looked for examples of other people who had faced perpetrators, for those with a comparable drive. Every time I searched, every time I plugged an item into

Google, the same result kept appearing: reconciliation. And attached to that result: South Africa. And the result scared me, for I had no interest in reconciliation, had no interest in some granola-caked forgiveness trek toward Mohammad. I just wanted to square the words "terrorist" and "sorry" so that I might be able to, once again, sleep through the night. Breathe.

But the result kept appearing. Reconciliation. The victims kept asking for it. The perpetrators kept allowing it. And so I decided to explore a South Africa on the brink of democracy, on the brink of a post-apartheid existence, in order to better understand the phenomenon that was growing within me,[9] a phenomenon Jamie didn't yet know existed.

South Africa: This is what I learned:

For over thirty years, white Afrikaners of Dutch descent – under the cover of the ruling white National Party (NP) – raped, murdered, segregated, and economically enslaved an entire population. And when their rule, and thus apartheid, finally came to an end in 1994, when a nation of victims rose to power behind Nelson Mandela's African National Conference (ANC), there was no state-sponsored revenge, no retribution, no rounding up of the fair-skinned perpetrators and burning them at the stake. Instead, there was a national, legislated process of reconciliation. Of truth-seeking. Of forgiveness. This process, this national attempt to heal through testimony, through dialogue, through understanding, would inform and influence my own burgeoning journey back to Jerusalem.[10]

An abbreviated tale. After years of international sanctions, years of a country crumbling under the weight of its colonial transgressions, South Africa's leaders knew in the early 1990s that the end was near. They knew that apartheid had lost its hold, and that the move to democracy was inevitable. Negotiations were established on how to structure a peaceful transition to democratic rule between the ruling NP and the opposition ANC, between the whites and the blacks, between the perpetrators and the victims. The NP still held control of the military, and this gave the party's leaders a position of strength from which to bargain. And so before agreeing to step down and allow for a historic election to take place, they demanded this: amnesty. They demanded absolution for all transgressions committed in the name of the state. They demanded get-out-of-jail-free cards. In return, the opposition – people who were victims or family and friends of victims of some of the most horrific crimes ever to be chronicled – demanded that they be given this: truth. The deal is immortalized in the last clauses of South Africa's interim constitution:

> *The adoption of this Constitution lays the secure foundation for the people of South Africa to transcend the divisions and strife of the past, which generated gross violations of human rights, the transgression of humanitarian principles in violent conflicts and a legacy of hatred, fear, guilt and revenge. These can now be addressed on the basis that there is a need for understanding but not for vengeance, a need for reparation but not for retaliation, a need for ubuntu [the African philosophy of humanism] but not for victimization.*
>
> *In order to advance such reconciliation and reconstruction, amnesty shall be granted in respect of acts, omissions and offences associated with political objectives and committed in the course of the conflicts of the past ...*[11]

As a typical American, oblivious to the detailed histories of other people, my mouth dropped upon first reading these sentences. *Amnesty?* No fucking way. I couldn't wrap my head around it.

How could a nation of tortured souls so easily have turned away from justice? How could truth replace justice? The thought of affording Mohammad such an opportunity, some metaphorical amnesty in return for testimony, for the truth, for an answer to the question – Why did you do it? – elicited nothing but a shudder, a shake of the head. There was no fucking way. Never.

I was not alone in feeling uneasy about such a trade: truth for absolution. Antjie Krog, the noted South African poet who, as a radio journalist, covered South Africa's reconciliation process, struggled with the very idea in her memoir *Country of My Skull.* How could truth replace justice? Through the creation of the Truth and Reconciliation Commission (TRC), chaired by Archbishop Desmond Tutu, the post-apartheid government was charged with carrying out an exhaustive "truth recovery process"[12] through public hearings that "would give victims an opportunity to tell the world their stories of pain, suffering and loss … and would question victimizers about how and why they had caused that pain, suffering and loss."[13] In that order. First the victims. For months telling stories impossible to believe. One after the other. And then the perpetrators. Explaining what had happened. Why it had happened. How.

Before the TRC commenced, Krog – anxious about the stories waiting to be unleashed by the scheduled testimonies, by victims sitting at tables with microphones and television crews and cameras rolling for month after month – struggled to wrap her head around the idea of it all. Around truth as an elixir. Truth as an equalizer. As a replacement for justice.

Initially, she was coaxed to openness by the Chilean philosopher José Zalaquett, whom she heard say, "It will sometimes be necessary to choose between truth and justice. We should choose truth … Truth does not bring back the dead, but releases them from silence."[14]

But soon the silence ended. The victims of South African apartheid approached the microphones, wanting to be heard, finally. Wanting first to dilute their traumas by having their stories recorded, acknowledged, validated. Wanting next to ask questions, know facts, know what had happened to the father who had been necklaced – ringed by stacked tires and burned – or to the child found hung from a eucalyptus tree, or the mother raped in her dead son's bed and then sunk to the bottom of a lake, stones tied around her crushed skull. They wanted to understand how, when, where, to know from those who knew best. And they wanted closure. Needed the perpetrators to end what they had begun. Needed them to lean into the microphone and say, "I'm sorry." To reclaim their humanity – their humanness – by forcing the murderers to reclaim their own, even if such reclamation efforts were contained only in the words spoken, words without intention. "I'm sorry." Words mattered. Articulation mattered. After years of silence, years of darkness, words were lights, illuminative.

Week after week, as the victims revealed their traumas and then sought the truth underlying these brutal experiences, Krog grew viscerally uncomfortable with the word – truth – a discomfort that manifested itself as a stutter, a significant stumbling block for a radio journalist:

"Your voice tightens up when you approach the word 'truth'," the technical assistant says, irritated. "Repeat it twenty times so that you become familiar with it. *Truth is mos jou job!*" ("Truth is your job, after all!")[15]

The victims' demands for truth I understood, the need to digest what happened as a reclamation effort – this I got. But I also understood Krog's hesitation, her uncertainty. Her stutter. Perhaps because I couldn't yet comprehend the victims' desire for a personal apology from the perpetrator. For what? Particularly when no immediate interest in forgiving existed on the side of the victims.

Was it a matter of control, reversing the roles? A form of revenge? *You destroyed me and my family, so now I'm going to do the only thing I can: put you on your knees. So go ahead. Ask, asshole. Ask for forgiveness. I'll determine if it's accepted. It's up to me now. I'm in control.*

Yet none of the South African victims spoke of this – of taking control – as a motivation, at least none in the testimony I found. Instead, they spoke of reconciliation, as though it was the natural by-product, or *the* product, of truth. Truth *and* Reconciliation. Truth coming first. Then the joining, the conjoining.

Reconciliation. The word began to breathe, began to represent something alive within the pulse of my daily research, a research I kept secret from Jamie. I started taking notes, wondering if the word was possible, if the truth which preceded the word was possible.

Still unsure of my own motivations, of the reason for my desire to convene a personal TRC with Mohammad, I knew one thing: this was larger than me.

15

Antjie Krog underwent a remarkable psychological transformation while covering the commission's events. In the beginning, she was the objective reporter, a disconnected professional, attending the commission's first hearings as nameless victims limped forward to tell how they had watched nameless men chop a brother's arms off, split their sister in two, asking now to simply be told where the bones were, to know where a body rested. Krog, the objective observer, dutifully wrote everything in a pad. But it didn't take long before it became impossible for her to remain distant, disaffected, for the stories were so shocking, so brutal, that she began to exhibit symptoms of Post Traumatic Stress Disorder. The truth made her crack. The truth made her a victim, another victim wanting her story to be heard, craving an audience willing to listen to the truth as she knew it. A truth called memoir – an internal truth and reconciliation process.

As I read *Country of My Skull*, I nodded, recognizing her disintegration on the page. I nodded when a psychologist told Krog, "The more you empathize with the victim, the more you become the victim: you display the same kinds of symptoms – helplessness, wordlessness, anxiety, desperation." And I thought, *Yes*, patting myself on the shoulder, thinking, *It's okay to feel as though you're a victim, even though you were eating pesto-coated pasta in the sunshine when Jamie's body was ripped open. It's fine that you have been compelled to chronicle these experiences, these stories. It's fine that you now seek to understand what happened, that you now seek the truth, that you desire some type of reconciliation. This is what happens. This is what can happen. This is happening.*

In the years after the bombing, attempting to resume a violence-free life in Washington, D.C., I had dismissed my growing psychological distress partially because I refused to acknowledge a personal claim to any form of victimhood. *Jamie was the one blown up*, I'd say. *She's the victim*, I'd say. *You have no reason to be such a fucking mess*, I'd say.

It wasn't until after reading Krog, after seeing someone unconnected by blood or relation crumble upon being exposed to the mere telling of a trauma, that I understood how far things could go. She gave me permission to be released from the illusion that I stood, definitionally, outside the word victim. I gave myself permission to release myself from myself, to let go of the collar and dust off the shoulders.

Me: I'm sorry about that. Didn't mean to press you so hard against the wall.
Me: It's okay. You kept me there a long time, you know.
Me: Sorry. Just had no idea you are a victim, too.
Me: Me either. Can I go now?
Me: Yeah, you can go.

I put down Krog's memoir and went to the library's databases housing psychology journals with names like *Traumatology*, *Journal of Trauma & Dissociation*, *Journal of Traumatic Stress* – in search of a name, a diagnosis, something to which I could point and say, *See, there it is. There's scientific proof. A name to your plight.*

Jamie could hang a hat on Post Traumatic Stress Disorder (PTSD) when things got tough, or at least could point to some of its chronicled symptoms, one of which is "restricted range of affect" – the inability to feel. Clinically, I knew I qualified for that one. I certainly wasn't feeling anything. But the diagnostic criteria for PTSD listed in the *Diagnostic and Statistical Manual of Mental Disorders*, Fourth Edition, Text Revision (DSM-IV-TR) were meant for a "primary" victim, someone who "experienced, witnessed, or was confronted with an event or events that involved actual or threatened death or serious injury, or a threat to the physical integrity of self or others."[16]

Jamie was the primary victim, not me. I was nothing.

Then I discovered an article entitled "Understanding the Secondary Traumatic Stress of Spouses" by Kathleen Gilbert. In it Dr. Gilbert of Indiana University's School of Public Health noted that a spouse often exhibits psychological symptoms mirroring those of the primary victim, so much so that a unique syndrome – secondary traumatic stress disorder (STSD) – had been identified and defined as "a syndrome of symptoms nearly identical to PTSD." She shared a striking case of STSD from a qualitative study done in 1988 on the female partners of Vietnam veterans, all of whom had been at home in the United States during the war. In interviews, the women claimed they were so affected by their husbands' stories of trauma that they often had panic attacks "set off by triggers similar to their husbands', such as 'the sound of helicopters, sudden noises, gunfire, [and] the smell and sound of spring rain.'"[17]

I imagined a housewife looking up from her shopping cart in the local Safeway parking lot and, seeing a traffic helicopter hovering overhead, being so overcome by the spinning blades that she dives under the nearest car, arms shielding a baby and a bag of groceries. And the thought gave me a strange sense of joy.

Not for the astonishing psychological suffering of this woman, her apples rolling on the asphalt, but because such a reality said to me, "If this can happen, then you too are allowed to be damaged."

And I thought, *Are such staggering psychological imprints temporary, or will they forever be branded into the psyche? Will this woman duck into the nearest building every time a helicopter hovers overhead for the rest of her life?* I wasn't so much concerned with this hypothetical homemaker, but the way in which she metaphorically represented my own suffering. And I thought, *Can I go back to the person I was before the terrorist attack, or have I forever lost that identity? Is it possible to "move beyond" or "overcome" a trauma? Or is such an idea mythical, a misleading cliché we repeat in order to survive?*

And I thought of South Africa, of the perpetrators seated before microphones, surrounded by rows of victims in the packed courtroom, and began to imagine what this would look like, Mohammad seated before me as I listened to the story of how he had become a butcher. I began to believe that true healing might only be achieved – if at all – through some type of reconciliation. I began to believe in the possibility of such an intuitively obscene construction actually doing something remarkable, something magical, as EMDR had for Jamie. And as I began to believe, with South Africa pressing me forward, the scores of victims – throwing justice aside for understanding – pressing me forward, an email arrived from Israel, an email for which I'd been waiting over five months, since I had first faxed off my request to meet with Mohammad:

Dear Mr. Gershon,

I deeply apologize for the delay.

Unfortunately, your request to visit Mohammad Odeh hasn't been approved by the Prison Services.

> *The reason is that the prisoner refused to give his consent, which is vital in order to approve the meeting.*
>
> *Respectfully,*
>
> *Ruti Koren*
>
> *Bureau Manager*
>
> *Ministry of Public Security*

Sitting in the UNCW library, surrounded by students, I read the screen with disbelief. Then, half-forgetting my coordinates, I muttered, "Fuck you, you fucking fuck. You fucking asshole," shaking my head involuntarily, quickly, the words coming out automatically, "No, no way, you can't do this, you prick." People started looking my way. The woman at the computer next to me pivoted and stared.

I rose and left and pounded my steps into the sidewalk as my mind absently fired rounds into the air. *You blow up my wife and then refuse to meet me? How can you still have control? You can't still have control. You can't refuse. You fucking have to be a part of this. I've traveled so far, worked so goddamn hard for this after what you did. Fuck you. You can't do this. I won't let you do this.*

The anger was forceful, knocking me off balance as I walked past giddy students, my first moment of authentic emotionality since the bombing coming unexpectedly in public.

Me: Fuck him.
Me: Hey, you're angry. Something within has changed.
Me: Shit – you're right.
Me: Nice going.

Taken aback by the taste of my venom, I lapped the campus, a do-it-yourself dose of bi-lateral stimulation, a bit of self-therapy, EMDR on the cheap. As my anger dissipated, I thought about

South Africa, about a nation committed to the process of healing, about how being immersed in history – in stories of reconciliation – had somehow reoriented everything, had become my only conceivable way forward. And I thought about my anger at the prospect of being denied a meeting with my perpetrator, the potential for which I'd only realized after reading other victims' testimony. But the anger ran deeper than that.

This anger was something I had sought for so long, an anger I had anticipated would accompany a desire for revenge, a desire for vengeance, for the chance to exact my will upon Mohammad as he had exacted his will on Jamie as she enjoyed a peaceful lunch with Ben and Marla in the Frank Sinatra Cafeteria that summer's day. But as I circled the UNCW campus, my anger transitioning to dull despair, I began to consider what had so suddenly triggered this emotional response after all these years of near-paralysis, after all these years of complete synaptic frigidity with regard to the bombing. What had made me so angry?

Me: It's South Africa. All your reading about the TRC, the hearings, the victims learning what happened directly from the perpetrators – the victims finding solace in the details and in the expressions of remorse from those perpetrators who gave them.

Me: But how did this make you so angry?

Me: Because you want it. It's evidence that you believe in it – in the restorative power of directly learning from Mohammad why he did it and why he's sorry for it. Or at least why he expressed remorse when, in all likelihood, none actually exists. If he even said such a thing.

Me: So you feel robbed?

Me: I think so.

Me: Isn't that naive?

Me: What?

Me: That you're giving such restorative weight to a hypothetical meeting with Mohammad?

Me: It's just hope. I believe in it because I hope it could be powerful. Have heard it worked with others. And you're forgetting something.

Me: What's that?

Me: The impulse to confront Mohammad came before reading about South Africa. The impulse was already there. It was there as soon as you read the word "sorry" in that AP article. South Africa simply put the impulse in context.

Me: And now you're angry because –

Me: Because he refused.

Me: Could it be that you're angry because his refusal shows he's not really sorry?

Me: That's possible. I mean, how could he be sorry and refuse to speak with you? I think it's both – if he's not remorseful, then there's no opening to speak with him and understand how all this happened. And I want him to be sorry. I want him to be remorseful. And then I want him to speak.

Me: You want control.

Me: I deserve it.

Me: So now what?

Me: I'm not sure.

When I got home that afternoon, Billy Jonas was turned up on the living room stereo, Noa shaking her little tochus to the song "Watermelon" –

Green on the outside, it's pink on the in,
Your tummy's gonna ache if you eat that skin.
You better spit the seeds out, sisters and brothers
'They're coming' out one end or the other![18]

Jamie was smiling and shaking Tamar on her hip to the folksy beats, Tamar letting out a giggle each time Jamie swayed.

"Hey," I said, closing the front door behind me.

"Hi."

Noa turned around and yelled, "Abba," running toward me, arms spread. She was a bird. She was soaring. They were soaring – Jamie and our two young girls – spreading their wings to the music, gliding across the hardwood floor. I dropped my bag and momentarily joined in, grabbed Noa's hands and twirled as the girls laughed, Tamar flapping to the beats, a syncopated response to falling from the nest. We'd begun falling from the nest, a tangled mass of spit, straw, and synaptic debris. It was above us somewhere. I could see it, knew it was there, knew I'd soon be returning to it, would be leaving them behind and flap up toward it when the music ended as I grasped Noa's hands, lifted her three-year-old body off the floor and spun it, her legs submitting to the centrifugal force, body straight, arms taught, the curve of her smile leaning into the circles we were tracing, rising, rising –

After dinner and putting the kids to bed, I slumped into a green sofa-chair. Jamie looked at me with the eyes of a raptor.

"What's wrong?"

"Nothing."

"You sure?"

"Yeah, just tired."

I sat down with Krog's book, from which I'd removed the dust jacket in order to keep my reading somewhat discreet. Jamie knew I was doing research. She knew I was preparing for something related to my writing. But she recognized this as my process, whatever it was, and was content to leave me to my own devices, motivated, in part, by her own desire to leave the attack in the past, where it belonged.

Opening Krog's book, I started to skim, my eyes eventually resting on a passage near the conclusion of the victims' public testimony:

> *We prick up our ears. Waiting for the Other. The Counter. The Perpetrator. More and more, we want the second narrative ... There can be no story without the balance of the antagonist. The ear and the heart simply cannot hold their heads above a one-way flood.*[19]

Jamie was sitting opposite me on our juice-splotched couch, reading Sarah Vowell and smiling to herself. *There can be no story without the balance of the antagonist*, I thought, and though Krog was speaking of something different – of the time in South Africa when everyone felt the weight of anticipation, listening to victim after victim chronicle their traumas, waiting anxiously for the perpetrators to show themselves – her words shook loose another thought: *What if Mohammad didn't really refuse the meeting?* After all, I didn't have his story, the story of the antagonist. All I had was a vague "I'm so sorry things didn't work out" from Israel's Ministry of Public Security. *Of course they don't want me meeting him. Why would they allow access to some writer looking to see if a terrorist had expressed remorse for his crime? Why would they approve such a meeting?*

I began to suspect that the Israeli government might not have given my request any consideration, that Ruti Koren, Bureau Manager, Ministry of Public Security, might have used Mohammad's refusal as easy cover. My suspicion was based on nothing more than an intuitive hunch. And I thought, *How do I even know if they asked Odeh? They probably didn't even approach him about it. Why would they?*

Rising from the chair, I went to the kitchen and grabbed a bag of organic Colombian coffee beans, the image of a rooster, our local independent coffee house's logo, stuck on the front. I felt like crowing. After putting on a pot of coffee, I brainstormed ways to verify that Mohammad had in fact refused my request to meet, knowing no satisfactory gestures would be forthcoming from the Israeli government. Hearing the pot's gurgling, Jamie came in and said, "You're not making coffee."

"I know it's late, but I kind of need it." We had a standing rule: I was allowed to drink as much coffee as desired, so long as it was consumed before three in the afternoon, on account of my insomniac tendencies. It was a rule I had approved after protracted negotiations, the original time offered having been noon.

"David, it's almost ten o'clock. Please don't."

"I'm going to be up tonight doing some research. I'll be fine."

"You have to do this tonight? You can't wait until tomorrow?"

"No. I'm thinking about something and want to dig into it a little bit, and I'm not going to be able to sleep anyway."

"Fine, as long as you can get up with the kids in the morning."

"I will."

"Seriously."

"I'll be fine."

"And be in a good mood?"

"I'll be fine."

"Okay," she said, willing to drop it, the conversation now ammunition to be used in the morning were I to remain buried under a foxhole of blankets when the alarm chimed or our kids awoke and started jumping on the bed, the latter more likely than the former.

Armed with a cup of coffee, I returned to the living room and opened up my laptop. *How do I do this? Who might be able to get an audience with Mohammad? Or his family?* And again the answer came, an answer that had been quietly planted in my synapses while reading about South Africa: peace activists. Israeli and Palestinian professionals and grassroots activists who were already dedicated to the cause of reconciliation. Those already on the ground, already enmeshed in the difficult task of creating dialogue among Palestinians and Israelis, would not only be capable of helping, but they would be passionate about doing so. I knew they would – knew at the very least they would show more interest, more responsiveness, than the bureaucratic channels in Israel among whom I had drifted for six months before being told that Mohammad had waved off a meeting.

From the beginning, attempting to procure an audience with Mohammad – the process itself – proved to be nothing short of maddening. My frustration with the Israeli government bubbled over immediately when first dealing with the Israeli Embassy in Washington, D.C. Under the illusion that good fortune had landed at my feet, I attempted to contact Israel's Ambassador to the United States, whose daughter I had taught at JDS for over a year and whose wife I had met countless times for parent–teacher conferences; his wife even knew me by name. She liked me, or, perhaps more accurately, she had bestowed upon me kind smiles indicating that I was not hated. I convinced myself that this would make the process easy: I had exactly the type of high-level connection that one dreams of having in such situations. Israel's top diplomat owed me a favor. And though I knew the difficulty of the request, knew that it was bold to expect gaining an audience with one of Israel's most renowned terrorists, who was held in a maximum security prison, I thought, *You've got this. Just call the embassy, explain who you are, get a phone number, and call the Ayalon family.*

But expectations and reality failed to converge. The embassy rightly refused to provide contact information. *We will forward on to the Ambassador anything you'd like to provide us.* So I sent personal emails to an embassy secretary who acted as my middleman, waiting for responses from her which only came after I pestered, annoyed, refused to go away. And the answer, when it did come, was always the same: no response from the Ambassador or his wife. After three months of being ignored by the parents of a child I taught for a year, I gave up.

I decided to bypass the embassy and manufacture my own high-level contact, gaining press credentials from David Horowitz at the *Jerusalem Post* and flashing them at Israeli officials, sending faxes to the Israel Prison Service and emails to the Israeli Ministry of Public Security with my credentials plastered boldly at the top. Repeatedly. I sent the same email daily to everyone who worked in the ministry for a solid month until finally receiving confirmation that my request had been received (over thirty times, actually). It took a similar barrage of insistent emails, of emailing the same email every day – Could you please update the status of my request to meet with Mohammad Odeh? – until eventually, six months after I'd started, I learned Mohammad had shaken his head. *Thanks, but no thanks.*

It was the response that had released my anger, a response I was beginning to realize might never have been given.

I sat down with my cup of coffee, propped up the computer, and went to work, searching online for organizations and individuals to contact about my situation. Peace Now. *B'tselem*. The Palestinian Center for Human Rights.

Clicking through the web pages, I realized that there was a time, not long before, when I would have viewed such organizations as anti-Israel, as anti-Semitic, a time when I would have looked upon reports critical of Israel coming out of such organizations – reports on, say, Israel's settlement policy or the economic distress of the Palestinians in Gaza – as nothing more than products of a terrorist sympathizer. I did not think of Palestinians as human – they taught children to champion martyrdom and spilled blood joyfully, dutifully, in the streets of Israel. All of them. I had written every one of them off. Fear and propaganda had urged me to write them off. An entire people. This despite my progressive sensibilities, the same sensibilities that triggered an automatic bristling anytime broad-stroked stereotypes in America were brushed over entire peoples. In America, I was enlightened, but in Israel, I was at war. Us against them. Us against a brutal people. An evil people. A people not worth considering, much less expressing concern over. They were murderers, and anyone interested in standing up for their rights or plights was a traitor and saboteur. For me, it was a zero-sum game. Either we won, or they did.

And so the irony: being personally affected by the inhumane brutality of Palestinian terror – of this murderous element woven into the outer fringes of their social fabric by ideological extremists – forced me to consider Palestinians' humanity. I read Peace Now's website, from an analysis of Israel's segregating barrier wall to a chronicle of ongoing dialogue initiatives, and grew aware of just how far my moral and political pendulums had swung. As I sought the assistance of these peace activists, I began to sympathize with their mission: working for the human rights of both Palestinians and Israelis. Things were not black and white, as I had been led to believe. It was not good versus evil. There were shades of brutality and benevolence on both sides.

Unlike the Israeli authorities, who sat on their hands for months as I sent futile inquiry after futile inquiry, requesting updates on the status of my request before I learned that Mohammad had refused, the response from peace activists was overwhelming and immediate. Twenty-four hours after I had sent emails to a few hand-picked individuals from a handful of the organizations I had found online, my inbox was filled with messages from people wanting to help, from those wanting to put me in touch with others whom they thought could help. They considered my mission theirs, so much so that my note was reposted on listservs, bulletin boards, blogs, co-opted by people who wanted this as much as I did.

Then I received a message from Leah Green at an organization called The Compassionate Listening Project. I had never heard of it. The name sounded painfully hopeful, painfully touchy-feely. She suggesting that she could help, then wrote, "I think we should talk by phone."

I had nothing to lose.

Before calling, I searched for the organization's website and was instantly impressed. Leah had founded an organization with a full résumé of reconciliation initiatives around the world, produced three documentaries about the Israeli–Palestinian conflict, and led delegations in Israel, Syria, Jordan, and Lebanon. I picked up the phone and dialed.

"This is Leah."

"Hi Leah, this is David. You emailed me – "

"David. Hi. I'm glad you called. How are you?"

"I'm good, thanks. I'm just curious. Can I ask how you found me?"

"I saw your request reposted on a human rights blog, and I think it's great what you're doing – very brave. I would like to help if I can."

"I appreciate your offer. I don't know exactly what, but anything you could do would be great, really. I'm just looking for advice or some direction on what I should do, because I'm a little lost at this point."

"You're looking for a path to somehow meet with the perpetrator, and have not been successful going through Israeli authorities, correct?"

"Yes."

Leah and I talked for a bit about the governmental structure in Israel, about those departments which were likely to be of little help. Then we talked about the professional contacts she had established over decades working in the region, contacts she seemed more than willing to use on my behalf.

"Listen. This is what I think you want to do. You want to make direct contact with the family of the perpetrator – Mohammad, right?"

"Yeah. The family name is Odeh."

"My advice is to make contact with the Odeh family and let them know who you are and what you're trying to do. If they're receptive, my guess is that they would be able to ask Mohammad directly if he would permit you to meet him in prison. I'm sure they have minimal visitation privileges. They would have the capacity to present Mohammad with your wishes and learn how he feels about you meeting with him."

"Wow. Okay. That's interesting advice, though I'm not exactly sure how to go about doing that. I don't speak Arabic or anything, and I have no idea how to navigate contacting a random Palestinian family."

"I believe you wrote that the family lives in the Silwan neighborhood in East Jerusalem?

"As far as I know – just what I read in a few newspaper articles."

"Well, I happen to have an extremely good contact in Silwan with whom I've worked before, a Palestinian official well-known and respected in the community. And I'm planning on traveling to Israel next month for something else. If you want, I could contact him and perhaps try to see if he knows the family. Maybe he would be able to arrange a visit with them for me. If so, I would be willing to go on your behalf."

"Seriously?"

"Of course. I'd be honored to help. What you're doing is important and brave."

"I don't know about that."

"It is."

"Well, thanks for your kind words and generous offer. I'm not sure what to say. I'm a little shocked right now that you'd be willing to do all of this for me. You don't even know me."

"This is my job, and it's a gift what you're trying to do. I think that – the best thing I think would be for you to write a letter to the family, something that tells them who you are and why it is exactly that you want to meet with Mohammad. Something that will give my Palestinian colleague an idea of what he's presenting to the Odeh family, and something that I could also read to them in person, should I have the opportunity to visit them."

"What should I write?"

"Just something that tells them who you are and why you're doing what you're doing. Direct it to them."

"Could I email you something so you could look it over and see if it's in line with what you're thinking of?"

"Sure, that sounds fine."

"Great. I'll write something tonight and send it to you."

"Sounds good. I will contact my colleague in Silwan and let you know when I hear back."

"Thanks so much."

"You're welcome, David. Good luck."

16

Me: What does a letter to the family of the man who tried to murder your wife look like?

Me: Sorry, what was that?

Me: I know, it sounds a bit crazy.

Me: Just a bit.

Me: No advice?

Me: Not exactly my area of expertise.

Me: Why are you always such a smartass?

Me: Don't start.

Me: Fine. I'm going to write.

Me: Good luck.

Aware that I needed to shed the sarcastic vestments tied around my waist, I sat down at our dining room table with my laptop and afforded myself the blank space in which to write from the heart, or at least from a heart I hoped existed, or could exist, a space which was difficult to locate. I began to type:

> *Dear Odeh Family,*
>
> *My name is David. On July 31, 2002, my wife was injured in the bombing at Hebrew University that your son, Mohammad, perpetrated –*

Jamie walked in. "Whatcha doing?"

"Nothing."

"Writing?"

"Yeah."

"What?"

"Nothing important."

She stopped and stared. "Then why did you have that look?"

"What look?"

"That look you have when you're focused or determined. You look like whatever it is you're doing over there, it's taking great effort."

"Are you trying to give me a hard time?"

"No."

"It's nothing."

"You don't have to tell me," she said.

"You don't want to know."

"Probably right."

It was the truth – Jamie really didn't want to know. If she'd asked at that point about the books I'd been reading, books about South Africa and the theoretical concept of reconciliation, I would have told her. I would have revealed my embryonic thoughts, thoughts of engaging in some type of reconciliation effort. But this? Writing to the family of the man who had caused her so much suffering? So much pain? I couldn't do it. At least, not yet.

Jamie opened a bag of Ghirardelli dark chocolate chips, signaling that she was taking a sensual escape from something. "What are *you* up to?" I asked, shifting our focus.

"Recovering."

"From what?"

"From Tamar – she was a little challenging today."

"Sorry."

"It's okay. How were classes?"

"Fine. My students don't talk. Literally. I think they're brain-dead."

"Just blame it on the beach."

"The beach?"

"All that salt corroding their brains."

"More likely the weed."

With that, she returned to the living room. I returned to my letter to the Odeh family. Deciding not to hold back, I suppressed all of my usual ironic impulses and wrote without pause:

> *I am writing to you now with a pure heart and a desire for understanding, a desire for reconciliation, a desire for peace. I have no interest in revenge, no interest in harboring feelings of anger, no interest in blame. Instead, I am only interested in listening, in giving Mohammad a chance to speak, to hear his story so that I may understand fully my own as I attempt to move beyond what happened ...*
>
> *I requested a meeting with Mohammad through the Israeli Prison Service, but he recently refused to meet with me. At least, this is what Israeli authorities told me. However, I cannot be sure that Mohammad truly does not want to meet unless I'm able to know from his own words.*
>
> *If you can find it in your heart, I ask that you speak with Mohammad and let him know why I would like to speak with him. And if you find my motivations pure, I humbly ask that you encourage him to agree to speak with me.*

After reviewing the letter, Leah wrote to say it was spot-on, and that she was in the process of contacting her associates in Silwan to lay the groundwork for a potential meeting with the Odeh family. Then, as an aside, she emailed me a link prefaced only with the following: "You might want to email her to find out more about her story … how it turned out." No other context. I didn't recognize the url – www.justvision.org – nor did I have any clue as to whom Leah was referring. I dutifully clicked on the link and found myself staring at the profile of someone named Robi Damelin. Confused, I read.

She was an Israeli. Had lost her son, a young Israeli soldier, to a Palestinian sniper. And now she was working toward some type of reconciliation, working toward meeting the perpetrator, toward speaking with the enemy.

And I thought, *Someone else is doing this in Israel. I'm not the only one.*

The profile page indicated that Robi had been featured in a recently released, award-winning documentary called *Encounter Point.* I pressed earphones into my ears, clicked on the movie and a trailer popped up, waiting to be viewed. I pressed play. The screen opened onto visions of hysterical crowds, people running in slow motion, the sounds of Israeli ambulances, Middle Eastern strings echoing in the background. The screen opened wider, swallowing the periphery with flashing images: a Palestinian man in his twenties showing a missile-induced scar running down his cheek; an Israeli man in his forties snorting absently after recounting the moment he learned of his daughter's death from a suicide bombing in Tel Aviv; a clip of Robi being interviewed on a prominent Israeli political talk show, the interviewer looking confused, asking, "I really want to understand this – you don't have anger toward the sniper?"

Then, for the first time, Robi's voice became audible, her South African accent echoing in the miniature speakers as images of the

Old City in Jerusalem scrolled across the screen. Stone in the foreground. A voice in the background, echoing against the stone, speaking of confronting the enemy, of channeling the will to do what most would never consider.

I listened to Robi address herself as she unknowingly addressed me: "So what do you do with this pain? Do you take it and look for revenge and keep the whole cycle of violence going, or do you choose another path?" Her voice was followed by more images of Israelis and Palestinians, all bereaved, all victimized by horrific losses, shaking hands, hugging, speaking with one another, trying to understand each other.

The screen flashed a text interrupted by barbed wire:

The most important story in the Middle East

is not being told on the nightly news.

When it went blank – when the trailer's music faded, leaving me staring into the pixels – I digested what I'd seen, feeling the weight of what I had decided to begin, what I was joining. This wasn't a game. This wasn't simply about personal healing. This was about the history of a region, a conflict, a struggle, into which my personal mission for recovery fit. Without warning, I felt alone, isolated. *Why hadn't I told Jamie about my letter to the Odehs?* I thought, understanding that my impulse to tell her was a selfish one, a desire to have the weight of this realization shared and shouldered by someone else. What I really needed was the company of the people I had just witnessed on the screen; I needed to converse with them and smoke with them and understand them in order to understand myself. *I need to see this film*, I thought. The website said the documentary was still being shown at film festivals around the world, but it wasn't yet available for purchase, and it had not yet been released. I reviewed the list of upcoming screenings. The only showing anywhere remotely close to us was at the Harrisburg Jewish Film Festival.

Harrisburg is where Ben was from, I thought, knowing his family, the Blutsteins, still lived there. The coincidence felt meaningful – an implicit message from an implicit force informing me that this trip needed to be made. *Leah's traveling to Silwan. So I'll travel to Pennsylvania. It only seems fair*, I thought, shrugging, a shrug that pulled me by the scruff and dropped me a week later five hundred miles away in the lobby of Harrisburg's Midtown Cinema, a small room filled with multi-colored plastic chairs and a barista serving up Green Mountain Coffee and entrance tickets.

Momentum was hurtling me forward quickly. It was disorienting. Never before had I been given over to such spontaneity. Such irrational abandon. From Wilmington to Harrisburg. For a movie.

Jamie was at home with our children and knew why I had traveled so far. She understood what the movie was about, and understood that I was beginning to consider a trip to Israel which would take me much farther. While she hadn't asked for details, she also hadn't objected.

"The movie's in Harrisburg?" she'd asked.

"Yes."

"And you need to see it?"

"Yes."

"Because you're considering doing something similar?"

I paused before answering, "Yes."

She didn't want to know anything more. It was enough. By the time I'd traveled to Harrisburg, she finally knew about my conversations with peace activists and visions of going back to Israel. She did not yet know, however, about the letter to the Odeh family, about how far I was going, how far I'd already gone.

As I waited for *Encounter Point* – the only movie in Harrisburg's Jewish Film Festival that I intended to see – I became skeptical about the wisdom of my journey. Something was off internally, something somewhere had misfired, leading me inexplicably to a room where a smattering of retired Rust-Belt Jews were schmoozing about grandchildren and Israel, waiting for the screening to begin.

Me: How did I get here?

Me: You're trying to do something that is unspeakably crazy – better get used to finding yourself in situations that don't make sense. This won't be the last.

Me: But I don't even know how to explain this. Driving from North Carolina to Pennsylvania for a movie is not something I would do. Ever.

Me: Of course not. But you're not you anymore. You're someone else, someone trying to visit the terrorist who attempted to murder your wife, and you've driven a distance you wouldn't normally consider because the film is about a similar subject, and you felt compelled to drive and see the film rather than wait six months for it to be released on DVD, would rather drive up the East Coast for an hour-long documentary about an Israeli woman who lost her son to a Palestinian sniper, lost him and responded by trying to reconcile with the sniper's family, would rather drive than wait. Because you're tired of waiting. And because you need to see how it's done before you leave to do the same.

Me: I drove through North Carolina, Virginia, and Maryland.

Me: You want to travel farther.

Me: I know.

I wanted someone to approach me and ask who I was. What I was doing. Why I was there. And I wanted to tell him, to tell everyone – these people who undoubtedly knew the Blutsteins, knew their story, the tragedy having been local – how I was connected, why I was sitting in this theater waiting for this film to begin. I now understood that it was my training for a journey to Israel I'd been planning, intent on confronting whatever there was to be confronted, without fully realizing it. The desire to be known felt liberating – being identified by those who would have responded with an *Oy vey*. They'd know about Hebrew University. They'd remember. They'd press my hand, touch my cheek, say, *Ayzah mizkein* – poor one.

But I remained anonymous, watching the hall empty as the double doors to the theater swung open, the barista taking tickets as the abandoned cappuccino machine gurgled to a belated stop.

17

Before traveling to Harrisburg, I had contacted the Blutsteins by email, wondering if they wanted to see me – wanted to see the side that survived, the side saved by chance. Ben's father immediately emailed back, inviting me to dinner, which made me nervous, a survivor's-guilt-induced anxiety. I was unsure whether it was a genuine offer or one motivated by some obligatory sense of courtesy.

After viewing the film, I became nervous for another reason, for it had concretized my path going forward. The images of mourning Palestinians and Israelis, reaching for each other out of desperation, out of exasperation, made solid the significance of the steps I had decided to travel. I was going to try being a reconciler – not a forgiver, a reconciler – and I knew I needed to reveal this to the Blutsteins. A scene flashed in my mind from the film I'd just seen of a Palestinian man, once imprisoned for a role in the Intifada, who was shunned by his community after engaging with peace activists upon his release. "Some people got to the point of only saying hi to me."[20]

Then I thought of Susan Sarandon, playing Sister Helen Prejean in *Dead Man Walking*, being tossed angrily from the home of a family bereaved of their daughter after learning Prejean had been counseling the killer on death row. "You brought the enemy into this house, Sister. You gotta go." And I wondered if I too would be tossed from the Blutstein home, afraid to call and confirm dinner for that evening, despite the family's insistence that they wanted to see me. But they didn't know about my attempts to attain a meeting with Mohammad, and I was unsure if they even knew his name, afraid of even mentioning it, of recalling images they undoubtedly had worked to blur over the years. And my thoughts of reconciliation? How could I possibly tell them about my desire to understand the enemy, to dialogue with the enemy? I imagined them responding, heard their internal thoughts, heard them say, *Sure, it's easy for you. You didn't lose anyone. Your child, your oldest child, wasn't murdered. You still have everything. Everyone. And to come into our home and evoke not only memories, but the idea of reconciliation with that monster – you shouldn't have come. You should go. Now.*

Finally, an hour before driving to their house, I called, hoping nobody would answer the phone. Someone picked up.

"Hello?"

"Katherine? Hi. It's David Harris-Gershon."

"Hi. It's Rivka."

Rivka, Ben's younger sister. The one who, when visiting Ben in Israel months before his death, never left her brother's side. Never stopped smiling. It was startling – I had never seen two siblings more in love. It was something Jamie and I talked about constantly during their visit, particularly this effusion of warmth emanating from Ben, someone I had previously viewed as sarcastic, prickly. Around Rivka, he was a puppy unrestrained. Jumping. Tickling. Laughing. So when she said her name, I froze on the line, unable to collect anything other than a memory of her burying a laugh in Ben's shoulder.

"Rivka," I said, a statement, not a greeting. "Um – I was just wondering if I was still meant to come over."

"Of course. We're looking forward to it. Five o'clock. You know how to get here, right?" Her voice was so kind, so exuberant. So disarming.

When I arrived, we stood around for a couple of minutes, hands in pockets, shuffling feet, before moving to the dinner table, where Richard had placed plates full of salads replete with asparagus, mushrooms, tomatoes, lettuce, and sliced strips of tenderloin. I picked at the abundance as we picked around the conversation until, unable to wait any longer, I said, "I know I emailed that I've been doing some research and a bit of writing about the attack, and I just want you to know that, if you have any questions about it, ever, or if you want to read some of what I've written, I'm willing to share. Not that I'm recommending it, but figured it would be best to let you know about it, and – "

I glanced up, saw their demeanors darkened. I couldn't muster the word "reconciliation," the word "dialogue." What I had said was enough. "And that's all. Just wanted to say it."

They looked at each other, and Katherine said, "How much do you know?" I wasn't sure how to interpret this question, so I didn't answer. She went on. "Because I don't know anything, haven't wanted to know anything about the attack. Just kept myself away from the details, I suppose, and I'm not sure I want to know them."

Fear as opposed to anger. It was a relief. "Well, I do know things."

"Oh," she said, eyes down. I knew she wanted to ask me, *Are you writing about Ben?* It's a question I was anticipating, the question they would have had every right to ask, the question I would have felt bad answering, *No, I'm not. He's mentioned, of course, sometimes at difficult moments. But no, I'm not writing about him.* But the question never came. Instead, recollections of Ben trickled out. Stories. And then Rivka dashed to her room and returned with a series of essays she had written about her brother. She handed them to me. Richard and Katherine added, "We were hoping you could look at them. We'd like to see them published. It would be nice for people to know the story, for them not to be blind to what happened, and anything you could comment upon would be appreciated."

"Of course, I'd love to."

Then Rivka said, "For a couple of years, I wrote imaginary letters to my brother in my journal. I wrote his responses back." She looked at me, smiled, said, "Life of the dead brother's sister" in a sarcastic, light-hearted tone.

I thought, *I want to see them*, saying nothing as I rose to leave, as they showed me oil paintings and charcoal drawings of Ben that Rivka had been working on, rendered from photographs that were resting on the living room floor. Looking at the images, our reflections lightly coloring Ben's face, I turned to Rivka. "You know, the difficult thing about charcoal is that you are never really finished – you can always lighten or darken at will."

I was amazed by their ability to talk openly about their bereavement, by Rivka's ability to display their loss, by her ability to create beauty from it. And looking at her portraits of Ben, the same feeling began to well that I had experienced while viewing *Encounter Point*, watching Israelis and Palestinians, mothers and fathers, trying to build connections across lines that had been severed, trying to plug the cord in somewhere else, somewhere meaningful, somewhere charged. Holding Rivka's essays rolled between my fingers, it seemed wrong to leave, to step out the door and begin the drive back to North Carolina. To shake hands. Say goodbye. Yes, I know how to get to the highway. Thanks. Yes, take a left at the light. Thank you for everything. I'll email Rivka about the essays. Goodbye.

When I drove the 477 miles to Pennsylvania for the opportunity to see Robi Damelin on screen, I was hoping to learn just how she did it – how a Jew prepared for a meeting with a Palestinian terrorist, before I traveled the 6,108 miles across the Atlantic to do it myself.

Me: This is for me. For my sanity.

Me: Even though you don't understand from where this desire for a meeting with the perpetrator is coming?

Me: Yes.

Me: Even though all the research on South Africa, searching for a connection between them and you in order to understand what seems to be a twisted desire – to confront Mohammad – has shed no light on the psychology of this? On why you're driven to do this?

Me: Yes.

Me: So even without understanding, you're going through with it?

Me: Yes.

Me: For you?

Me: Yes.

Me: You're crazy.

Me: Perhaps.

All of it was for me. Thoughts of reconciliation, of confrontation, of traveling across the world to confront the other – all of it was driven in large part by selfishness, by a personal need to somehow move beyond the trauma by going to the source. But after seeing the film – after watching bereaved Palestinians and Israelis struggle through personal pain to further the chance for political resolution, for peace between two warring peoples – something shifted inside me. I walked out of the theater and was no longer able to look upon my efforts through the tiny, solipsistic frame within which they had been housed, a frame ripped open and replaced by a window that looked out upon history. My journey was not just a narrative of personal healing, but a larger, historical narrative of two peoples clawing at each other, of those trying to change this narrative, trying to pare the nails, stop the fighting. A narrative I was entering at the edges. Unwittingly.

Most striking was the film's focus on the Parents Circle – Families Forum, an organization which brought together Israelis and Palestinians who had lost immediate family members in the conflict. It brought them together simply to talk, people torn open by grief who were willing to make themselves vulnerable again, to see the other side and accept a previously unrecognized humanity as a necessary step in reclaiming their lives and their own humanity. In the documentary they wept and hugged and marched arm-in-arm down city streets, and watching that in a dark theater in Harrisburg did something that all my research on South Africa and all my emails with peace activists – with Leah – had failed to do: revealed the context of my journey.

Perhaps the size of the screen had widened my frame of reference, revealing my place on the far margins of a burgeoning peace movement among Israelis and Palestinians that had previously been hidden from me. This was no longer just about me, about my desire to stop yawning intentionally in order to breathe. A meeting with Mohammad would have wider reverberations. I wasn't sure how. But *Encounter Point* resonated so strongly that I began to consider the potential power of what I was doing, thinking, *What if this personal act isn't so personal?*

18

Leah emailed. The Odeh family wanted to learn more. Wanted to learn more about my motivations from Leah, whose trip to the Middle East had been delayed until the summer. She would visit the family in the sweltering desert heat, would sweat in their home – an invitation having been extended – her perspiration evaporating while Jamie and I perspired in the humid hills of southern New England, perpetually drenched.

We had chosen to spend the summer working at a sleep-away camp, a Jewish enclave situated on old farmland in Northwood, New Hampshire, where the kids ran wild. Jamie taught Jewish studies and I wore two hats: athletic director and writer-in-residence. Each morning, I sat before an open window and pecked away at my laptop, occasionally lifting eyes toward the fields, picking up binoculars to check on the boys playing basketball on the blacktop or the girls on the diamond playing softball.

Often, a thought would come: *I am hungry*. Gazing upon swarms of campers buzzing around granola bars and bug juice, unfinished sentences scattered on the desk, the words malnourished, starving, I mouthed this often, a whisper, barely audible. "I am hungry." In any other context, it would have been metaphoric, an expression of some profound longing, some desperation. But at camp, despite the stack of chocolate chip pancakes and two bowls of Raisin Bran I normally downed at breakfast, it was elemental. I wanted to eat constantly. To be fed.

They came quickly at camp, such feelings of hunger, where for hours at a time I forgot entirely about Mohammad, about Leah's impending trip. And the spoken word came just as fast – you said what you meant, plain as day. And often, even saying all that you meant was profligate. "Juice" meant "please pass the pitcher of juice." "Quiet" meant "close your mouths for an important announcement." And "here" signified any number of things: "pass me the ball; give me back my hat; get over here this instant." I warmed quickly to such economy, such simplicity.

Many of my afternoons at camp were sweat-filled festivals. Example: after losing a heated game of dodge ball, then challenging middle-school boys to some pick-up basketball after taking some cuts during a Wiffle ball home-run-derby, I would look around for a group of kids needing inspiration. Often, my gaze would fall on a gathering of young girls, doing cartwheels or chatting in a circle on the soccer pitch. One afternoon, I jumped in front of a goal post, yelling, "You score, you get chocolate." Limbs flapped frantically, a flock in sudden disarray flying into lines, girls poised to fire shots from all angles, penalty kicks reaching the net in rapid succession as they yelled back, "We get chocolate."

One evening, I sat down with my laptop in the administrative building as counselors secretly planned *Maccabiah* – the camp's Jewish version of a color war. Logging in, I found a narrative waiting in my inbox, a story generated by my story, a story which I had temporarily forgotten amidst all the ice cream and games of four square. Leah had traveled to Israel, and her trip was chronicled in several messages strung together, messages which, for days, had been sitting there, waiting to be opened.

After landing in Israel, Leah found the *mukhtar* of Silwan, Fakhree Abu Diab, whose family was related to the Odehs, a particularly large and eminent clan in East Jerusalem. After speaking with Mohammad's mother and reassuring the Odehs that Leah was friend, not foe, Fakhree arranged for a visit. The deal: he would accompany her, acting as a chaperone and sentinel, not for Leah's benefit, but for the family's. His presence served as proof that no revenge was about to be exacted upon them. The next day, as Fakhree sat in the Odehs' living room, preparing them for Leah's visit, explaining in clear terms her role as surrogate for me – for the one whose wife was injured by Mohammad's act – the mother turned pale and unsteady, then quickly turned ill. Fakhree called for a doctor, who instructed the family to rush her to the hospital at Hebrew University. To the place Jamie was rushed, scorched and bleeding, after Mohammad's bomb went off.

When Leah arrived at Fakhree's home with her friend and translator Mariam – a Palestinian teacher – they all sat down to tea. The meeting would be postponed, Fakhree said. The father died twenty years ago, he said. The mother's heart has been broken by the actions of her son, he said.

A day later, the mother had returned home from the hospital. She was ready. The family was ready. And so Fakhree picked up Leah and Mariam and rattled over the bumpy side roads of East Jerusalem to the Odeh home, where Mohammad's mother greeted everyone weakly, cautiously.

Inside were two of Mohammad's brothers, seated, and tucked in the corner, eyes averted, was Mohammad's wife. Everyone was nervous, uncertain what, exactly, to expect from the other. So Leah, with Mariam translating her English into Arabic, sat down softly and began explaining the purpose of her visit. Sunlight streamed through some gauzy, white curtains that led to a stone courtyard, where Mohammad's two children played outside. She glanced at the wall, where there was a poster cataloguing Mohammad's sentence – nine concurrent life sentences, one for every person murdered. Looking back to the family, Leah tried to set them at ease by chronicling her seventeen-year history working with Palestinians, hoping to gain their trust, to pry them open. After she spoke the word – *reconciliation* – the family shifted in their seats, their defensive postures relaxed. Then the stories, the pent-up emotions, poured out. An avalanche.

They spoke of shock. Of disbelief after learning what had happened. Felt as though they themselves had gone through a trauma. Not the same, of course. But a trauma.

They spoke of sadness for the gravity of it all.

They spoke of what-ifs and regret – that they would have stopped Mohammad had they only known. That he was no hero. Not to them.

They spoke of Mohammad as the gentlest of the family. Always the most sensitive. The most vulnerable.

They spoke of rough experiences with the Israeli army, about how, when Mohammad was fourteen, he was first imprisoned. Then again at sixteen, for throwing stones. Something all the kids did out of anger and humiliation.

They spoke of how he was not considered ultra-religious, of how he liked to pray at Al-Aqsa Mosque – it was a ten- to-fifteen-minute walk from their home.

They spoke of how the soldiers would mistreat and humiliate him, sometimes beating him.

They spoke of how he must have reached a point where he just broke under the pressure that his older brothers might have been better able to handle. He must have silently shattered. It's the only explanation.

They spoke of the children. Of how his girl was newly born when he entered prison. About how he's unable to hold her, so they kiss each other through the glass.

And they spoke of his supposed remorse. Of how they see Mohammad twice a month. How he tells them everything. That he's filled with remorse for what he did. And that if he could roll back time and remove his actions, he would.

The family told Leah that they were sure Mohammad never received any requests to meet with a victim of the bombing, and that they were certain he would have agreed to any such meetings. Then they told her, as Mariam tried to keep up with the flow of Arabic pouring out, that Israeli intelligence interviewed Mohammad two weeks prior and asked him if he thought he should be on the list of prisoners to be released in the prisoner exchange for Gilad Shalit.

And what did he say? Leah asked.

He said yes, they said. He said yes.

19

From Leah's emails, I gleaned that the meeting with the Odehs went better than anyone could have anticipated – that the connection was genuine, the family lovely, and the outcome beyond expectations. She reported that the family welcomed me with open arms. Told Leah they wanted me to come. That I should come and meet them. And that they would ask Mohammad, on their next visit, about meeting me. That they would ask him personally and tell Mariam, the translator, Mohammad's answer.

Upon reaching the end of these emails, my head spinning, I closed the computer and walked to the old farmhouse where we stayed. Noa jumped off the porch and ran toward me screaming, "Abba, Abba. You said we could go to the *agam*. Can we go to the *agam* now? Please? You said. You said."

"Yeah, we can go swimming," I said. "Go get your bathing suit on."

"Yipee," she yelped, skipping up the stairs and into our room.

"And do a last potty," I yelled, following.

"But I don't need to."

"She hasn't had anything to drink all day," Jamie said, rocking on the porch.

"Why not?"

"I don't know, she just hasn't."

"We have to make her drink, Jamie. It's hot."

"You make her drink."

"I mean get her something."

"Her bottle is right there," she said, pointing to the railing.

I sighed as Noa ran toward me, jumping. I turned to Jamie. "Hey, don't open my computer."

"You have nothing to worry about."

"I mean, there's Israel trip stuff on there that I need to deal with when I get back, and I know you don't really want to deal with the details and stuff right now."

"Thanks for the warning. I won't look at it."

Though we had not talked about my journey to Jerusalem in any detail, nor intimately discussed my reconciliation plans, Jamie understood the essence of what I was attempting, and had been wholly supportive, being invested in my healing. However, she also did not want the psychological burden of another recovery on her hands. Understandably so.

I picked a towel off the laundry line and walked Noa down a gravel path to Travis Pond, plopping down on the sand as she ran into the shallows, particular phrases churning to the surface. *Considered the gentlest of the family / filled with remorse for what he did / wishes he could roll back time.* None of it made any sense, and I didn't know whom to trust – an enemy welcoming me with open arms or the Israeli government bent on dragging its heels. I wanted to believe the Odeh family, wanted to trust their words, but it seemed too clean, too perfect, having come to expect nothing but obstruction and insincerity. I knew better than to accept as reality that which others projected – that the Israeli government really wanted to help, or that a Hamas murderer wanted to roll back time. And yet my intuition kept leaning toward the enemy, kept nudging me and saying, *Why would the family lie about this?*

But I knew they had already lied about certain things, if only for the purpose of self-preservation, lies they needed to repeat in order to survive, still viewing Mohammad as kind, as gentle. *They all feel that if you meet Mohammad you will see his humanity and his heart very clearly.*

Me: They're delusional.

Me: They have to be.

Me: Seriously. He's a murderer. I'm not the least bit sorry he can't hold his kids. Tough shit.

Me: Yes. But it is sad for the kids.

Me: It's horribly sad, but fuck if I'm going to feel sympathy for him. He robbed parents of their children. He should now be robbed of his own.

Me: Not exactly the words of a reconciler.

Me: I'm willing to talk with them, understand them, learn about them. Make that effort. Consider them in ways I'd never conceived. But I don't have to forgive.

Me: No you don't.

Me: I'm not going to.

Me: Then don't.

20

Back in Wilmington, after settling into the autumn semester's routine, I walked into a classroom in Morton Hall one morning and sat amidst my creative writing students. I placed a cell phone on the conference table and announced to the assembled masses, "I just want you guys to know, before we start, that I may be getting a call from Israel that I have to take. Probably won't, but it's due, so I apologize in advance if it happens."

Weeks earlier, Leah's translator, Mariam, had written to me, reporting that the family had visited Mohammad in prison. They had asked pointedly about my request to meet with him. He had responded, and they had in turn relayed his response to Mariam, hoping it would be passed along to me:

> *at first Mohammad was hesitant and did not understand why someone whom he has hurt would want to meet him but then as they discussed your visit and told him about your intention which is reconciliation, he agreed so Mohammad is more than willing to meet with you*

The words felt true, they felt honest, that this man wouldn't understand my request, that he would have been perplexed as his mother pleaded with him to meet with me, to meet with someone who should want him dead. I imagined his mother crying, begging, Mohammad having already caused too much pain for her, for the family, and him leaning into the glass and agreeing to do it, saying, "I'll meet with him," even if he didn't mean it, even if they were just words to pacify a broken mother, to make her stop sobbing. It didn't matter. Regardless of his intention or sincerity, I believed the words were spoken – "Mohammad is more than willing to meet."

I decided to hold him to it. I decided to believe in the *possibility* of holding him to it by making two determinations:

1. Armed with new evidence to wave at the Ministry of Public Security, I would re-open my request for a meeting, asking for Israeli authorities to check with Mohammad again.

2. It was time to return to Israel.

My students gave me curious looks as I tried to focus on the task of teaching, unable to help but wonder what the complexion of this trip to Israel would look like, the complexion of which I wouldn't know until the final verdict on my request came from the Ministry of Public Security. The verdict I had been expecting. The verdict my cell phone was anticipating. My students wanted it to vibrate. They wanted it to dance on the faux oak tabletop and interrupt class. They wanted it to sing.

"If they call, are you going to speak in Hebrew?"

"That would be so cool."

"Say something in Hebrew right now."

I told them to shut their mouths – *stohm et ha'peh* – which they found exceedingly entertaining, before beginning to workshop an essay written by Alice, a thirty-something single mom doing her best to juggle school and life among beach-clinging sorority girls and surfers. Ten minutes into a discussion on the structural integrity of her piece, the phone buzzed. I scanned the incoming number.

"Guys, I'm so sorry." Everyone smiled.

"Hello?"

A woman on the other end spoke in Hebrew. "David, this is Hadar Cohen from the Ministry of Public Security."

"Hello Hadar."

"David, I'm calling about your request to meet with the prisoner."

"Yes?"

"I'm afraid it has been denied again. The prisoner has refused to meet."

"He has."

"Yes, David. I'm very sorry about this. If there is anything I can do, I will try to help."

"But I've spoken with the family of the prisoner. They say he wants to meet. How am I supposed to view what you've told me?"

"I don't know what to say about that. It has been passed on to me, to tell you, that the prisoner has refused, and that no meeting can take place without his approval."

"Why not?"

"It is a law."

"Is there anything I can do differently?"

"You could try sending him a letter, maybe?"

"To the prisoner?"

"Yes."

"Through the Prison Service?"

"Yes."

"I don't think so. Listen, this is what I've decided. I'm going to travel to Israel anyway, and I want to meet with people to learn firsthand what I might be able to do. Can you arrange a meeting for me with someone from the Prison Service?"

"Umm. I can try to do this, yes. When do you plan on traveling?"

"The first week of December. It would be much appreciated if you could do that. Oh, and I also want to meet with someone from the Ministry of Public Security. Maybe I can meet with you?"

"You want to meet with me? Why?"

"To talk about things I can do while I'm there."

"David, I would be happy to meet with you. But I'm not the right person – I don't know if there will be anything I can do."

"That's fine. I just want you to show me in person that my request has been rejected. I just want to see the written denial. Do you have a file?"

"No."

"How do you know?"

"I've been told by my superior."

"Avi Dicter?" I asked, referring to the Minister of Public Security and one of the most prominent politicians in Israel. The line was silent.

"Never mind. Can I send you an email to review what we've discussed about my trip and everything?"

"Of course, David."

"Great. I'll also give you the details of my travel schedule once it is set."

"Okay, David. Is there anything else I can do?"

"No. Thanks for calling and helping again. I appreciate your efforts."

"I'm happy to help."

"Okay. Goodbye."

"Bye."

I closed the phone and returned to the world of perplexed undergraduates watching me.

"That was Hebrew?"

"Yes."

"Cool. What did they say?"

"That they were happy to help."

Happy to help. No government official in Israel has ever, since its formation as a bureaucratic state, been happy to help. Even on the rare occasions when someone actually *is* happy to help, culturally it is a requirement to feign displeasure and boredom. This isn't meant as derogatory – it's simply the way things operate, generally. (There's a reason Israelis collectively have referred to themselves for some time as *Sabras* – prickly cacti that have a sweet pulp hidden beneath a rough exterior.) It's not really all that surprising once you get to know the country, which is, in essence, one large, dysfunctional family – for Jews, at least – the family that survived Nazi Germany, pogroms, and global anti-Semitism to arrive on a sliver of land where they now fight simultaneously for survival and the right to a good wireless plan. Combine Old World Jews, with their *shtetls* and collective traumas, with Middle Eastern disorganization and machismo, and you have the foundation for a maddening, twenty-first-century techno-village filled with God's chosen clan, my clan, a clan I know fairly well. So when, after the hundreds of emails I'd brazenly sent to Hadar – functioning as continuous taps on the shoulder, waiting for her to turn around and respond – she said dryly, "I'm happy to help," the words dripped with irony. And it was this irony that made me suspicious. Which words were true? Was she happy to help? Had Mohammad refused to meet? Had the Israel Prison Service refused to ask him? The answer alone wasn't particularly important, except that it directly impacted my ability to attain a meeting with Mohammad, a chance to face him and ask, *Why?* To trade justice for truth.

After hanging up with Hadar and finishing my class, I headed to a computer lab on campus, resolved to begin choreographing my trip to Israel, hoping to find a path toward some elusive and blurry idea of reconciliation.

If I can't face Mohammad, I want to meet the family, I thought, remembering Leah's words, the family welcoming my efforts with open arms, inviting me to visit them, an invitation I was now eager to accept. I sat down and composed a letter to Mariam, asking if she could try to arrange a visit, and if so, whether she would be my interpreter in the event the Odehs actually meant it. A few days later, I had my response:

> *david i am glad you are coming and of course i will be with you …*
>
> *i contacted the family again*
>
> *mohammad has no objection what so ever to meet with you and talk*
>
> *you are more than welcome to visit the family in december*
>
> *i am planning to spend my xmas in egypt but do hope to be here when you come as i am personally looking forward to meet you*
>
> *anyway i am now sure that the family and mohammad want to meet you and i dont know why the prison keeps giving a negative response*
>
> *take care*
>
> *Mariam*

Part IV

Collective History

21

The history of Jewish suffering has been etched into my memory since birth. It began subconsciously with the first pin-prick of pain felt at my circumcision, at the moment my covenant with God was consummated. It was a warning: *Don't worry, there's more where this came from.* In Sunday school, as a wide-eyed kindergartener, I first learned about the stories of slavery in Egypt during Passover and the tales of near-genocide during Purim. Then there were the stories of the Holocaust that I gleaned when family members felt comfortable sharing them – stories spoken in hushed tones about relatives I'd never met, the ones who had been lost to the ovens. These came together to form a lineage of victimization stretching back centuries. It seemed as though I was told, again and again, that I was descended from the weak, the helpless, the few lucky enough to survive. As a result, the one thing I truly understood about my Jewish identity while I was growing up in the suburbs of Atlanta was this: as a people, we were always on the brink.

This history of suffering was concretized while Jamie and I were living in Israel. The daily images on television of carnage, of innocent Jews exploding while drinking coffee, validated my lifelong sense of vulnerability. And then Jamie was thrown to the floor. And we became the narrative. We became Jewish suffering. We became a part of this history.

But it was a history skewed by our collective traumas. The full range of our vision had been obscured over the years by bandages and blinders. In my mind's eye, Jews were the eternal victims – the people everyone wanted dead – which made anyone associated with our suffering a mere implement of history's anti-Semitic, machine-like march. Never had I considered the humanity of Palestinians. Never had I considered *their* history. They were animals, terrorists, the contemporary incarnation of Amalek. They were just the latest in a long line of people wanting us dead, lined up throughout history: Arabs, Germans, Russians, Romans, Greeks, Persians, Babylonians, Egyptians.

And here then was the definition of irony: becoming a victim, becoming a footnote to a footnote in the history of Jewish suffering, led me to consider for the first time the history of Palestinians, the history of those who were ostensibly responsible for our becoming footnotes. It was a history which had been invisible, irrelevant to me. A history I had ignored. But in order to move beyond the trauma wrought on us by Mohammad's action, I chose to turn history on its head. I chose to move toward him in order to understand him. I chose to consider him and his people and the historical chain of events that led to the moment the bomb went off in the Frank Sinatra Cafeteria, the moment Jamie was thrown to the ground.

And in understanding Palestinians as a people, I thought that, perhaps, a new history could be written. I thought that such an understanding might lead to a different life, a life devoid of hyperventilating and nightmares. A life like the one that existed before the bomb exploded.

I purchased a ticket to Israel knowing that the Odeh family was preparing for my visit. *I need to prepare as well*, I thought, visiting the university library and its musty, cavernous bowels where information was hiding within the intestinal walls of its closed books.

The eighties carpeting and beige, metal stacks called to me, said, *This will be your training ground*, said, *These walls will guide you.* Feeling obedient, I listened, spending weeks under the humming fluorescent lights combing through volumes of history and psychology. First, those on my own people. And then, those dealing with the other side, with the Palestinians, with the collective traumas we've shared for a century.

Over time I constructed a regional tragedy I had never fully understood, a tragic narrative that began with the story of my own people thinking, *We've got to get out of here.* It was a thought that arose out of European anti-Semitism and the mind-numbing horrors it visited upon Jews in the nineteenth century. At that time, most of the world's Jewry lived in an area called the "Pale of Settlement" in Russia's vast, frozen empire. And life there was hell. Jews were singled out and treated as sub-human – they were forbidden to own land, were restricted in their movements, and were: "subjected to a brutal system of twenty-five year military conscription, which occasionally entailed the virtual kidnapping of their children … and their attempted conversion to Christianity by the authorities in special preparatory military schools."

Then came the pogroms, the mobs wielding scythes and torches, raping and murdering and decimating entire Jewish towns. And from this suffering came Zionism's call – the desire for Jews to return to their biblical homeland. Out of these traumas came a secular, political movement, a movement to return to the land of Israel, to find a sanctuary. To live.[1]

But when the waves of Jewish immigrants fleeing Europe arrived in Palestine, the Palestinian Arabs didn't see victims standing before them. Instead, they saw European Jews trying to gobble up their own homeland. Which, in truth, is what they were doing; as soon as the immigrants arrived, the mass-purchasing began. Jews – most of whom weren't allowed the basic right of land-ownership in Europe – were now clutching the soil, kissing it, claiming it. They wanted to transform the land into a Jewish one, to redeem it.[2]

For Palestinians, this meant a wave of dispossession, as farms were bought up by these financially backed, white-skinned newcomers. For Palestinians, Jewish "redemption" meant becoming invisible. They were asked to watch as colonizers carrying the slogan "A land without a people for a people without a land" gained both momentum and acreage over a soil that was plenty populated already. They were asked to witness a Zionist movement that looked straight through them and saw nothing but open space. Property disputes were inevitable; so were violent clashes. Arab peasants, dispossessed and aggrieved, began to attack Jewish settlements, striking out, the seeds of conflict planted in this sandy soil.

Despite the Zionist slogan, Palestine was far from "a land without a people." Just before World War I, Ottoman-controlled Palestine's population was more than 700,000, with just 60,000 of those living in the region being Jews.[3] Given that they were massively outnumbered, with Arab landowners rebelling around them, it's not surprising that Zionist leaders sought outside help in their quest for a national homeland. It was a quest not only precipitated by necessity – by the pogroms and hatred from which the Jews had fled. It was a quest fed by spiritual visions of a redemptive history, fed by the promise that biblical Israel was not just a land, but a fertile woman beckoning the Jewish people back to where God wanted them. A land calling out to be reclaimed, to be rescued from captivity and released from the temporary grip of her captors, to have her soil tilled according to biblical commandments, by the hands of those fulfilling biblical commandments, by those who understood destiny.

The Zionist leaders, desperate for land and intoxicated by this spiritual vision, nudged destiny forward by seeking help from the

British government, which, after the Allied powers' victory over the Ottoman Empire in World War I, had taken administrative control of Palestine. In a letter now known as the Balfour Declaration, Britain's Foreign Secretary, Arthur James Balfour, wrote to Lord Rothschild, a leader of Britain's Jewish community, confirming that Britain would not, in 1917, stand in destiny's path:

> *Dear Lord Rothschild,*
>
> *I have much pleasure in conveying to you, on behalf of His Majesty's Government, the following declaration of sympathy with Jewish Zionist aspirations which has been submitted to, and approved by, the Cabinet:*
>
> *"His Majesty's Government view with favour the establishment in Palestine of a national home for the Jewish people, and will use their best endeavours to facilitate the achievement of this object, it being clearly understood that nothing shall be done which may prejudice the civil and religious rights of existing non-Jewish communities in Palestine, or the rights and political status enjoyed by Jews in any other country."*[4]

What was remarkable about the Balfour Declaration wasn't that the British government came to defend the nationalist rights of the Jewish community; it was that the letter negated the existence of any nationalist rights for the nearly 650,000 Arabs living in Palestine, calling them "non-Jewish" communities that would be granted civil and religious rights, but not nationalist ones. The British government, it seemed, didn't consider the Arabs in Palestine as a people.[5]

This view would, in part, keep Palestinians from realizing their dreams of an independent country for themselves, a view perpetuated and sustained for decades with such staggering tenacity that more than forty years later, in 1969, Prime Minister Golda Meir could state with a straight face, looking into the mirror of history standing before her, that "There was no such thing as Palestinians … They did not exist."[6] And indeed they didn't – at least according to the Western world after World War I. For when the League of Nations carved up the Ottoman Empire and drafted the Mandate for Palestine, which officially gave control of Palestine to Britain, the document included the text of the Balfour Declaration and recognized "the historical connection of the Jewish people with Palestine and … the grounds for reconstituting their national home in that country."[7] Yet not once in the twenty-eight articles of the mandate was there mention given to a Palestinian people. Instead, they were referred to as "the inhabitants" and "natives" and "non-Jewish."

The sudden introduction of a European, nationalist paradigm into what was once Ottoman-controlled, Arab land compelled Palestinians to think of themselves as a people in newly realized political terms, to think of themselves as a nation.[8] By denying Palestinian nationalism while championing the nationalist rights of the minority Jewish community, the British government unintentionally inspired Palestinians to stand up and demand their collective, political rights and identity as a Palestinian people. They weren't just some native, faceless entity. They too were a people with a destiny. Zionism forced Palestinians to look down upon a land to which they were connected, both religiously and historically, and see it anew: not just as their home, but as their country. And so Palestinians began demanding political rights just as they were learning how such rights functioned among Western nation states.

And here is where I learned the story of Palestinian subjugation began in earnest. After the British took control of Palestine, they denied Palestinians any form of administrative autonomy. Palestinian leaders, frustrated, demanded that Britain give them some form of representation and self-determination.[9] British officials responded with a smirk, reaching out to the Palestinians and saying, *Don't be silly. Of course you can have your representation. Simply accept our Mandate, and poof – representation you shall have.*

Accepting the Mandate, Palestinians knew, would be political suicide. It would signal their "recognition of the privileged national rights of the Jewish community in what they saw as their own country, and formal acceptance of their own legally subordinate position."[10] Palestinians balked at such preconditions. Britain tsk-tsked back with wagging fingers and said, *You ask too much of us; nothing can be done.* Then, just to make their point clear, they granted the Jewish community "fully-fledged representative institutions, internationally recognized diplomatic representation abroad … and control of most of the other apparatuses of internal self-government, amounting to a para-state within, dependent upon, but separate from, the mandatory state."[11]

The march toward establishing a Jewish state, with no consideration for the nationalist rights of Palestinians, was on. And the logic that led this march was best articulated by Foreign Secretary Balfour himself, who wrote in a 1919 confidential memo that "Zionism, be it right or wrong, good or bad, is rooted in age-long traditions, in present needs, in future hopes, of far greater import than the desires … of the 700,000 Arabs who now inhabit that ancient land."[12]

Jews' blood, in other words, was redder.

It pains me to admit this, but there was a time when I thought that Jews somehow populated a different spectrum in God's moral universe. After years in Israel, in the Holy Land, studying mystical texts from mystical teachers subtly suggesting that we – Jews – mattered in unimaginable ways, I couldn't help but believe.

After all, who doesn't want to think of themselves as unique, as special in some ethereal way? And the evidence that the rabbis brought to prove this point seemed compelling. "There must be a reason we've survived so long," they'd say. "There must be a reason the world focuses a disproportionate amount of attention on a people which make up less than .01 percent of the world's population," they'd say. "It must be that we indeed are a light unto the nations," they'd say. I couldn't help but believe.

But the story of Palestinian oppression began to complicate such pedestrian notions. The story of Palestinian suffering began to cloud my worldview, one which had cast Jews as good and Palestinians as evil. But the words "good" and "evil" were suddenly difficult to dole out with a child's simplicity, as I had done in the past. Even if I had wanted to believe in the simplicity of such false absolutes, the words no longer allowed it, parsing themselves, splitting in the air and reconfiguring before me, "evil" becoming "veil," wrapping itself around "good" and hiding all that had previously been clear to me. Palestine's history complicated matters because the Palestinians were my enemy, both theoretically and practically. And Palestine's history complicated matters because I couldn't stomach the brutal ways in which my enemy was, in part, created.

After World War I, Britain and France were handed control over a number of territories that the League of Nations recognized as "independent states." These were Arab territories "deemed to be in need solely of a period of external advice and assistance" until they could be turned loose as nation states in their own right. Such territories included Iraq, Lebanon, Syria, Transjordan, and Palestine.

Now consider this: of these Arab territories, all – save the Palestinians – were given some form of governmental representation by the British and the French during their training-wheel years, and by 1946 all of these Arab territories – save Palestine – had become full members of the international community as free, self-governing states. In Palestine, the Jews were given the Jewish Agency, which served as a pre-state government, while the Palestinians were given virtually nothing. Sure, the British had offered them a similar Arab Agency, but only if this agency supported the terms set out in the Balfour Declaration, which gave national rights only to the Jews. That left the Palestinians as the only group with "no international sanction for their identity, no accepted and agreed context within which their putative nationhood and independence could express itself, and their representatives had no access whatsoever to any of the levers of state power."[13]

Why were Palestinians the only significant population of people in the Middle East not granted nationalist rights in the early twentieth century? And why is this still true nearly one hundred years later? One hundred years: five generations of political suppression, colonial occupation, brutal violence, and shame.

I had never known any of this history – had never cared. But the more I read, the more I thought, *Man, they were fucked.* Yes, some of their plight came down to incompetent and corrupt leadership – as is so often the case – but the reality was that the Palestinians were victims. The British government had chosen to champion a competing victim, my people. Zionist leaders gained the sympathy and support of British officials, principally Balfour, after years of lobbying in the early 1900s. And in recognizing not merely the Jews' tragic existence in Europe but their dream – the necessity – of a homeland in Palestine, the British government made the people already inhabiting Palestine invisible. It was a zero-sum game, and in the end, we won.[14]

I could no longer feel the jubilation of that victory.

None of this mitigates the unspeakable traumas experienced by European Jews, including my grandmother and grandfather, out of which the State of Israel arose. After the pogroms, after the

Holocaust – where nearly half of my family was turned to ash – there was a legitimate need for a Jewish homeland. A Jewish refuge. The Jewish immigrants who descended upon Palestine after the wars weren't buoyed by waves of enthusiasm. They were treading currents of desperation. And after World War II, when Hitler's murderous regime was fully revealed, there was no doubt that Israel would be established. Not as a colonial enterprise. But as restitution for the sins of history.

However, Israel's establishment became a defining moment for Palestinians – a defining trauma. Every year, as Israelis celebrate Independence Day, Palestinians mark *al-Nakba* – the catastrophe.

Before Israel was born in 1947, both Jews and Palestinians suffered. Jews had struggled against anti-Semitism and genocide in Europe, and Palestinians had struggled against a lack of self-determination and colonial suppression – two very different victimhoods. Victimhoods which can be noted, side by side, but cannot be compared. Nor should they be. Yet noting them side by side offers a glimpse into the lens through which each people was looking when 1947 turned to 1948. A lens tinted by bitterness and sorrow, by injustice and suffering. A lens through which it would have been impossible to consider the needs and desires of the other side with any clarity or empathy.

When the time came for me to fully consider the birth of Israel, I thought, *This is just about understanding my enemy. I have no interest in judging the circumstances around which Israel was created. I have no interest in exploring why Palestinians refused the United Nation's partition of Palestine into two states in 1947 – one Jewish and one Arab – or how the war started between the two sides in 1948 and ended with Israel claiming nearly eighty percent of Palestine. There are already too many who-shot-first arguments, too many who-is-to-blame explorations; there is no need for another. Yes, multiple Arab armies simultaneously attacked Israel the moment it defeated Palestinian fighters and declared independence. Yes, Jewish para-military forces conquered Palestinian lands and kept them. But I'm not interested in finger-pointing, I'm interested in the result, in what happened to the Palestinians and their society after the war, in why they consider themselves the true victims of history.*

What I had not known, what I could no longer ignore, was that the original Arab–Israeli war ripped a majority of Palestinians from their homes and scattered them across the region. It altered the landscape to such a degree as to make it wholly unrecognizable, with the most vibrant Palestinian cities, such as Jaffa and Haifa, conquered and subsumed into the new Jewish state. I learned that:

> *[a]t the beginning of 1948, Arabs constituted an absolute majority of the population of Palestine ... approximately 1.4 million out of 2 million people. They were a majority as well in fifteen of sixteen subdistricts of the country ... [and] owned nearly 90 percent of the country's privately owned land.*

After the war, over half the Palestinian population had become refugees as Israel conquered and seized seventy-eight percent of what was once mandatory Palestine (up from the fifty-five percent offered to Jews in the UN Partition Plan). Overnight, those Palestinians who remained in the new State of Israel became a super-minority, with everyone else either huddled in the twenty-two percent of Palestine that was left to them or living in camps elsewhere.[15]

During our time in Jerusalem, Jamie and I lived right in the heart of some of this subsumed land; many of the stone homes that surrounded us, now occupied by Jews, had been abandoned by

Palestinian families in 1948. Living there, it was difficult to imagine the neighborhood differently than it now stands: a wealthy, vibrant Jewish area full of synagogues and falafel stands and boys with yarmulkes playing football in the streets. But beneath our lives, a Palestinian neighborhood had disappeared, with someone, somewhere in Gaza or the West Bank or East Jerusalem, telling their grandchildren in hushed tones about the ways things used to be before violence forced them to leave their dishes and bedding and family photographs, before they were forced to abandon their ancestral homes.

Even with the passage of over sixty years, emotions remain raw. Claims to the land remain tenuous, fragile. Ask an Israeli casually whether an old house here or a domed structure there used to belong to Palestinians – as I did innocently on occasion – and you'd risk an angry look, as if the question alone suggested that things could or should be given back, that the country could be pulled out from under their feet. And when the words came from a Palestinian – "That was my childhood home" – they were taken by some as a provocation, a threat.

David Ben Gurion, Israel's first Prime Minister, was stunningly honest about what a realistic Palestinian perspective on things might be:

> *If I was an Arab leader I would never make terms with Israel. That is natural: we have taken their country. Sure God promised it to us, but what does that matter to them? Our God is not theirs. We come from Israel, but two thousand years ago, and what is that to them? There has been antisemitism, the Nazis, Hitler, Auschwitz, but was that their fault? They only see one thing: we have come here and stolen their country. Why should they accept that?*[16]

We have taken their country. I learned that there were some in 1948 who wanted to take more than seventy-eight percent. After routing the Egyptian army, Yigal Allon – a thirty-year-old commander and future acting Prime Minister – wanted to push his soldiers all the way to the Jordan River and take what is now the West Bank (or the Occupied Territories, depending on which side of the divide you're on). He wanted to reclaim a "Whole Israel." Allon's reasoning was partially strategic – taking this land would widen Israel's narrow waist – but Ben Gurion rejected the idea because he didn't want to absorb the West Bank's Arab population into Israel; he wanted a Jewish state with a Jewish majority.

Allon's desire to grab the West Bank was not merely rooted in military strategy. It was also rooted in a desire to redeem every inch of biblical Israel for Jews, a desire propelled by United Kibbutz, an organization that represented much of the kibbutz movement in Israel, a movement which played a central role in the development of the state. In 1955, United Kibbutz pushed the idea of a "Whole Israel" for "the Jewish people ... and the Arabs living in the land." The Palestinians as a people were invisible, again. United Kibbutz, following the lead set by European entities before them, "treated the Jews as a nation, and the Arabs as individuals without national rights."[17] The kibbutz movement cultivated a system in which collectives could take over large swaths of agricultural land. It provided a path to a future in which every inch of Palestinian soil could be planted by Jews, and defended by Jews. However, for Palestinians, it was the continuation of the discrimination they endured under British rule, to put it lightly. While it might be argued that the new Israelis, traumatized by history and fighting for survival, were simply defending themselves by pursuing their best interests at the expense of another, this truth cannot be ignored: it was at the expense of another.

Once, I witnessed the following conversation between an Israeli teacher and his seventh-grade student in Washington, D.C.:

Teacher: As you can see, Israel's national anthem is one that represents the spiritual hopes and dreams of an entire nation.
Student: Wait, does everyone in Israel sing this?
Teacher: Yes.
Student: I think maybe some people wouldn't sing it.
Teacher: Everyone sings it.
Student: What about the Palestinians –
Teacher: I said it's for the nation, not for the Arabs.

The teacher then asked his class to rise and listen as the Israeli national anthem – *Hatikvah*, "The Hope" – was played. These American students, twelve and thirteen years old, knew the words, had them memorized in Hebrew, though many of them had never visited Israel, and might never press the grit of its sandy soil between their fingertips.

As long as deep in the heart,
The soul of a Jew yearns,
And towards the East
An eye looks to Zion,
Our hope is not yet lost,
The hope of two thousand years,
To be a free people in our land,
The land of Zion and Jerusalem.[18]

Of course, *Hatikvah* isn't an anthem for everyone living Israel; it's a song for those whose dreams in that country matter. It's a song for those Jews who dream of freedom in "the land of Zion," the word "Zion" – traditionally interpreted to mean biblical Israel – never spoken lightly. And while from 1948 to 1967, the country's borders never stretched to the Jordan River, there were those who still dreamed that one day it would happen, choosing to ignore the massive Palestinian population standing in the way.

It was this yearning, perhaps, that led to what happened in the Six Day War of 1967, during which Israel seized the Gaza Strip and the West Bank (along with the Golan Heights and Sinai Peninsula). As the noted historian Gershom Gorenberg put it, once Israeli troops crossed into the West Bank, "the logic of the avalanche took over. On the ground, commanders seized opportunities. In the cabinet, politicians renewed dreams unconnected to defense"[19] – those dreams of claiming (or reclaiming, as many Jews would say) all of the Land of Israel. And when Israel's army decimated Jordanian troops so easily that the land stood bare, empty of enemy soldiers, Israeli politicians couldn't resist. Thus, the Old City of Jerusalem was stormed and taken. The West Bank was flooded and taken. The reasons weren't strategic. They were spiritual, irrational, based on two thousand years of longing. Moshe Dayan, the Defense Minister who oversaw Israel's capture of East Jerusalem in 1967, later described the West Bank as "part of the flesh and bones – indeed the very spirit – of the Land of Israel."[20]

But the flesh and bones of Palestinians were ignored. Again. That is, until Israel awoke and suddenly realized it was responsible for millions of Palestinians living in the now-occupied West Bank and Gaza.

In 1967, there were minority voices in the Israeli government, the voices of leaders who couldn't stomach the idea of Israel taking these lands. The Minister of Justice at that time, Yaakov Shapira, said, "In a time of decolonialization in the whole world, can we really consider [controlling] an area in which mainly Arabs live?"[21] Such voices were overruled when Jordan seemed unwilling to negotiate with Israel for normalized peace. And so, the Israeli government chose a wait-and-see strategy, uncertain what to do with the West Bank but unwilling to relinquish it.

Dayan, for his part, wasn't worried about the Palestinians, as evidenced by the infamous way in which he described matters to the Palestinian poet Fadwa Tuqan:

> *The situation today resembles the complex relationship between a Bedouin man and the girl he kidnaps against her will … You Palestinians, as a nation, don't want us today, but we'll change your attitude by forcing our presence on you.*[22]

The situation today. Forty years later, Israel continues to force its presence upon a stateless Palestinian people. While Dayan was one of the first to correctly identify Palestinians as a nation – "You Palestinians, as a nation, don't want us today" – he incorrectly assumed that they would fulfill the awful imaginings of his metaphor and submit to his military.

He was right, though, that the Israelis would force their presence on the Palestinians, and that this would change Palestinians' attitudes toward their oppressors. Today, the identity of Palestinians living under Israeli occupation is defined as much by their everyday interactions with Israeli security forces as by their interactions with their own family members. For Palestinians, there is no such thing as a routine drive to the store, no such thing as a quick jaunt to the doctor or the post office or the bank. The West Bank – the Occupied Territories – have been carved up by protruding Jewish settlements that reach deep into Palestinian areas. They are like fingers pressing into an inflated balloon, bisecting neighborhoods, communities, and even cities.

While these fingers of Jewish settlement – and the private roads feeding them – have cut off such economic centers as Bethlehem and Ramallah from each other, it's the hundreds of temporary and permanent military checkpoints that are most disruptive, transforming a ten-mile trip to a friend's house into a straitjacketed journey of several hours, punctuated by soldiers drawing guns at each passing car.[23]

These checkpoints are the places in which Palestinians are forced to confront their subjugated status and feel the shame of submission on a daily basis. As the noted historian Rashid Khalidi writes in *Palestinian Identity*:

> *The quintessential Palestinian experience ... takes place at a border, an airport, a checkpoint: in short, at any one of those many modern barriers where identities are checked and verified. What happens to Palestinians at these crossing points brings home to them how much they share in common as a people.*[24]

After coming across Khalidi's words, an image surfaced in my mind. It was from a video of a Palestinian–Jewish dialogue group, a roundtable discussion in English held at the University of Minnesota, posted online, in which a Palestinian man recounted his checkpoint story: He and his wife and children were trying to drive home when they were stopped at a military roadblock by some Israeli soldiers. The family was asked to exit their car. The uniformed soldiers, guns drawn, just teenagers, started asking their checkpoint questions, harassing the family. They weren't seeking information. They were looking to shame them. "But it didn't really matter to me; they were just playing games with us," the man recalled in the video. But then the man looked down at his son. The boy's teeth were chattering violently and his pants were soaked, the piss running down his legs into a puddle in the sandy soil at his feet. The barrel of one of the soldiers' M-16s was absently pointed between the boy's eyes. The man, realizing what was happening, pushed the barrel away from his son's face and screamed, "What the hell is wrong with you?"

The soldier – just a kid, just a stupid teenager who probably knew family or friends or fellow soldiers who had been killed by Palestinians – pointed at the man and sneered, "You're a Palestinian. Tell him to get used to it."[25]

For nearly a hundred years, Palestinians have been expected to "get used to it," have been expected to submit to a greater power – first Britain, now Israel – while subjugating their political rights, their humanity, and their identity as a nation. And the accompanying economic, geographic, and social devastation wrought upon the Palestinians during this time has trickled down from generation to generation. For too long, they've been under the thumb of an undemocratic, military legal system in the Occupied Territories. For too long, they've suffering through indefinite detentions, indiscriminate raids, home demolitions, and missile attacks. For too long, they've watched soldiers visit violence upon them for the temerity to protest nonviolently, within the borders of their own villages, Israel's expanding settlements. This has been their inheritance. It was Mohammad Odeh's inheritance.

Which is not to justify Mohammad's murderous act – I'll never be callous or naive enough to explain it away so conveniently. There's no justification for the murder of innocent men, women, and children. None. No reason can be given to legitimize such brutality.

Reading historical volumes in the university library, I refused to justify Odeh's crime. But I also refused to ignore the context surrounding it. I refused to ignore the historical backdrop out of which an East Jerusalem man with a newborn infant, who came from a decent, moderate family, could willingly place a bomb in a university cafeteria and think, *This is good.* Think it was good and then express remorse.

And I refused to acquiesce when fellow Jews, hearing of my plans to meet Mohammad, would look at me, shake their heads, and say, "There's nothing to understand," their eyes silently saying, *Poor, poor David. He wants to know why the bombing happened. It's because those people are pure evil, that's why.*

I often looked at such people, unwilling to acknowledge the suffering of the Palestinians, and would say nothing, unable to mouth a response. Instead, I would look beyond them and see my impending return to Israel, to Palestine. I would see an image of Mohammad's mother staring back at me, her expectant face lined with worry, but willing to talk. And I would think, *May this trip give me something to say to her, to them, and to myself.*

Part v

Reckoning

22

A trip does not begin at the moment of departure, when grooved wheels start spinning upon asphalt or crunch over gravel. It does not begin when landscapes scroll peripherally, when geographies shift and political borders are crossed, revealing themselves to be nothing more than lines drawn with invisible ink.

A trip begins at the moment of conception. It begins when a desire for movement vibrates firmly in the mind, when anticipation becomes an itinerary.

I sat prostrate in a booth at JFK, waiting to board my flight to Tel Aviv. I knew my trip had already commenced, but wanted to pinpoint its beginning, to hear a gun go off; I needed language to tell me that, yes, it has started, the marathon has begun. And so I paid the airport's internet access fee and looked up the word "trip" online. Definitions. Parameters. These were what I needed.

The first entry I found said, "journey or voyage," a definition I could accept, a definition that emerged some time in the 1600s out of the Middle English word *trippen*, to step lightly.

I was stepping lightly.

Scanning the etymology and history of the word, I wondered if someone, stepping lightly hundreds of years ago, had caught a toe on an exposed root and fallen face-first – an action which allowed for the definition of trip to include "a stumble, a misstep."[1] And I thought, *Am I stumbling? Is this trip a misstep? Am I a fucking idiot?* Here I was, moving toward an Israel I wasn't sure I actually wanted to enter, moving closer to a Palestine that scared me, moving toward the source of things.

Finally, the airline staff called for passengers to board Delta flight 148. As I passed through the gate and neared the plane's open hatch, New York's December chill seeped through the gangway's molding, marking my fear. A fear that propelled me forward, quickened my pace. The gun had gone off. It was time to start running.

In some ways, my trip had begun when I first received word from the Israel Prison Service that Mohammad had denied my request for a meeting. I was immediately suspicious. Mohammad's refusal was so tidy, automatically invalidating any need for a decision from government bureaucrats. And when Mariam confirmed such suspicions by writing, "The family and Mohammad want to meet you," I was unable to let things rest. These discordant answers seemed to be a tumorous outgrowth of the conflict between Palestinians and Israelis, a conflict so pervasive it was able to invade and occupy the truth. Someone was lying, and I was intent on finding out who – not for the sake of some ethical principle, but to remove the cancer.

Weeks before leaving for Israel, I tried contacting prominent figures in Israeli intelligence circles, people with connections, people capable of checking the status of my request to meet Mohammad from within. I was determined to find if I'd been given a convenient answer by the Ministry of Public Security, an answer which needed no explication or justification from prison officials. In the weeks before my flight, I stayed up many nights sending email after email to Israeli politicians, strategic fellows, journalists, and professors, searching for someone on the inside willing to do some digging for me.

When the responses arrived, they came from Knesset members, former ambassadors, renowned scholars, and foreign correspondents stationed in Jerusalem. I was awed by the outpouring of interest from these people of consequence, whom I had basically spammed. But for all the well-wishes and notes of encouragement, nobody seemed willing or able to help. The journalists didn't want to risk alienating their governmental connections. The professors claimed impotency. The politicians suggested I turn to the Ministry of Public Security, the very people I did not trust. Then I received a note from Mordechai Kedar. The message was brief:

> *Dear David,*
>
> *I highly appreciate your efforts. I'll try my best to enable your visit.*

I'd written to dozens of people within the Israeli security apparatus, but had no memory of sending an email to this man, a research associate at the Begin-Sadat Center for Strategic Studies claiming the capacity to "enable" a meeting with Mohammad. I poked around online and found his biography:

> **Dr. Mordechai Kedar (PhD Bar-Ilan University) served for twenty-five years in IDF Military Intelligence, specializing in Arab political discourse, Arab mass media, Islamic groups and the Syrian domestic arena. A lecturer in Arabic at Bar-Ilan, he is also an expert on Israeli Arabs.**[2]

This guy's the real deal, I thought, emailing back a formal note of gratitude and wishes for continued correspondence.

But nothing else came. The line went silent.

Well before dawn on the day of my departure, I awoke to my cell phone vibrating beneath the pillow. Someone had left a message. Groggy and worried, I thumbed in the phone's password and listened. A deep, coarse voice speaking English with a Hebrew accent crackled through, the cadence slow and cautious:

> *David. This is Mordechai. Now it is 4:30 in your place. Can you call me? The Prison Authority want your passport number and if you are coming alone. If not, who wants to visit the prisoner and everyone's passport number. If you don't call, I'll call again. The bagel and lox are waiting for you.*

The bagel and lox are waiting? Trying to clear my head, I rose and rooted around for my international calling card. It was well worn from dozens of calls to various Israeli government offices.

The phone buzzed again.

"Hello?"

"David. This is Mordechai. You got my message, yes?"

I rubbed sleep from my eyes and nodded. Then I remembered to speak: "Yes."

"David, my contact at the Prison Service is ready to help you. Can you give me passport number of anyone who want to visit?"

I pulled the passport from my external-frame Kelty backpack and read the number aloud, vaguely recalling Kedar's email, but still not exactly sure with whom I was speaking.

"I give this number to him and we see what happens. When do you come?"

"Tomorrow. I arrive tomorrow."

"Okay. This is soon. Do you have phone in Israel?"

"I'll be renting one, yes."

"Then you will call me when you are here?"

"Of course."

"Okay, David. Have a safe trip. We will speak soon."

[Click.]

I returned to bed and fell into the sheets. But later that morning I awoke in a panic. "Shit, shit, shit. Jamie, I think – I'm not sure, but maybe I might have done something bad last night."

Jamie raised an eyebrow as our girls crawled into bed. "What on earth are you talking about?" she asked while our oldest pecked her cheek with kisses.

"Last night I gave someone from Israel my passport number. A man called and asked for my passport number. So I gave it to him. If it's the person I think it is, it's someone trying to help. But now I don't know who I gave it to."

"Who are you worried you might have given it to?"

"I don't know. What if it was somebody from the government? What if they don't like what I'm doing? Fuck, I hope there's no one waiting for me at customs. What if they don't let me in? Can they do that?"

"Why'd you give someone your passport number?"

"He asked. I don't know. It was four in the morning."

I pulled out the phone and listened to Kedar's message again, then pressed it to Jamie's ear. "Listen to this."

"Bagel and lox?"

"Yeah. I know."

"Sounds like he's trying to help. Do you know who this is?"

"I think it might be the big intelligence guy who emailed me. Remember him?"

"So go email him and ask if it was him."

I emailed Kedar and waited, hoping something would pop up in my inbox before leaving the country. But no message had arrived by the time I closed out of dictionary.com's window and was herded onto my flight by Israelis wearing Delta's red, white, and blue uniform.

As I navigated my way through the jet's cramped aisles, brushing past burly Chasidim and teenage tourists, I wondered if I would be denied entry into a country I feared to enter, a country I needed to enter.

Once we were airborne, I distracted myself with an in-flight magazine article on Roman cuisine. While reading, I began to sing. "It's the hard-knock life, for us. It's the hard-knock life, for us. Instead of treated, we get tricked. Instead of kisses, we get kicked. It's the hard-knock life."

My girls were addicted to musicals, at least those classics to which they had been exposed by Jamie and a host of well-meaning gift-givers. At the ages of four years and eighteen months, their addiction had grown acute. First it was *The Sound of Music*. Then *Mary Poppins.* Just days before I left Wilmington, the girls had been given the soundtrack to *Annie* by a friend and poet who doubled as a sometime-babysitter. When we put it on for the first time and pressed play, they immediately began chanting, "Annie! Annie!" Grasping our hands, they danced around the living room and tugged us toward some ethereal joy.

I caught myself singing audibly – feeling a sudden loss, an absence at the memory these lyrics elicited – and looked over to find a woman seated on the plane glancing my way. She smiled. I shifted my eyes down and lowered the hymn to a whisper, moving my lips to the song's rhythm, a song that felt essential. I had never left my children for more than a day, and was holding them within the lyrics, holding my place amongst them with each syllable.

I sang hoping to survive this journey to Israel about which I had deeply embedded fears – fears I knew to be irrational, despite the fact that the last time Jamie and I were there, she had almost been taken away.

So my lips kept moving, reciting the lyrics as we banked toward the Atlantic, toward the Mediterranean, toward the known past and the unknown future.

I've never been able to sleep on airplanes – something about the ridiculous height, the opportunity for free-fall without warning, keeps me alert during even the most dreadful stretches of sleep deprivation. On international flights, when the lights are lowered and most passengers turn onto their sides, pull miniature blankets up to their chins, and sleep with open mouths, when the brain sends out tentacles of dopamine, instructing the limbs to fan out and relax – even then, my mind refuses to relinquish control over its surroundings, refuses to make such allowances. Sleeping pills have no effect. Melatonin-inducers have no effect.

So I remained awake during the sixteen-hour trip from New York to Rome to Tel Aviv, singing the soundtrack to *Annie.*

As the flight attendants extinguished the cabin's main lights and passed through the aisles, distributing tea, I thought, *Why must things be so hard?* The question sounded bombastic, overly dramatic. It made me cringe. And yet, despite the ironic impulse to dismiss it, the question reflected my true state, providing cover both for the personal obstacles that had surrounded my attempts to confront Mohammad as well as the larger political struggle squeezing both Israelis and Palestinians. I felt sandwiched between a conflict with no perceptible solution and a psychic conflict wholly subservient to the blood being shed in the land to which I was flying. Seeking my own form of reconciliation had forced me to consider the failed attempts at a greater reconciliation in Israel and Palestine. It forced me to consider how this journey fit within a much larger struggle.

I had delusions, to be sure, for I thought that my decision to meet with the Odehs might somehow shift the balance, such that Palestinians and Israelis, hearing of my brave efforts, would decide to stop shouting for a moment and talk. I knew it was foolish to think in these terms, to believe that my own attempt to heal by confronting "the other" might inspire others to follow the same path. But I also refused to believe differently. *This has turned into a mission*, I thought, understanding I had chosen to merge the personal and the political, that I had fashioned a selfish quest for sanity into something larger, something unrealistic. As the survivor, I was now trying to take everything that had happened – Marla's death, Ben's death, Jamie's suffering, my hyperventilating – and transform it, place it all in a chrysalis and let it grow wings, grow something that could emerge and fly, pollinate, pulsate in the air, make the desert bloom. The cliché was so tired it kept me awake.

I knew I was being guided by hope, by a hope that a resolution could be brought on all fronts, a hope which expanded from the knowledge that the two peoples, Israelis and Palestinians, or more specifically, Jews and Muslims, share the same mythical forefather: Abraham. And they – I should say we – share more than just a father. We share a common experience: abandonment.

Abraham's son, Isaac – the one who was bound and almost murdered by his father – wasn't the only child Abraham failed at God's behest in the Book of Genesis. There was also Ishmael, whom Abraham fathered with his maidservant Hagar after Sarah was unable to produce a child. Ishmael, Abraham's first child, was eventually rejected – cast into the desert with his mother and a water bottle when rivalry erupted in the household, Abraham showing them the door after God instructed him to do so.

Neither son saw their father again until Abraham was dead of old age, wrapped in a shroud. Neither son returned home until their father was unable to harm them any longer.

If anything, Jews and Muslims should have rallied against our common enemy. We should have protected each other throughout history from a devious deity and a father who abandoned us both. We should have followed the example set by Isaac and Ishmael, rival siblings who re-united to bury Abraham upon his passing, to bid him good riddance.

Instead, we've suffered through a bloody sibling rivalry, one played out on a grand, tragic scale, with both sides paralyzed by the psychological traumas induced after years of conflict, years of victimization, years of extremist ideologies overshadowing those who just want to watch a good soccer match in peace. *Instead of kisses, we get kicked.*

Flying to Rome, I considered the history of Palestinian and Israeli suffering, the mutual perpetration, the victimization. Both sides have been scarred and hobbled by the weight of it all. Israel devastated by the specter of giant, Arab nations clutching at its borders, by Palestinian bombs and threats of martyrdom, by the inescapable shadow of the Holocaust. Palestine in turn ravaged by the paralysis of colonialism, by an overwhelming, brutal military force, and by the suffocating shame a lifetime of occupation brings.

As the plane leveled and began cruising, I bent over to extract my backpack from under the seat in front of me, where it had been stuffed in a space far too small for something so bulky. Before takeoff, I had hidden it from an edgy Israeli flight attendant, worried she would force me to stow it overhead. But when I tugged at the bag, my body pinned between the window and an overweight, grey-haired woman sleeping next to me, it wouldn't move. It was stuck. I angled my head between my knees and peered down to see what was wrong; the crown of my head butted sharply into the seat before me. A man peered between the seats as I mouthed, *Sorry*, then felt around and discovered that one of the bag's buckles had locked onto the seat's metal casing. I tugged, holding my breath, grimacing from the strain. When the strap finally came free, my elbow snapped backwards, the funny bone angled directly at the sleeping woman's head. In the fraction of a second before impact, my mind slowed and recognized the potential damage. I imagined the woman's nose crunching under the force of my elbow, the brittle cartilage popping easily, naturally, as the bone fractured, the blow's force dispersing across her face, now shattered and bleeding, her breath labored, the crew rushing to our row, the call for a doctor, the emergency medical landing. Then, in that fraction of a second, while I imagined all this, I was somehow able to adjust the trajectory, to tuck my arm in slightly, my elbow hitting her headrest instead.

I was astonished by how hard it hit, how traumatic the force. The woman's head bounced, lost contact with the seatback, and returned to a resting position. Her eyes fluttered and her arms rose in self-protection, instinctively, and then – she fell back asleep. No one had noticed. Everyone was oblivious to the violence I had almost committed. I couldn't believe it.

It was such a small moment, an infinitesimal alteration of a swinging elbow, just tenths of a second on an airplane traveling five hundred miles per hour, thirty thousand feet high above Greenland's coastline where, down below, narwhals cut through frigid Arctic currents and fishing boats were anchored, the day's work not yet started. The world was immense. The moment was small. But it was a moment that had changed the course of history, at least for the woman sleeping soundly next to me. And I thought: *You are powerful.*

Shaken, I reached into the backpack and pulled out a folder stuffed with loose pages – academic articles from psychology journals, its pages intending to rationalize the irrational conflict to which I was returning in Israel and Palestine. These scholars proposed to explain why the conflict hadn't ended, and why it might never end, by exploring not history, but neurons and synapses.

I opened the folder and began reading.

Pages: Hey.
Me: Hi.
Pages: Ready?

Me: Sure.

Pages: Then let's get on with it. We've been in this folder too long.

Me: Okay, okay. Let's see, which article are you?

Pages: I'm "Why Does Fear Override Hope in Societies Engulfed by Intractable Conflict, as It Does in the Israeli Society?" by Daniel Bar-Tal.[3]

Me: Oh yeah. Nice title. And a good question. I don't know the answer. Why does fear override hope?

Pages: It's because fear is an automatic emotion, grounded in the perceived present and often based on the memorized past. Hope, in contrast, involves mostly cognitive activity, and thus is based on creativity and flexibility.[4]

Me: So fear is an automatic, unconscious emotion that surfaces without warning. This seems intuitive – the adrenaline pumping automatically at the sound of a scream or sight of a masked gunman. But what does it mean that hope is cognitive? That it's not an emotion, but a thought? I've felt hopeful. I feel hopeful right now.

Pages: Oh, sorry. Hope is an emotion, but it more resembles a state of mind in that it's only brought about by cognitive thoughts, by perceived goals or outcomes that could be achieved in the theoretical future.[5]

Me: So hope is goal-oriented, and thus cognitive. I have to think to be hopeful. I have to want something, to envision something, envision the possibility of something to feel hopeful, to experience such a state of mind. Sounds like an exhausting emotion. So much preparation. So much work.

Pages: It is.

Me: So it's not even a fair contest, then. Fear sounds automatic, involuntary. Like blinking or breathing. Fear just rises in the throat without warning. But hope? You have to prepare for it? You have to think it? You have to desire it?

Pages: More or less. And because hope is based on thinking, it can be seriously impeded by the spontaneous and unconscious interference of fear.[6]

Me: And there's so much to be afraid of. So much has happened. Palestinians have been dominated by foreign nations for nearly a century. They have been dispersed repeatedly, and have been under the thumb of a powerful military occupation for as long as I can remember: checkpoints, trigger-happy soldiers firing tear gas and live ammunition, drones dropping bombs on apartment buildings, cars, schools. And Israelis, despite having the most advanced military in the Middle East, have seen images on the news of suicide bombers blowing themselves up, rockets falling from Gaza, and Arab leaders screaming for the destruction of the Zionist regime. And all this against the backdrop of the Holocaust and a two-thousand-year history of persecution and exile. It's no wonder both people feel victimized. Both are afraid of being wiped off the map. Both fear extinction.

Pages: Yes. And this fear, based on both the distant and immediate pasts of both peoples, is recalled reflexively, the brain short-circuiting with fear, a fear which bypasses the thinking process. It's a mechanism of adaptation meant to protect life and homeostasis, but often operates irrationally and even destructively at the moment it is invoked.[7]

Me: It sounds like a failure of evolution, this primal fear triggering violence as a protection even when it's not necessary, which leads to a violent, defensive response: more violence, more harm, more destruction. Which is why it's so cyclical. One side attacks, making the other side afraid, which in turn attacks, perceiving a need to protect itself. All of it just leading to maladaptive responses.

Pages: You've got it. When in fear, human beings tend to cope by initiating a fight, even when there is little or nothing to be achieved by doing so. It's an evolutionary appendix, a lingering flaw.[8]

Me: But what about hatred? Terrorists don't just kill innocent civilians out of fear; soldiers don't shoot at unarmed, nonviolent protesters out of fear.

Pages: Hatred is often generated by fear, being an emotional response closely related. We often hate that which is threatening to life or the reflected world presumed to be valuable, ethical or necessary – the world as it should be. Hatred is simply fear with the helmet strapped on, the pads laced, the body juiced with some performance-enhancing injection. Hatred is fear ready to explode after an expletive-filled speech from the coach, imploring everyone to hit the other side in the mouth. Hard.

Me: So how do Israelis and Palestinians overcome the fear and hatred, the cycles of violence that are both generated by fear and the cause of more fear? How do they overcome this automatic emotional response rooted in real, traumatic histories?

Pages: May I introduce you to my colleague for that?

Me: Sure.

Pages: This is "Psychological Correlates of Support for Compromise: A Polling Study of Jewish-Israeli Attitudes Toward Solutions to the Israeli–Palestinian Conflict" by Ifat Maoz and Clark McCauley.[9]

Me: Nice to meet you, "Psychological Correlates."

Pages: Pleasure's mine.

Me: You sound complicated.

Pages: Not really. I'm simply a study on different attitudes Israelis and Palestinians have toward one another, and how those attitudes affect the potential for them to, as you put it, "overcome the fear and hatred" in order to achieve a solution to the conflict and reconcile.

Me: Isn't it obvious? The better the attitude toward one another, the better the chance for resolution?

Pages: It's not that simple. And it's totally fascinating. You'll see.

Me: Okay.

Pages: By the way, this study was actually done in July 2002, just before the Hebrew University bombing. So the results were gleaned at exactly the moment Mohammad Odeh struck. Not that this affects what I'm about to tell you, but it is interesting nevertheless.

Me: [Sigh.]

Pages: Ready?

Me: Sure.

Pages: Okay. Have you heard of something called zero-sum threat perception?

Me: Not exactly, though I could guess.

Pages: No need. I'll explain. Conflict and violence between groups often arise from the perceived threats presented by the other, and these threats to a group's safety produce fear.

Me: And this fear – or any perceived threat that causes this fear – prohibits dialogue and reconciliation?

Pages: Hold on. Only in the specific circumstance we're getting to. Don't interrupt.

Me: Sorry.

Pages: Now, negotiation research has identified a form of threat perception that appears to be particularly powerful in blocking mutually agreed upon solutions between individuals with conflicting interests. This is the zero-sum game perception – the perception that each side can profit only to the extent that the other side loses, that there is no possibility of an agreement that would leave both sides better off.[10]

Me: Okay.

Pages: In Israel, we have a situation where each side feels threatened, each side feels as though the other might be bent on its destruction. We measured this amongst Israeli Jews, who responded strongly when asked whether Palestinians hated Jews and would destroy Israel if possible. A significant proportion believed this, felt this to be true. And in a situation where such a threat perception exists, it's not surprising that few Israelis who felt this way were interested in compromise or resolution. And how could they be? How could you compromise with somebody you think wants to destroy you? Compromising just gives the other side an upper hand, a better place from which to stab you in the back. Ultimately.

Me: So this perception of threat creates a competitiveness. If one side gains, the other must lose. Israelis who see Palestinians as wanting to destroy them have only one response: hit Palestinians in the mouth long enough and hard enough until the threat goes away, until they lose. There's little room for compromise.

Pages: That's one way to put it.

Me: But what about fear? Is it created by a perceived threat, or does fear create the perception of being threatened?

Pages: That's a chicken-and-egg question that I'm not interested in. But we did look specifically at fear, and found something really interesting.

Me: What's that?

Pages: We thought that fear – the fear one group has toward the other – would similarly engender resistance to any compromise or resolution to the Israeli–Palestinian conflict.

Me: It didn't?

Pages: It did. But what's interesting is that fear only corresponded to a resistance for compromise when Israelis feared for the group, for their people, for the State of Israel. When there was a fear that Israel could be destroyed, when the threat-perception was near zero-sum regarding the group, there was little motivation for compromise with Palestinians. However, and this is the really interesting part, fear for personal safety had absolutely no relationship to such resistance in our study. Israeli Jews who expressed fear for personal safety were just as likely to support compromise solutions. These results suggest a specification of the role of fear. It is possible that fear for one's group is a source of resistance to compromise, whereas fear for personal safety is not.

Me: That makes so much sense. I've never understood how Israeli leaders could perpetually undermine avenues toward peace when public polling in Israel shows majority support for some type of resolution to the conflict. The Israeli government just seems to behave so pathologically, always unable to take its finger off the trigger, even as the populace grows restless. And maybe it's because leaders, responsible for the country, for the fate of the country, can't help but view things as a zero-sum game, can't help but fear for the safety of the entire people. It's their job. It's their responsibility. It's why Yitzhak Rabin said, "In every generation they rise up to destroy us, and we must remember that this could happen to us in the future. We must therefore, as a state, be prepared for this."[11]

Pages: Which makes Oslo so remarkable – that Rabin could have overcome this threat perception as Prime Minister to seek a compromised peace with Arafat.

Me: So if Rabin could do it, if Rabin could view Palestinians as the next people ready to rise up and destroy Israel, could have that fear and threat perception etched beneath his skin, and then turn all he knew on its head and envision a future of two states existing side-by-side – if he could do it, how might it similarly be done by others? How do we move past all the fear and perceptions of threat and all the automatic, unconscious responses and utilize a nascent hope? Not a naive hope, but a cognitively sophisticated, calculated hope?

Pages: Our results indicate that willingness to compromise – to hope for and envision a situation in which both sides can reconcile for the good of everyone – depends both on sympathy for the other and on the perception that there is a possible future in which both groups are better off.[12]

Me: So what then? How can this be done?

Pages: How do you increase sympathy for someone?

Me: Know them? Learn about them? Meet them?

Pages: Exactly. Meet them.

Me: So, is what I'm doing a part of that?

Pages: Could be, though you're not Israeli, and so don't fit into our rubric.

Me: But I'm Jewish.

Pages: True.

Me: If an Israeli heard or read about my efforts, that would perhaps increase sympathy for Palestinians, right?

Pages: Sounds like a stretch. It could, perhaps. Depends how intimately you plan on getting to know Palestinians.

Me: If an Israeli leader read about my efforts –

Pages: Don't hold your breath, kid. We're scientists, and thus realists.

Me: Fine. At least tell me that what I'm doing – on this plane, hurtling toward Israel at five hundred miles per hour – has the potential to shift things slightly, has the chance to not only be self-serving, but to possibly increase sympathy for all sides among those who hear about it.

Pages: You need such a justification?

Me: I'd like it.

Pages: Why?

Me: I'm afraid of being killed.

Pages: By Palestinians?

Me: Yes. Shouldn't I have reason to fear given what's happened? Even if the fear is irrational? Isn't it automatic?

Pages: Of course.

Me: So then?

Pages: And so you need justification that your efforts may have meaning, may have an impact outside yourself, because … ?

Me: Because it would give me hope.

Pages: You already have it. Otherwise you wouldn't be on this trip.

Me: I know. But I'm afraid of the fear. I'm afraid of its capacity to kick in automatically, to take over the synapses. Just tell me what I'm doing could have meaning outside myself. Just give me that hope.

Pages: Fine. What you're doing fits into the spectrum of things, into the spectrum of what might be needed for reconciliation and compromise between Israelis and Palestinians to happen. It could help. It can't hurt.

Me: Thanks.

Pages: You're welcome.

23

When the plane touched down in Rome, I exited and wandered the empty, angular hold of Leonardo da Vinci–Fiumicino Airport. At six in the morning, only an espresso bar was open near the international gates. Red-eyed travelers crowded around the counter, some sitting in elevated chairs, others standing, elbows propped against the bar, chatting. The scene, filtered through my sleep deprivation and the surrealism of trans-Atlantic transport, appeared dream-like. Here were small, porcelain cups with miniature, oval handles no larger than a penny. Here were Italian men sipping and conversing, accenting indecipherable words on the backbeat while fingering the handles with a thumb and finger, holding lattes as I would hold a dirty tissue or refuse. And here was Italy, a way station, its boot preparing to punt me into the Mediterranean as our plane took on fuel and the espresso machine screamed.

I bought a latte and took a table overlooking the parked planes. Runways stretched symmetrically in the distance, the geometry something I thought da Vinci would have appreciated, something he would have sketched. I sketched my conversation with Mordechai Kedar, my mind numb from reading academic articles on the plane, wondering if all the preparation would lead to nothing more than an inhospitable encounter with airport security in Tel Aviv.

I hoped Kedar was who I thought he was.

I hoped they'd let me in.

Four hours later, our plane touched down in Israel as everyone in the cabin clapped collectively – a tradition, or intuitive outpouring, that has always struck me as endearing. It wasn't like the applause that sometimes breaks out spontaneously in America after a pilot sticks a particularly choppy landing. This was something else altogether: Jewish Israelis and diaspora Jews applauding the fact that such a landing could be possible, that Israel itself could be possible, the applause not really for the pilot so much as for God, for history. Clapping and thinking, *Can you believe it?*

After disembarking, I streamed with the rest of the passengers through an elevated corridor overlooking an expansive atrium. Below, Israelis reclined, reading and sipping and eating before a manmade waterfall. It was all new. I recognized nothing. In my absence, the country had continued to advance at light speed, to play catch-up with Europe and America, to stake its claim on a first-world status.

Nothing was familiar until, passing through a vestibule, I saw the Israeli customs officials sitting in their booths, the lines forming – citizens to the left, visitors to the right. Taking my place, I fingered the passport in my pocket and began rehearsing some lines:

Ani mvaker yadeedeem.	I'm visiting friends.
Esah l'America b'shavuayim.	I'll return to America in two weeks.
Lamadati ivrit k'sheh garti b'aretz.	I learned Hebrew when I lived here.

Toeing a black strip on the ground not to be crossed until given permission to do so, I waited anxiously until hearing, "Next."

"Hi." I slid my passport under a Plexiglas window to the female soldier manning booth No. 23.

"What is the purpose of your visit?"

"I'm visiting friends."

"Where do they live?"

"In Jerusalem."

"Can you tell me their names?"

I told her.

"And what is their address?"

"Um. I'm not exactly sure. I might have it in my bag somewhere."

She looked up and stared as I started rooting around. "How do you plan on visiting them if you don't know this?"

"I have their phone number. I have to call and get directions."

"You didn't get directions before you arrived?"

"No."

"Why would you travel here without knowing where you're going?"

"I do know where I'm going. I just have to call and get directions."

"What's their number?"

I fumbled through my pockets, knowing the number was actually in my email inbox. "It's in my computer."

"You don't have their number with you?"

"I do. It's just in my computer." I pointed to the backpack over my shoulder.

"And how long do you plan on staying with these friends?"

"Two weeks."

"This is a long visit for friends, yes?"

"I guess. They're good friends."

I could feel the sweat pooling under my arms. She was making me nervous, her questions and demeanor taking on a more severe tone than that to which I was accustomed. Eyeing my passport, she riffled the pages and then scanned the barcode. I waited for some flags to pop up on the screen, for her to look up at me and then raise the phone and call security. *Do not permit entry*. I had given Kedar my passport number. It had been entered into the system – the barcode would give me away. I thought about how stupid I was, how ridiculously stupid.

She reached toward a handle and, raising it, stamped the passport. "Enjoy your visit." After sliding it back under the window, I grabbed it and exhaled deeply, crossing into the main terminal.

I was in.

I entered a commercial atrium where people were waiting for relatives and friends and lovers to emerge from baggage claim; an artificial wall of bubbling water soothingly separated them from those who had just disembarked, the wall unintentionally satirizing Israel's separation barrier. On this side, us. On the other, them. I picked up my rental cellphone from a kiosk, settled near a coffee shop, pulled out my laptop and connected the 230-volt power adaptor. As far as the computer was concerned, we were in Europe – in Italy or Germany or France – where 230 volts was the going electrical currency, rather than the 220 used nearly everywhere else in the Middle East. It was an infrastructural code for where Israel stood, where it felt it stood, despite the pesky problem of geography.

I checked my email. Nothing from Kedar. I clicked "compose:"

> *Julie,*
>
> *I've landed. My rented cell is: 057-743-8350.*
>
> *Call me when you arrive.*

Julie was the woman coming to save me.

Before deciding to make this journey to Israel, I had feared the psychological difficulties it promised to present. I feared the power of sensory recall and how it could dislodge all the traumas that remained compartmentalized, remained firmly in place. I feared the smell of falafel frying in vegetable oil, the army of white Mercedes taxis zipping around sand-swept streets, the three beeps played on the radio every hour, on the hour, on all radio stations, indicating a scheduled news update, beeps which, when heard, would stop most people in their tracks, fingers reaching toward the dial to increase the volume.

This fear of returning to the source of things elicited what, for me, was an unusual response: I asked for help. I emailed a select group of friends, titling the message "A travel invitation you'll probably refuse," and requested something unrealistic, something quite unfair. I asked for companionship, for protection, for someone willing to spend a thousand dollars on an international airfare to be my guide, to help navigate the self-constructed maze awaiting me in Israel.

Julie responded immediately: "I want to come with you." It was a response I hadn't anticipated, having asked the question with similar expectations an inexperienced archer has when picking up a bow and looking down the arrow's shaft at a target one hundred yards away, thinking, *What the hell?* before releasing the cord, knowing the target would be missed, knowing the arrow would likely be lost in the woods or buried in the grass, but firing away regardless, because that's what one does when holding a loaded bow.

So I fired. And Julie moved the target, said, "I want to come."

I had befriended Julie in Israel during our time at Pardes before the bombing. A short, folksy intellectual in her twenties, with unconventional sensibilities that bordered on anti-establishment, I was drawn immediately to her flowing, cotton pants and tweed hats, to her quick wit and sharp tongue. Not long after arriving at Pardes, Julie developed a reputation as something of a dynamo in Talmud class, picking up the nuanced arguments and logical puzzles with admirable speed. *She's impressive*, I thought. *We should know her.*

Once, during a lull in the day's learning, I challenged her to a game of chess, rolling out a regulation-sized, matted board with ivory and black weighted pieces. Julie grinned, recognizing the territorial claim being staked by the personal board, the invitation to play on my home turf. She slid a chair forward and said, "Good luck."

From that moment, we developed an obsessive rivalry, playing during lunch, on weekends, late into the nights when Jerusalem's stray cats screeched and mortar shells echoed off the Judean Hills. Sometimes, Julie would visit our apartment unannounced, and as we lounged and chatted, she or I would inevitably eye the board, nod, and set it up without a word. Jamie would roll her eyes and say, "Let me know when you guys return to this world."

I finished the email to Julie, who had signed on for everything: she would follow me wherever I went – to Jerusalem, to points past the Green Line, to the home of the man who started everything. I packed up the computer and waited for a call from the two friends with whom I was staying, James and Debbie. They happened to be passing through Tel Aviv and had arranged to pluck me from the airport and drive me back to their home in Jerusalem.

When they pulled up, I waved and casually approached their green sedan as a police officer prodded me to pick up the pace, *Yallah*. I embraced Debbie quickly and threw my things into the trunk as the officer impatiently waved us away, our departure feeling like an evacuation.

As we made our way along Highway 1, I looked out the window and saw Israel – the narrow, rectangular license plates, the road signs in Hebrew and Arabic, the grassy, coastal plain – and exhaled wistfully. I was surprised by the strength of my longing, by the sense of desire, as though I had finally returned to the arms of a belligerent lover.

"How are you?" Debbie asked in her British accent, leaning over from the passenger seat, a knit scarf wrapped around her neck falling into the open space between our seats.

"I'm good."

"It's really good to see you."

"I know. It is. It's crazy, but it feels good to be here."

"We're so glad you're here," said James, a tall, lanky scholar and determined mystic.

"I am too."

It surprised me, this response – not so much its utterance, but the sincerity with which it was uttered, the authenticity of it. *I am too.* It was true, I *was* glad. Happy. Even giddy. It was a response utterly in conflict with the fear that I had anticipated would take hold upon landing in Israel. *Weird*, I thought.

It was the same sensation that surfaced during Jamie's initial recovery at Hebrew University's Hadassah Hospital, when, speaking with friends who had come to visit – those friends she permitted to visit – Jamie projected an effusiveness that was somewhat unsettling. People would step into her room, holding their breath, expecting to encounter an outwardly broken woman, and were greeted instead by a smiling chatterbox. It was unnerving for them, and for me: Jamie's outward projection was so counter to what seemed appropriate or natural. But nothing was natural about what had happened, and as I would come to understand later, Jamie's effusiveness during those first days of recovery belied an internal brokenness. It was an instinctive, emotional disconnection from what had occurred in the cafeteria, a disconnection that was necessary in order for physical healing to take place. She was not mourning. She was not grieving. She was healing – her body burned, her intestines sliced and stitched back together, her psyche shaken. And in order to heal physically, it was necessary for Jamie to focus only on the immediate, on the faces of friends and the opportunity for engagement – for an escape from the world she had escaped.

Which is perhaps why I felt giddy, sitting in the back seat as James navigated Highway 1. And while I thought, *This is strange*, experience told me that it really wasn't. I knew the fear would come, that it was coming, that I could do nothing about its pending arrival. But in that moment, in the presence of friends who had been in Israel with me when the bomb went off, I felt at ease. I was comforted by the memories of studying with Debbie before the bombing. Every morning, after getting our caffeine fix, we would sit across from one another in the shelter of the *Beit Midrash* and learn together. The light would filter onto our book-riddled table, where we would alternate reading aloud, puzzling over obscure legal decisions. Our learning sessions were always marked by an intriguing imbalance, with Debbie – the painter, sculptor, and abstractionist – lifting intuitive understandings from the Aramaic as I, the literalist, conjugated verbs and looked up the precise meaning of phrases, the rational mind tying itself into knots, trying to keep up with the conclusions Debbie felt.

As we approached Jerusalem, getting closer to Mount Scopus and East Jerusalem and the West Bank, closer to confronting the past that I was working so furiously to jettison, I felt surprisingly calm. Debbie glanced my way and said, "I think what you're doing is so brave."

"Thanks."

"It's amazing. Really."

"I don't know what it is, really."

"Well, I think it's really brave. How did you decide to do this? Can you tell me the story? We're both really curious to know. Is it okay to ask?"

"Of course it's okay," I said, explaining how I'd read the reports of Mohammad's expression of remorse, and about Leah's visit with the Odehs. Then I mentioned Robi Damelin, featured in *Encounter Point.*

"We know her," said Debbie, "she's James's cousin." James nodded.

"We haven't seen her in a while; we should call her up and invite her over for a meal."

"Oh, don't do anything like that for me," I said, stunned by the connection, the compressed community of people in this place. "I plan on calling her anyway – we've been in touch a bit."

"It's not a big deal. She's family."

We hit heavy traffic and slowed to a stop. The sky had darkened. We were in the hills rising up toward Jerusalem, the limestone apartment complexes clinging to the steep slopes overlooking the highway. Some of the windows flickered with candlelight as brake lights flamed before us.

"It's Hanukah," I said, thinking aloud.

"Yes," said Debbie.

"I'd forgotten."

"You must be tired."

"I don't know what I am. I feel ready to begin."

"Begin what?"

"Everything."

"You're going to be busy, hmm?"

"I hope to be. I don't know what's going to happen. But at least I'll be busy."

"Well, how about tonight we feed you and let you sleep. There's an office we've cleared; you can sleep on the floor. Tomorrow you can get up and begin whatever it is you've got planned."

"Sounds good."

"We'll give you a key – we both leave for school early. Just come and go as you please. Don't worry about us."

When we arrived at their apartment, it was late. I unloaded my things into a side room while Debbie and James tinkered with a *Channukiah* on the coffee table. There were nine candles in place.

"It's the last day," I said.

Debbie gave me a bear hug.

James lit a match, set it upon the *shamash*, and began swaying, chanting, singing the blessings, moving the flame from left to right as each candle caught easily. They began harmonizing, singing *Ma'oz Tzur* – "Rock Fortress." The words were an allusion to God, the God of miracles who supposedly inhabited this land, a divine occupation I didn't believe in but felt nonetheless as Debbie sang and James swayed and our images reflected in the living room's glass door. I saw past my reflection and looked upon the angular, stone homes in the distance, where others were lighting *Channukiot*, thanking God for the miracles that had already occurred and praying for miracles that had yet to be.

It was late.

"Do you want something to eat?" James asked.

"No. Thanks. That was a nice way to end the day. I should crash. Thanks, seriously, for letting me stay with you for a bit." I looked around at the cramped space, the living and dining room mixed together just off the main entrance, affording guests the ability to kick off their shoes onto the stone floor and, in one continuous motion, step in, shut the door, and sit down for dinner.

"I hope it'll be okay for you."

"Are you kidding? It's perfect."

"The bathroom's just off your room."

"Gotcha."

"Have a good night. We'll see you when we see you."

"Goodnight, guys."

I closed the door and crawled into a sleeping bag already spread out on the floor. The clock showed that it was after 10 p.m. – too late to call Kedar. I emailed Mariam, letting her know that I had arrived, and that I would be in the country for two weeks. "We should arrange a visit to the Odeh family," I wrote. Next, I sent an email to Ian Domenitz from the Israel Prison Service, confirming my arrival, and another to Kedar. Then I called it a night. Lying down, I thought of all the loose ends waiting to be tied, wondering what the knots would end up looking like, from which angles the strings would be pulled, hoping that whatever ended up being formed would prove permanent, sturdy – knots with which you could trust your life.

24

When Kedar called, it was early. I had just emerged from the shower – a square of tiled floor in the bathroom set off from the sink and toilet only by a plastic curtain hung from the ceiling that reached down to my knees.

Dripping, I answered the phone. "Hello?"

"David, Mordechai Kedar. I get your messages. How was your trip?"

"Hi, Mordechai. Fine, fine. Thanks. Thanks so much for calling, I know you're busy."

"No problem, David. I give your passport number to Prison Service."

"Thanks so much. I really appreciate the help."

"I'm afraid news is not all good."

"Oh."

"We could meet if you like. Do you have car here in Israel?"

"No, unfortunately not. I'm not sure what your schedule is, but maybe we could meet in Jerusalem sometime when you are available. If you will be here."

"I'm very busy, David. No time for travel. But you are welcome to come to Ra'anana and visit me at my home in the afternoon."

"Sure, of course. I can come. When were you thinking?"

"Today, David."

"Oh."

"You can come today, yes?"

"Yeah, sure," I said, having no idea how far away Ra'anana was or how I might reach it.

"I leave soon to go teach at the university, and have presentation to give to police station here at four in the afternoon. Come for lunch at my home at two. We can talk then." Kedar gave me his address, and told me to call upon arriving at the central bus station in Ra'anana.

"Okay, I'll give you a call when I arrive."

"Good. I see you in the afternoon."

[Click.]

I dressed and shuffled into the kitchen. The stone floor's chill seeped through my socks as I filled an aluminum kettle and warmed some water for coffee on the gas burner. Rubbing my hands involuntarily over the steaming water, I wondered what it was Kedar had learned, and why a personal appearance was required to acquire it. Images of Israeli officials formed ranks in my mind, all of them shaking their head and mouthing, *Ee'efshar* – impossible.

Moving to the dining room, I sat with my scalding cup of Nescafé and unfolded a map of Israel upon the table. Morning light streamed through the sliding glass doors and highlighted Ra'anana, situated near the coast, somewhat north of Tel Aviv. I knew how to get from Jerusalem to Tel Aviv – taxi vans called *sherut* (or service) lined up in an alley downtown at all hours. Banking on there being a similar way to reach Ra'anana from Tel Aviv, I estimated the trip would take two, perhaps three hours, if things went well.

I caught a taxi downtown to Jaffa Street and got out near the intersection of Ben Yehudah – the city's cobblestoned, commercial center for tourists, where discount jewelry stores and ice cream stands coexist with Burger King and Kentucky Fried Chicken. The vans to Tel Aviv were off a side alley, and after locating them, I squeezed into the lead vehicle beside some Palestinian laborers and nodded, *Ma nishmah?* – How's it going? The Hebrew came out sharp and gruff, as though awakening from a deep hibernation, the gutturals emerging from the cavernous recesses of a past life to forage in my jet-lagged synapses. When the van reached its capacity, I called to the driver, *Yallah, hasherut maleah* – Come on already, the van's full.

When the driver hopped in, we passed our fares to the front – forty shekels, approximately ten dollars – and settled in for the winding, hour-long trip from the hills of Jerusalem down through the coastal plateau, the trip ending in central Tel Aviv at the country's largest bus station, housed in the belly of a tiered shopping mall. Once there, it was time to find a way to Ra'anana and Kedar. I walked past pierced Israeli punks who feigned their marauding before bass-thumping music stores and itinerant Thai workers who huddled behind upturned collars along the curb, waiting for rides to the fields. Spotting a police officer directing traffic, I asked, "*Yeish sherut l'Ra'anana?*" – Are there vans to Ra'anana?

"*Aiyn.*" – There aren't.

I could have taken a bus – several lines ran steadily between Tel Aviv and Ra'anana. But I had promised Jamie I'd stay away from them; so I turned instead toward the idling taxis. The phone buzzed.

"Hello?"

"David?"

"Hi Jamie," I said, pressing the phone to my skull and plugging my free ear against the din.

"How's your trip?

"It's good."

"Where are you?"

"I'm actually in Tel Aviv, at the bus station. I'm trying to figure out how to get to Ra'anana."

"Where's that?"

"It's about a half-hour from here."

"Why are you going there?"

"Mordechai Kedar invited me. I'm going to his house."

"Is he that big intelligence guy, the one with all the connections?"

"Yeah."

"Sounds like you're making progress."

"Eh, I don't know. He sounded pessimistic on the phone. How are you guys?"

"We're fine. It's snowing here."

"Cool."

"You're not taking a bus, right?"

"Of course not."

"Take taxis. Don't worry about the cost."

"I am," I said, moving toward the line of white Mercedes. I could hear a muffled conversation commence on the line.

"Can Noa say hello?"

"Yeah."

"Okay, here she is – "

I stepped into a cab. "*Ra'anana, b'vakashah.*"

"*120 shekel.*"

I nodded and put the phone back to my ear as the driver put the car in gear.

"*Abba*?"

"Hi Noa. How are you?"

"*Abba*, it's snowing in Pittsburgh."

"Wow. That's amazing."

"Are you in Israel?"

"Yes. I'm in Israel."

"Is it the day?"

"Yes."

"We just woke up here."

"I know."

"Isn't that funny?"

"Yep. It sure is."

"*Abba*?"

"Yes?"

"Tamar's allergic to the cats here."

"Oh, is she stuffy?"

"Yes."

"Aw. That's too bad. Is she keeping you up at night?"

"*Abba*?"

"Yes, Noa."

"When are you coming home?"

"I'll be home next week."

"Is that long?"

"It's not too long."

"How can I know how long it is until you come back?"

"I have an idea. Maybe you can make a chart with *Imma* that has the days of the week on it. And each day you can color in a box to see how many days are left."

"Does *Imma* know how to make a chart?"

"I'm sure she does." The phone muffled again as Noa turned toward Jamie and repeated the plan. "Noa?"

"Yes?"

"Can I talk to *Imma* now?"

"She says she can make a chart."

"Great – can I talk to *Imma* now?"

"Bye *Abba*, I love you – "

"I love you."

" – hey David. What kind of chart does she want?"

"Just one that has the days until I come home. You can cross off a new day each morning, just to give her a visual of how long until I come back."

"Oh, okay. That's a good idea."

The driver leaned over as we approached Ra'anana and said, "*La'an rotzeh?*" – Where do you want?

"*L'tachanah ha'merkazit.*" – The central bus station.

"Hey Jamie, I think I should go and make sure this guy's taking me to the bus station."

"That's okay. I have to make the kids breakfast anyway."

"How are you holding up?"

"We're fine. Everything's fine. Let's just say single-parenthood isn't something I'm hoping for, but don't worry about us. We're doing what we need to do, and you just do whatever it is you need and then come home."

"Thanks. I love you."

"Love you too, I'll call soon."

" 'K – bye."

The cab pulled up to Ra'anana's central bus station, which was nothing more than a parking lot with seven or eight shelters huddled beneath Microsoft's headquarters in Israel – a looming, glass structure encased in green, reflective windows with the company's logo stretched across the top. *Strange*, I thought while shuffling across strips of asphalt and rubble. It was December. The sun was surprisingly hot. I ducked underneath the awning of a bus stop where soldiers holding M-16s, blue-collar workers holding empty lunch bags, and single mothers holding fidgety infants were waiting. A few stray children tossed rocks into a gravel pitch behind us. I tucked myself into a corner of the shelter and called Kedar.

"Hallo?"

"Mordechai? Hi, it's David. Just wanted to let you know I'm in Ra'anana at the bus station."

"David. Welcome. You are early; I'm still at university, but I can meet you at my home. Do you mind walking, David?"

"Um, not really."

"My home is just a mile from where you are."

"Okay."

He provided walking instructions, then hung up abruptly. I looked at the phone and gathered myself, repeating the directions internally as a young, brown-haired woman turned to me and said, "*Atah Americai*?"

I nodded and she smiled, tucking her chin playfully to her chest and looking down briefly. I glanced up at Microsoft's headquarters, a glistening symbol of American prosperity and commercial domination. I squinted and said, "*Lama*?" – Why?

She shrugged. It was a shrug of loneliness, of impossibility – a shrug I felt crawl into my cartilage. I turned away and walked toward Kedar's, feeling the chill of an everlasting shrug,[13] thinking, *You know what he's going to tell you. You know what to expect.*

Beyond the shadow of Microsoft, I entered a surreal suburbia. Meticulously manicured lawns and contemporary apartment buildings. Medians lined with palm trees, creating a green, coastal canopy. I was disarmed – by the charm, the peacefulness, the choreographed serenity. I found myself at Mordechai Kedar's apartment complex a mile later, enveloped in a serene side street in this family-dominated neighborhood.

A car pulled up and parked. It was Kedar. I recognized him from his profile on the Begin-Sadat Center for Strategic Studies website. As he approached – a gray-haired intellectual in his fifties wearing slacks and a blue dress shirt – I noticed a gentle confidence in his gait. He greeted me warmly with a handshake accompanied by a backslap. His only words: "I see you made it okay."

He led me into the building, and once we were inside his apartment, Kedar gestured with an index finger for me to sit at the kitchen table as he rooted around in the refrigerator. I gazed upon the view, an expanse of desert hills and, in the distance, beige apartment blocks rising out of the desolate sand.

"You like potato kugel?"

"Sure."

"Good. We have plenty," he said, setting down a baking dish and sliding some food onto a plate. After insisting I eat – "eat, eat" – he sat across from me, sliced kugel onto his plate and dove straight into the business at hand, the reason for my arrival.

"When I started to look at your request, I did it normal, and went through normal procedures with prison service. When it came to Yossi's desk, he saw my name and called me, wanted to know why I not call him about it and wanting to know what this David person was about. When I told him, he immediately agreed and that's when I called you asking for passport number."

He was moving too fast. "Who's Yossi?"

"My friend Yossi is one of the people who deals with who visits prisoners. He makes some of the decisions," Kedar said as he sliced another piece of potato kugel and slid it onto my plate without asking.

"Why did you go through the normal bureaucratic process instead of calling your friend? I'm just curious."

"I knew it would get to him. I have to save my favors, yes?"

I nodded in faux understanding, scooping up the kugel and politely shoveling it in, despite being anything but hungry. "So your friend Yossi agreed that my request was a legitimate one?"

"Sure, of course. So as I said, Yossi checked. Spoke to the prison chief at – your Mohammad is now at Rimonim, he was moved to another jail – and the prison chief told Yossi that prisoner refuse. He not want to meet with you."

It was the same story I had heard before. Kedar poured orange juice into my glass and said, "There's nothing to do. He can't make the prisoner meet with you. I'm sorry."

There was nothing for me to say. *This is what I've traveled all this way to hear?* I thought.

"Want to know why this is?"

"Why what is?"

"Why you can't meet with this Mohammad?"

"I thought you just told me why."

"No, I mean why prisoner gets to choose."

"Oh. Okay."

"It's very interesting. Muslim women sometimes attack soldiers. They take out knives and jump at them. At first, we were confused by it, because these women are not what you would say is a terrorist, or jihadist. And then we realized what they were doing: they wanted to go to jail. They were trying to escape revenge killing from family, and saw jail as the only way to live. Jail became refuge for these women. And then we found when they were in jail, family members would try to visit this woman. We worried that they wanted to harm them or kill them. So they make a rule that prisoner does not have to meet with anyone without his permission. This is why you cannot meet with your Mohammad."

"But I don't plan on hurting him. This is clear to everyone, right?"

"Of course, but I'm telling you a rule. It's rule for all prisoners to protect them."

"I understand this. But I guess I just don't understand why he wouldn't want to meet, particularly if he really did express remorse about what he did, and knows I'm not looking for revenge. Especially since his family claims he's told them he welcomes a visit from me."

"He is Hamas, yes? What does he gain from meeting with you, David? Not much. But if it is learned in jail that he meet with you, it could cause him trouble. Maybe Hamas does not appreciate it. Maybe someone in jail doesn't like the idea of him meeting with you. He could put himself in danger. This is what I think."

I looked down, confused. "This is what I don't understand. Why would he tell his family, aloud, in prison, that he would meet with me if he was afraid for his safety? Wouldn't he be afraid to even say such a thing to his family? It doesn't make any sense. Of course I understand why he would refuse, given a situation in which he's afraid of the repercussions should the meeting be found out, should Hamas learn of it and not like it. But I would assume in such a situation Mohammad wouldn't articulate aloud to his mother that he would like to meet with me. Why would he say this?"

"I don't know why, David. Maybe he lies to his family."

"Is it possible he's not the one lying?"

Kedar shrugged. I had gone too far.

"David, you should know something about your Mohammad. Or something about what Palestinian society was like when he committed attack. Want to hear a joke?"

"A joke?" The conversational turn was puzzling. "Um. Okay."

"Why is price of Kleenex going up in Jerusalem?"

Kedar waited for me to play along. "Why?"

"Because East Jerusalemites are wrapping stones with tissues before throwing them."

I didn't get it.

"This was a popular joke in the West Bank during time Mohammad committed the attack, a joke that shows very much about that time. There was much anger amongst Palestinians in the West Bank against those living in Jerusalem. They would tease them and say that Israeli Palestinians liked their comforts – their state-provided health insurance and citizenship – more than the

Intifada. And this caused much shame in East Jerusalem. Many Palestinians felt much shame about having money and living good lives. They had much shame about being seen as not fighting. Not getting dirty. I'm sure your Mohammad felt shame – "

We were interrupted by his cell phone, into which he immediately began speaking in fluent Arabic. Cupping a hand over the speaker, he leaned in and said, "Just a student. She have trouble registering for classes of mine."

I thought about the joke, about its questionable value as an informative kernel of sociology serving as a possible backdrop for Mohammad's actions, but it had absolutely nothing to do with how I might gain an audience with him. I wanted an audience, not a punch line. When Kedar hung up, he looked out the window. We both sat quietly for a time, watching an Egyptian vulture circle against the blue sky. He turned to me and said, "David, I have a friend. His son was kidnapped and murdered by Hamas, and he is today a peace activist. I will never understand why he is peace activist after something like this happened. It is not something I could do. It is not something I can understand or judge. But he is a friend."

Suddenly, I understood why Kedar had invited me to lunch. "You don't understand why I'm trying to meet Mohammad, then."

"No. I'm perplexed by these motivations you speak. I do not understand."

"Then why have you done all of this to try and help? Why did you make all the efforts, contact the prison service, call me in America for my passport number, and invite me here to be with you if you don't really have a stake in what I'm doing?"

"I not always like or understand my friend's peace actions, but he is my friend. And so I help him. Because I can."

I nodded. It was enough.

"Do you understand why you're doing these things, David?"

The question's tone was tinged by curiosity, by a desire to learn something elusive, exotic. But it was the one question I couldn't answer. "Some things are done without understanding why they need doing. That's all I can say."

He nodded as I rose and thanked him for inviting me, for attempting to assist me despite such uncertainties. Then I left, walked out of the home of one of the preeminent scholars in Israel on Palestinian society, a man with connections in the Israeli security apparatus. I walked out of his home and passed over the threshold separating hope from ambiguity. My chances of meeting with Mohammad seemed slim. That much was obvious.

What wasn't clear, as I caught a cab back to Tel Aviv, was what this meant for me. Was this attempt to remove psychological debris from my path now officially a failed one? Simply because I couldn't meet with the perpetrator? After all, Jamie had been the one caught in the blast. Not me. And she was still alive. I still had her, could still cling to her, didn't need to grip the murderer's shirt, just below the collar, and shake her out of him. And anyway, I *was* uncertain about my desire to meet with Mohammad. There was nothing intellectual about it. What could Mohammad possibly say to me? *I'm sorry?* I couldn't accept it, knew that I wouldn't be able to accept it.

In Jerusalem, I flagged down a taxi and was received by a clean-cut Israeli in his mid-forties with a closely shaved head. He was strong and athletic, with a powerful jaw line and dark, deeply intelligent eyes. A business identification card posted beside the cab's window read: *Moshe Ben-Tzion* – Moses, son of Zion. As his car descended into the center of the city, he asked my profession. Without pause, I told him I was a writer, after which the question came, "*Ma atah oseh b'Yerushalayim*?" – What are you doing in Jerusalem?

I decided to be forthright. “My wife was injured in the terrorist attack at Hebrew University in 2002. I’ve come to try and understand what happened. In a couple of days I’ll be visiting the family of the terrorist who tried to kill her.” I chose not to mention the idea of actually meeting with Mohammad, an idea which suddenly seemed likely to earn a swift kick to the curb if articulated.

“Why would you want to do something like this?”

“I need to understand them, need to understand how someone from a good East Jerusalem family could do something like this.”

“There is nothing you can learn from such a meeting,” he said, eyeing the road, head shaking.

“You might be right, but I’m going to try.”

“Let me tell you something,” he said, briefly staring at me in the passenger seat, his face clenched, serious. “The only possible outcome is that you will be more upset after meeting them than you were before. Nothing good can come of it. Nothing.”

His face turned sad, and I intuited pity. “You think I’m naive, don’t you?”

“You don’t want to know what I think.”

“Yes, I do.”

“My views are extreme. You will not like them.”

“I want to hear.”

“Do you know what I did for twenty years? I’ll tell you. I specialized in Palestinian relations for the IDF. I can speak, write, and read Arabic fluently. I know their customs, their society; I know Palestinians better than they know themselves. And I will tell you this: give a Palestinian your hand, and he will shake it. Give him your back, and he will kill you.”

I wondered silently if it was my fate to meet every self-described expert on Palestinians living in Israel. The taxi driver launched into a long soliloquy meant to supplement his claims, describing his years of patrolling, his years of getting to know Palestinians, of joking with them, of eating meals in their homes and attending weddings and escorting them to work. Of how he knew that if he had ever let down his guard, only for a second, one of his Palestinian acquaintances would have shot him dead without a second thought.

"Look," I said forcefully through a smile, "I've lived long enough to know the limits of what I'm doing. But I've also lived long enough to know who to trust."

"Very well. You go and meet your Palestinian family," he said, grinning back and handing me his card from the dashboard. "And after your visit, I want to hear about it. I want to hear about how I was correct. I'll buy you lunch, we'll go to the *shook* and I'll buy you a huge meal at one of my favorite places and you'll tell me how I was correct and you were mistaken. You'll tell me how you were wrong over the best meal of your life."

Taking the card, I nodded in agreement. "I'll call you."

"Promise. Don't be like most Americans who speak kindly because they want to seem kind. Mean what you say."

"I'll call you, I promise," I said as we stopped. "I'll call you."

25

After several calls to Mariam's number had been placed without a response, I began to worry. Her emails were marked by an unmistakable willingness to arrange a meeting with the Odeh family, but they'd all been accompanied by vague, unsettled ideas for when such a visit might happen. The sticking point appeared to be Fakhree, a prominent Palestinian businessman from Silwan who was trusted by the Odeh family, so much so that his presence would signal for them that the meeting was safe, that I could be trusted, or at least not feared, as would be normal given the circumstances. The family was wary of my intentions, afraid that I wanted to slaughter them in an act of revenge, an act of honor. Mariam, serving as both my translator and logistical coordinator, had said that Fakhree was hard to pin down. So I waited for her to call, thinking, *Two weeks. Don't worry, you have two weeks.*

Stuck in this holding pattern, I decided to call Robi Damelin, sensing the need for guidance, or a guide. Weeks earlier, Robi had been put in touch with me by a peace activist who learned of my impending journey. She had emailed me and described the loss of her son and her ongoing efforts to gain access to the perpetrator. "I am going through a similar process as you, and that is the reason for my writing," she had confided.

When I had watched her struggle on the screen in Harrisburg, I recognized something familiar, her unspeakable need to find closure by opening the doors leading toward those whom everyone thought she should hate and fear. When Robi emailed, it was because she too had recognized a shared purpose, a shared vision upon hearing my story. She was on my team, was the only person I knew in Israel who was engaged in an attempt to meet face-to-face with a Palestinian who had violently harmed a loved one.

So I called.

"Robi?"

"Hello?"

"Robi? Hi, this is David Harris-Gershon. We've traded emails – "

"Hello David, yes, I remember. How are you?"

"I'm good. Is this an okay time?"

"Sure, it's fine. So you are in the country?"

"Yep. I'm actually staying with a relative of yours." I explained about James and Debbie, at which point Robi chuckled, saying she didn't even know they were in the country. Then the phone buzzed. It was Mariam. *I'll call her back*, I thought.

"So have you made any progress in your journey?"

"Well, not so much. I'm having real trouble trying to find a way to meet with the Palestinian perpetrator in prison. The one who did the Hebrew University bombing."

"I remember that bombing."

"Yeah. Well, anyway, I was – "

"Your wife was injured, correct?"

"Yes."

"And she's fine now, correct?"

"Yes, thanks. Yeah, she's doing well."

"I'm glad to hear."

"Thanks. Anyway, I plan on at least visiting the terrorist's family. Just waiting to hear back about it."

"David, when do you plan on visiting this family?"

"Um, I'm not sure, exactly, but I hope sooner rather than later. I'm just waiting for things to be finalized."

"And who's doing this finalizing? Who is going with you? If you don't mind me asking."

"A Palestinian translator and a well-known businessman in Silwan."

"A businessman? Why a businessman? Is there nobody else going as well?"

"Not that I'm aware." The phone buzzed again. Mariam had left a message.

"Why these people, David? Do you know them well?"

"Umm … No."

"You don't know them? You've at least met them, right?"

"Well, not exactly."

"Wait, what? David, this isn't a game. If you think this is a game, it's not. Are either of these people trained mediators?

"I don't think so."

"How are you even connected with these people?"

"They went with someone who already visited the Odeh family on my behalf, someone from the Compassionate Listening Project."

"This is shit. Excuse my language, but this is total shit. I'm sorry, but this is how I feel. Compassionate listening is not mediation. You don't know these people, they're not trained mediators. You think this is a good idea?"

"It was until now. I hadn't really considered it. Everything was fine with their visit last time on my behalf, so I just figured – "

"David, I'm going to ask you a question, and I want you to think about it seriously: would it be the end of the world if you didn't meet with the Odeh family on this trip?"

My heart stopped, the words *excuse me?* on my tongue. "I don't know. I haven't thought about this – "

"Because David, and I'm just being honest here, I don't think you should go. It's a huge mistake. A huge mistake. You don't know what you're getting yourself into. You think you can just walk into their home and talk without a trained mediator who knows how to navigate such emotional interactions? You don't have a clue what can happen. Will you be visiting just the family? Or will the whole village be showing up to confront you? You have no idea how these things can work, how these things can become political."

A mixture of confusion and anger gripped my body as she continued. "My advice to you is not to go. Don't go unless you have a trained mediator that you both know and trust, David. What you are doing is crazy, absolutely crazy. Promise me you won't go unless you have someone with you who can navigate this meeting in a professional, skillful way. You might think you can do this on your own, but you're wrong. You can't. You can't just walk in and think it's just a conversation. It's not. And you're putting yourself in danger if you think you can do this on your own."

She then began giving me the names of people to contact, a list of approved, professional mediators in the region she insisted I'd need in order to avoid having a meeting with the Odeh family turn into a destructive, traumatic confrontation. She asked me to promise her again.

"Promise me you'll think seriously about not going."

I shook my head. I couldn't promise. Here was a person like myself – a woman who had publicly shaken off her fears and launched a quest to reconcile with the other side, to speak with the other side – now injecting me with doubts. A woman who had actually *lost* her son, telling me I was vulnerable. That I should be prudent. That I should be afraid.

I couldn't promise. I said something non-committal – "thank you" and "I'll think about all this" – then hung up the phone, still shaking my head, feeling angry and frightened and confused. *What the fuck was that?*

Looking down, the phone's screen read: New message. I fingered the code and listened, pressing the phone to my ear:

> *David, this is Mariam. I just speak with the mother of Mohammad. The family would like you to come Saturday in the afternoon. This is in two days, very soon. I speak with Fakhree finally. He will come with us. So it is set. We should take advantage of this and go when they like. The family want to meet before the Eid al-Adha holiday, so this is good time. Please call me and tell me you got this message and I can tell family yes or no.*

I chuckled at the message, at the odd simultaneity, these two conversations pulling me in opposing directions, these charged magnets sliding across the floor, repelling each other. *Yes or no.* I was no longer sure, wanting to say *yes* but afraid of the repercussions, worried that I was being horribly rash, was being set up for something – what, I couldn't know. But Robi was right. I didn't know Mariam. Didn't know Fakhree. Didn't know where exactly I'd be traveling. How we'd be getting there. Or what Eid al-Ahda was – why its impending arrival necessitated I travel to the family so soon. *Fuck, that's the day after tomorrow*, I thought, needing time to think, to consider things. I searched for Eid al-Ahda on Wikipedia. It was the celebration in Islam of Abraham's willingness to sacrifice Ishmael.

Stupid site, I thought, *It's Isaac, not Ishmael. Isaac was the one who was almost sacrificed*, realizing as the words crystallized the degree of my ignorance, just how unfamiliar I was with the Koran, with Islam, with the ways of the other side. I marveled at the absurdity of it all. Here was a story so familiar to me, turned on its head. In the Koran's re-telling, Isaac had been traded for Ishmael, filicide becoming a psychic backdrop for Muslims, just as it is for Jews. *We've been competing as victims since Abraham,* I thought, *wanting to be the ones under the knife, always thinking we're the ones under the knife.*

The image was easy to conjure – being under the knife, feeling my throat tickled by an imaginary blade. I scratched it away and pulled at my goatee, my nerves pulled taut. I closed my eyes, envisioned a meeting with the Odeh family, and dialed Mariam's number.

"Hello?"

"Mariam? Hi. This is David. I just got your message."

"David. Hello, hello. Welcome."

"Thanks."

"I'm sorry it take so long to be in touch."

"It's okay. I really appreciate everything you've done and are doing."

"It is my honor, David. So you heard what I said in the message?"

"Yes. I was just thinking. See the thing is – "

"You can't do this meeting on Saturday?"

"No, well. Here's the thing. My friend Julie, who wants to come with me, who I want to come with me, doesn't get in until tomorrow, and I'm nervous that if she is delayed or something happens that she'll miss it. It's okay if a friend comes, right?"

"Of course. Yes. You already asked in email. The family said it is fine."

"So I was just thinking – "

"I'm sure she will make it. It will be fine, David. We should visit them Saturday. The Eid is coming, and after that we might not find time to go."

"But is it possible to do it after the Eid? I'll still be here."

"All I know is the family invited you to come before holiday. They ask that you come before."

"I know."

"David, you sound afraid. Are you afraid?"

"Maybe a little. I guess a little."

"Aww, David. Don't be afraid. There's nothing to be afraid of. Everything will be fine. Everyone is very nice."

"I guess I just wish I could meet you and Fakhree first beforehand – it would make me feel more comfortable."

"David, don't be afraid. Leah knows me. I will take care of you. I promise. The meeting with Leah was very nice. The family is very nice. There is nothing to be afraid of. I will be there with you to help if you need."

"I know. I know. Okay."

"Okay so you will go?"

"Yes."

"So I tell the family you are coming?"

"Yes."

"Wonderful. David, do you know where the *Tayelet* is?"

"Sure."

"Can we meet there on Saturday? Is it okay? I can drive you to the Odeh family from there."

"Sure, no problem."

"Okay, can we say 3:30?"

"Sure. 3:30."

"Good. I'll meet you there. Then we'll go to visit. Are you sure you are ready?"

"Yes. I'm sorry. I just got nervous, that's all. This is all very complicated."

"I understand, David. What you're doing is a good thing. Don't worry. It will be fine."

"Okay. Thanks, Mariam. I know this is all extra work for you, and I appreciate your generosity. You've been very generous."

"I'm happy to be help. It is good. So I see you on Saturday, okay?"

"Okay."

The phone clicked. It was done.

26

What does one buy the children of the man who tried to kill your wife? This is the question I silently repeated while wandering the cluttered aisles of Toys "R" Us, looking at Elmo talking dolls and semi-automatic squirt guns sporting Hebrew stickers that read *B'chaniah*. On sale.

It was Friday afternoon. The store was empty, and the staff were ready to close up shop, the metal security gate suspended halfway above the ground, warning tardy shoppers not to bother.

Hours before, Julie had slipped into the country, barely making it in before most modes of affordable transportation had shut down for Shabbat, and then she slipped into Debbie and James's apartment, pushed quietly through the door and smiled at me. After we had embraced, laughing at the melodrama of the situation, I pushed Julie back at arm's length, holding her at the elbows, and said, "Ready to go to East Jerusalem?"

"Am I ready to go? I just got here."

"Might as well dive right in, eh?"

"Right now? We're not going right now, are we?"

"No. Tomorrow afternoon."

"Shit. Are you serious?"

"Yep."

"Okay." She inhaled, her bags still draped over her shoulder.

"Sorry to hit you with this now, but you can take it. You're tough."

"Tomorrow, huh? Wow. How are we getting there?"

"Shit. I didn't even think about it."

"Think about what?"

"You don't travel by car on Shabbat, do you?"

"I'm going, David."

"I didn't even think about it. I'm sorry. I'm so sorry. Can you go?"

"It's fine. This is what I came here for. I'm going with you."

I pointed to the Toys "R" Us bag on the couch. "Want to see what I bought for Mohammad's children?"

"Toys?"

"Yeah."

"Maybe let me unpack first."

"Okay."

"Why toys?"

I shrugged. With the trip to East Jerusalem for a meeting with the Odeh family a sunrise away, I had decided that an offering would be appropriate, having no idea whether such a gesture would translate as being generous or offensive, whether the family would be pleased or taken aback by such gift-giving.

Earlier in the day, unable to sit still while waiting for Julie to arrive, I had polled Debbie and James for help as the sun made its slow descent. I didn't have much time.

Me: I think maybe I should buy some gifts for the kids. Do they do things like that? Or expect gift-giving from guests?

Them: How would I know?

Me: I don't know. It's a nice idea, right?

Them: Yeah. Sure. Buy them gifts. Can't hurt.

Me:	Are you sure?
Them:	No.
Me:	Then should I not buy anything?
Them:	Do you want to buy something?
Me:	I don't know. I mean, when someone invites you over to their home to host you, don't you usually bring something as a common courtesy?
Them:	I'm not usually hosted by people who might want me dead.
Me:	Fuck, come on.
Them:	You're nuts. Go to the store already, will you?

A Toys "R" Us employee approached wearing a button with a smiling giraffe and asked, "*Rotzeh ezrah?*" – Need any help? I shook my head. *If you only knew*, I thought, returning to the shelves, looking for something modest, something small that had nothing to do with pink ponies, lily-white princesses, or monster trucks. *What should I buy them?* I stared at a wall of Western toys made with American children in mind, now being marketed and sold in Jerusalem, New York's sixth borough, as the city is sometimes sarcastically called. I tried to focus on what the child of a traditionally Muslim, Palestinian family would appreciate.

After thirty minutes of fondling pieces of plastic made in China, I finally came upon a section in the back reserved for simple gifts, the type of items American parents buy to stuff in birthday favor gift-bags handed out to a bunch of tots attending little Johnny's bash at Chuck E. Cheese's: translucent rubber balls; pencils shaped like candy canes; smiley face stickers. I needed something for an eleven-year-old boy and a five-year-old girl. The store was closing. Sifting through the bins, I found a modest stencil set wrapped in plastic. No pop-culture figures pasted on the front, just five colored pencils and a pink protractor with geometric shapes cut into it for tracing. It felt right. *For the girl.* Then back to the bin. I tossed aside talking key chains and sheets of temporary pirate tattoos as the giraffe-emblazoned clerks made signals that they were shutting for Shabbat. On the shelf in front of me, a small Rubik's Cube materialized. A puzzle, the red and green sides visible, colors contained in the Palestinian national flag waving before me. *Of course*, I thought, plucking it from the shelf. *A riddle.*

When I awoke the next morning, the apartment was empty, its other inhabitants having crept out at dawn to attend Saturday morning services at various *shuls* in the neighborhood. Shuffling to the kitchen, groggy from a restless sleep, I made myself some instant Nescafé. Stirring the black, dry crystals into a mug of steaming water, I waited for the miracle of dissolution to occur, then took a sip, cringed, and searched for some sugar to dilute the stale, pungent grounds. Opening a drawer, a red Swiss Army knife slid to the front and glared at me. I glared back and thought, *I might need you*, grabbed the knife and my coffee, and walked onto the *mirpeset* – the balcony overlooking a small, side street. I knew it was ridiculous to take the knife. My fears were baseless, and this one-inch piece of sharpened metal would do nothing for me if I actually found myself in a dangerous situation. But this didn't stop me from pulling it out, folding open the longest blade, and experimenting with it by stabbing the table's wicker frame. I wanted to know if I could stab without worrying about the blade folding down on my fingers, and so I played with a few different techniques. First, holding the blade parallel to the ground, I poked the table with sharp, downward thrusts. That worked well – the blade was steady. Then, turning the sharp edge skyward with my hand gripping the handle from underneath, I stabbed the table's frame with upward jabs. This worked as well, and after some practice rounds in which I shredded a small patch of the wicker, I decided that, yes, this would do. I would hold it from underneath. Besides, I thought, if I found myself in a pinch, opening the knife quickly would land it in this position anyway. And since I'd be holding it with my life on the line, unable to think about how best to strike, things were pretty much settled: blade up, hand beneath.

Then, still holding the knife, enjoying the sun and the quiet of a Jerusalem Shabbat, I read an article from the Friday paper about the Israeli psychology establishment's outdated reliance on Freud and psychotherapy.

Before everyone returned home for Shabbat lunch (James and Debbie had prepared it the day before and placed it on a *blech* to warm), I rose from the *mirpeset* to get dressed. The question of what to wear was a difficult one. I knew to dress respectfully, but had no idea what the Odeh family's economic standing was. Were they poor? Well-off? Was Silwan a destitute neighborhood, or economically mixed? I didn't want to offend anyone by looking like a *shlump*, which was how many would characterize my day-to-day appearance. But I didn't want to overdress either, both out of a sensitivity to my guests as well as a fear I might be mugged by Palestinian kids for my leather shoes or suit jacket, a ridiculous, offensive fear fed by stories I remembered from my childhood of inner-city teenagers being murdered in Atlanta for their Nike Air Jordans. My suitcase open on the floor, all I saw was a neurotic equation: *blue tie + pink dress shirt = a blunt object to the head.* I scolded myself for such thoughts – *You're an asshole* – and chose black dress pants, a grey wool sweater, and a white T-shirt underneath. Respectable. Sharp. But not overdone. And sandals with black socks. *Perfect.*

The plan was to meet Mariam, my translator, at the *Tayelet* – a scenic overlook in northern Jerusalem – approximately a ten-minute walk from James and Debbie's apartment. By three o'clock, after the lunch crowd had slid from the dining room table to the futon and a few scattered chairs, Julie said she couldn't stand my nervous tics any longer: the tapping feet; the constant nose-scratching (often unjustly misdiagnosed as nose-picking); the chronic time-checks. She leaned over to me on the futon and finally asked, "You want to leave now?"

"Yeah, I think we should go."

"Then let's go."

We waved goodbye, descended the stairs, and proceeded north, my heart in my throat.

"Are you nervous?" Julie asked, matching my pace.

"Nervous? I don't even know what I am anymore."

"I don't think there's anything to worry about."

"You're probably right," I said, fingering the knife tucked away in a pocket. "But last night was a bit too much for me."

Julie nodded in agreement.

The night before, after Friday evening dinner with friends, Julie and I had made our way to the home of Rabbi Landes, the *Rosh Yeshiva* (director) of Pardes, where Jamie and I had been studying when the bomb exploded at Hebrew University. He was the one next to whom I had nervously chuckled after botching the Psalms reading as Jamie lay sedated in the operating room and our friends lay dead. Rabbi Landes was traveling out of the country after Shabbat, and wanted to see me before his departure. I had not seen him in five years. He knew what I was attempting. I had been summoned.

When we arrived, Rabbi Landes' wife, Sheryl, greeted us at the door and led us to the dining room table, where Rabbi Landes was seated – a curiously imposing and fiercely intellectual bear-of-a-man who was once described to me as a cross between Robert De Niro and Karl Marx. The dinner dishes were still out.

After we had taken our chairs, he leaned over and said bluntly, "So, what's the story?"

"Now wait a minute, Danny," Sheryl said, rising to clear the dishes, "I want to get some tea and dessert out before we get into his trip. Could we catch up with them first?"

"Fine," he replied in a gruff, playful manner, grinning over at his daughter. She had recently finished army service and was now completing her university studies. "How's your family?" he asked me.

While Sheryl bustled in the kitchen, we bid our time by running through the obvious topics of "what have you been doing with this" and "how are things going with that" until, dessert plates out, Rabbi Landes took his cue, leaned over again, and said bluntly, "What's the story?"

The story. I ran through it again. From Mohammad's reported expression of remorse in 2002, to my attempt at securing a meeting with him in prison, to tomorrow's visit with the Odeh family in East Jerusalem. When I finished, Rabbi Landes wasted no time. "I have two responses. First, as a rabbi, I want to ask: have you let anyone smart know where you will be tomorrow?"

"Debbie and James know," I replied.

"No. I'm not talking about someone who's good at analyzing mystical texts. I mean someone who knows what to do if you get into trouble."

"Umm. The exact details of where I'll be and when? Kind of. Not exactly."

"Do you know someone who you *could* contact? Someone who *knows* things? Knows how to get you out of trouble if you were to find yourself *in* trouble?"

"I do have a few contacts in the intelligence community who know what I'm doing. There is someone I could contact, I guess."

"Then this is my response as a rabbi: I'm giving you a *heter* to call someone tonight or tomorrow and let them know where you'll be and when you expect to be back. Call someone and let them know. Promise me you will do this," his finger pointed at my temple.

I was numb. A *heter* is a legal allowance to do something that otherwise would be forbidden according to Jewish law, and which rabbis can grant on a case-by-case basis when the need arises. Using the phone on Shabbat is strictly prohibited, and doing so would be considered "breaking" the Sabbath, something only allowed in a life-and-death circumstance according to most traditional views. Meaning: Rabbi Landes thought my life might be on the line, and as a rabbi felt obligated to give one of the boldest, most radical legal pronouncements possible. He was imploring me to break Shabbat. The starkness of his words began to sink in. Julie looked over. He continued.

"As for my commentary, I'll say this: no private act is strictly private. In this context, it's also public. I think you realize this."

I nodded. I did. It was the reason I had been so hesitant to inform my circle of friends from our time in Israel what I was doing – those friends who knew Marla and Ben, those who stood on the tarmac at Ben Gurion airport in Tel Aviv as their bodies were loaded into the belly of a plane and flown to be buried in America. I didn't want them to know I was attempting to speak with the enemy, and so I kept it private. I didn't want them to think that I was switching sides. And so for the year that I had wrestled with Israeli authorities to gain a meeting with Mohammad while coming to terms with my need for some sort of reconciliation with the Odeh family, I mentioned my efforts to only a select few, and asked those who did know to keep it confidential. The whole effort was personal – psychological – not political, and I feared what people might think: that I was attempting to dilute the severity of what had happened at Hebrew University; that I was looking to excuse the murder of our friends by seeking to understand the murderer. I feared this because in Israel, the private is always public, always political, and actions, even those taken by ordinary citizens, have always been seen as more than actions, but as statements of position in a massive, national tug-of-war. On one side the smaller, liberal left screaming *Human rights!* and, on the other, conservatives and the religious right shouting *Jewish survival!* "Terror Victim Wants to Understand Family of Terrorist" spun differently becomes "Victim of Palestinian Liberation Effort Supports the Palestinian Uprising."

I nodded at Rabbi Landes, who looked at me and said, "I think you know that this meeting of yours tomorrow might become a public gesture. And that concerns me. I'm afraid that you might be taken advantage of."

"I understand. I really do. But you should know that I have no designs on forgiveness. I have no interest in excusing what happened. I simply want to try and understand who these people are. That's all. I'm just trying to understand."

"We're just worried about you, and want you to be safe," said Sheryl.

Safe. I wasn't sure what safety meant any longer, overwhelmed by the official, rabbinic request to break Shabbat. By the implication that I needed to consider the political damage a visit with the Odeh family might bring. When Julie and I left, Rabbi Landes escorted us down five flights of steps and out to the building's entrance – mirroring, as is traditionally done by some Jews, Abraham's hospitality when angels visited him and Sarah to announce the impending birth of their son Isaac.

When we were on the street, the night sky luminous and expansive, Julie and I looked at each other and breathed heavily. "Holy shit," she said.

"I know."

"That was intense."

"I know."

"What are you going to do?" she asked, shaken, considering the impending meeting in East Jerusalem with the family of the man who had attempted to kill Jamie and had killed our friends. I didn't know where they lived. Where exactly the neighborhood of Silwan was located. Whether I was being taken to meet a family, privately, or whether an entire village would be greeting me at the door, as Robi had suggested. Was I really going into this unknown landscape guided by a Palestinian translator and businessman I had yet to meet?

"Are you still coming with me?" I asked.

"Yes, I'm coming. It's why I'm here."

"Good. At least I won't die alone."

Climbing the steep, olive tree-lined hill to the *Tayelet*, the knife jiggling in my pocket, I had thoughts of turning back, sweating through my wool sweater, laboring more than necessary as we neared the hill's crest. The Dome of the Rock and the Old City, a mere mile away, appeared before us, floating on a current of antiquity, a current of impossible politics. The separation barrier wove across the horizon in the distance as Western, limestone high-rises nodded at the bleak collection of concrete homes crammed on the eastern side of the hills. It was the side into which we would soon descend, where smoke was rising from fires burning, somewhere, for some reason.

The *Tayelet* is a stunning overlook, with a cobblestone walk that spans a quarter of a mile and a thin, green park running alongside it. As Julie and I walked, it became clear we had no idea where to meet Mariam. Would she be wandering the path, as we were now? If so, how would we recognize her among the crowds enjoying Shabbat, picnicking in the grass, playing Frisbee, walking dogs? We decided to head toward the northern-most parking lot. There we spotted a tall, sophisticated woman with dark curls, a black leather jacket, and wrap-around sunglasses standing on a short retaining wall, hands over her eyes, head swiveling back and forth, on the lookout.

"That's her," I said, pointing.

Julie nodded. "I think you're right." We walked over and stood before her.

"Mariam?"

"David," she said sweetly, smiling, my name punctuated by an Arabic inflection that made it sound like I was a beautiful, exotic flower. I exhaled. *I trust her*, I thought. *There's nothing to be afraid of.*

Julie extended her hand as I introduced her, told Mariam she'd be coming with us, if that was still okay.

"Of course. Of course. Come, let us get into my car. I am sorry for the mess," she said as we climbed into a silver Peugeot sedan, Julie taking the front and I the back.

"We have to meet Fakhree before we go to the family," Mariam said, picking up her cell phone as she hit reverse and turned left out of the parking lot toward East Jerusalem, with its fires and concrete and secrets – Fakhree the Silwan businessman who would be accompanying us, the one who the family trusted, his presence ensuring that the visit would be safe.

"He's not answering," Mariam said, weaving around potholes as we snaked through a maze of Palestinian villages. *Jabal Mukabar. Beit Sahur.* The names were all unfamiliar.

I pulled the toys out of my backpack and waved them before the rearview mirror. "Mariam, I bought some small toys for the children." The miniature Rubik's Cube and cheap stencil set bobbed in and out of her view. "Do you think it's appropriate to give?"

"Sure. Yes. Why not?"

"I just didn't know if it would be inappropriate or something that shouldn't be done."

"I don't know 'inappropriate.' You don't need to. But if you want, then give."

The winding road cut through steep hills, with stone homes scattered sporadically along the edge. Julie pointed out the window at several groups of yarmulke-clad men trekking uphill, their *tzitzit* swaying.

"Oh, you always see Jews walking here on Shabbat," Mariam said indifferently.

My mouth hung open as we passed the bearded, black-coat-wearing men out for a Shabbat stroll. How could they feel safe, walking on the edges of East Jerusalem wearing religious regalia? How could they be so brazen as to walk on the edge, each step an unspoken claim, each clap of the heel saying, "This, too, is ours?" Mariam didn't give it a second's thought as she began describing her job teaching English at the local Palestinian middle school. A cross dangled from the rear-view mirror. *She's not Muslim,* I realized.

"This is Silwan," she said as we bottomed out and moved slowly down a commercial lane unlike anything I'd seen on the western side of Jerusalem. The road, while paved, was dusted with a sandy film, making it seem as though we were on a dirt path. Open shops flanked it. Garages. Taxi offices. Grocery stands. Clothing stores. People were milling about in entrances, sitting on folding chairs, bits of litter being pawed at by gangs of cats. Children chased the cats with raised sticks. Men chased their children with raised arms as women chuckled in doorways. Mothers held their infants peeking out from behind the opaque hijabs sheltering them. Everywhere, fingers played with worry beads and lips lifted from cups of tea.

We stopped and parked in front of a small produce market as Mariam attempted to call Fakhree again. He didn't answer.

“Prince Fakhree – always forgetting. I call him this morning to remind him. I said, ‘We’re meeting at four. Promise you’ll be here.’ And he said, ‘Sure, sure. I’ll be there.’ And now what time is it? After four. And where is Fakhree?” Mariam shook her head. “Always late.”

Some Palestinians strolled by the car and looked in. I watched them watch us, expecting at any moment for a door to be opened abruptly, for calloused hands to grab my collar and rip me out onto the street, for a gun to be placed at my temple and a forearm across my carotid artery, hands pulling me away from the car, my heels dragging in the dirt while being backed into an open door. I was hooded, dragged upstairs and tied to a chair, hearing other voices just as the first blow landed, the back of my head –

Nobody batted an eye as they passed the car. They couldn’t have cared less about us. We were invisible. I was invisible. *They don’t see me.*

When the proprietor of the produce stand emerged and began glaring at Mariam, she started the engine. “We need to leave. He doesn’t like me parking in front of his shop. Bad for business. Would you like a tour of Silwan?”

Just then the phone rang. It was Fakhree. We pulled out, Mariam speaking quickly and, it appeared, playfully in Arabic. She cupped a hand over the phone and said to us, “He’s here” as we pulled into traffic and headed to the town center. Once we’d stopped, Mariam instructed us to get out and led us to a waiting car. *Why are we getting in another car?* A man was sitting behind the wheel, the car running, as Mariam pointed to me, then the front seat, as she walked around to the other side of the car and sat behind Fakhree. Julie slid into the back with a smile as I shrugged and opened the door. A large, well-dressed man extended his hand and took mine with unanticipated force. “Ahlan,” he said. *Hello.*

“Ahlan.”

Fakhree pulled away and began weaving through alleys squeezed between concrete homes that were stacked vertically up the surrounding hills. The car shuddered over potholes and gravel, and as the car shook I heard something fall. Fakhree turned to the noise, which I suspected was just a rock kicking up into the wheel well. Julie tapped my right thigh with a finger. I looked down, and there was my knife in her hand, pressed flush against my side. I took the handoff, discreetly slid the knife deep into a pocket, and turned. She shook her head subtly, rolling her eyes. I looked at Mariam – nothing. Back to Fakhree – his eyes were on the road.

Chance: Julie sitting behind me instead of Mariam, her reflexes quick, reliable. Jamie bending to reach for a folder, head shielded from the blast. *You should be thankful*, I thought. My wife was alive. *Alive.* She had been saved. Spared. And yet I refused, heading to see the Odeh family, not a thought of revenge in my head but a knife tucked in my pocket, not knowing what was to come. Not knowing anything. Knowing that had Mariam seen the knife, or Fakhree – the one guaranteeing this meeting's safety – it might have been canceled. *Give thanks, you fuck.* But for what?

Mariam looked up and said, "We're here."

We weren't *there*, at the home of the murderer's family, but at the bottom of a steep residential slope. We climbed the stone steps, our heels clicking against the uneven rocks, passing courtyards and kitchen windows cut out of concrete, passing doorsteps colonized with scrubby weeds and welcome mats, the rise beginning to feel precipitous. Then the stairs emptied onto a stone patio bordered by a low wall at the slope's peak. A home stood before us. Fakhree stepped onto the patio and, standing still, clapped his hands ceremoniously. I had never seen anything like it. No calling. No knocking on the front door. Fakhree simply clapped, each slap echoing off the stone loudly until a woman covered by a white hijab emerged from the house and approached cautiously. There was a greeting.

I nodded. And then we were led inside into a brilliantly lit room bordered on three sides by a long, olive-green sofa. It must have been twenty-five feet in length and formed a long U along the walls. We were invited to sit, and I plopped down, expecting to be absorbed by its cushions. Instead, I bounced up a foot. The sofa was a trampoline.

I looked around. A finely carved wooden cabinet held a T.V. and stereo speakers. The walls were covered with ornate pictures of Jerusalem and Mecca. In the middle stood a low table meant for tea, which was immediately delivered by a young, cheerfully rotund woman in a full, white hijab, who gestured for me to partake. *Shukran*, I said to the server – thank you. The old woman, the mother, sat down across from Julie and me. She turned to Mariam, seated nearby, and spoke in Arabic as I brought the small, ceramic cup to my lips, the smell of warm sugar strong in my nostrils. I closed my eyes and ceremoniously burnt my tongue.

"She says that Mohammad's brother will be coming soon."

I turned to Mariam. "They know who I am, right?"

"Yes, they know."

"Should I say anything?"

"Wait until others come, and then we start."

The thumping feet of children approached. I reached down into my bag and began rummaging. "Is this a good time to give my gifts to the kids?" I asked Mariam.

"Sure." She turned to the old woman, who bellowed toward the window behind her, "Sajidah! Hamzi!" The scurrying of feet on the front stoop intensified until, suddenly, two children stood before me. As they stared, smiling quizzically, the old woman pointed in my direction. I wondered what they had been told, if they understood. And so I asked.

"No, the children are too young. You are a friend of their father's. This is what they know." Mariam's words were gentle.

Her tone suggested that this message did not belong to her – this notion of friendship between me and Mohammad inflected softly to reveal disapproval, or perhaps empathy.

This is what I knew: they were the children of a murderer.

And this: I was not their father's friend.

And this: they were beautiful.

Hamzi, eleven years old with short, cropped hair, baggy jeans, and a mischievous grin, stood a distance away as I pulled a Rubik's Cube from my bag. "When I was a child, I was given this puzzle as a gift," I said, more to the family than to him. "But I could never solve it, and so I would peel off the stickers, re-arrange them, and proudly show the solved cube to friends and family. But they knew what I was up to, because the stickers were crooked. So don't peel the stickers. You won't fool anyone."

Everyone looked to Mariam, then back to me. And then there was laughter. The family began pointing, and Hamzi approached, lifted the toy from my hand, and nodded a thank-you. Then he darted out of the room. It was Sajidah's turn, and she shuffled shyly toward me, stopping two feet away, smiling widely. Then she shuffled a bit closer and stopped again, as if playfully checking the ground for a trap door. When she moved forward again, her legs brushed against my knees and her tiny hands were cupped below my chin. I placed the stencil set down into her palms and watched her receive it. Brown eyes open wide. Wisps of dark hair falling over her face. Mouth pressed into an embarrassed grin.

There was chatter. "The family says she loves art," translated Mariam as Sajidah pivoted and clasped the plastic to her chest, then hopped on one foot out of the room.

I am not your father's friend, I thought, overwhelmed by their normalness.

Then, Samar, one of Mohammad's brothers, entered the room. He was wearing a black, athletic jump suit – looking casual and relaxed – and a women in a full hijab was with him. She sat close to the door, as far from me as possible. The woman looked sunken, her face withdrawn inside the fabric hugging her head, her dark eyes staring at me, unblinking. *Mohammad's wife.* I feared her immediately, fingering the knife in my pocket.

"They say they're ready. You can begin," said Mariam.

I looked at them – Mohammad's mother and Samar looking perplexed but expectant – and said, "When I tell people I'm coming to meet you, they often call me brave, which I sometimes think is strange. But I do think you are brave, inviting me into your home, knowing who I am, knowing what Mohammad did to my wife and friends."

They nodded. *We are glad you have come.*

"I want you to know that I'm not here for revenge, that I have not come here out of anger. I simply want to understand you, to understand better Mohammad and how he could have done something so horrible. Whether we like it or not, we are connected by Mohammad's actions. And rather than think of you as enemies, and forget about you, I've decided to try and understand who you are and how this could have happened."

There was silence. Nothing.

Then an eruption of Arabic cracked sharply across the room, as Samar and Mohammad's mother began to speak urgently. Mariam tried to keep up:

His mother says, "Mohammad was a sensitive boy. So quiet. We didn't know. Never knew. We would have done anything to stop him, if we only knew –"

Samar says, "He broke. He would watch scenes of Palestinians being beaten on T.V., would sit and watch for hours. He would just sit –"

His mother wants you to know that "he was jailed several times as a teenager. Throwing rocks and the usual Intifada things.

Twice. Once when he was fourteen, and again at sixteen. And he never talked about it. But we could see he was affected. He was so sensitive –"

Samar says, "Mohammad liked to pray at the Al-Aqsa Mosque. He wasn't all that religious, but he liked it. And he would see his friends beaten by Israeli police. Old people. He was humiliated by them, hassled by them. He just broke. He –"

His mother thinks that "his other brothers were stronger. They could handle all of it. But Mohammad. I don't think he was strong enough. He wasn't strong enough. But if you could only know him, you would see he is a good person. A kind person. When they came and told us what Mohammad did, we didn't believe it. We thought it was lies. But we didn't know. We didn't know what he was doing. Don't blame us, we would have stopped him if we knew. We were in trauma for three months after –"

I raced to sort fact from fiction, the authentic stories of Mohammad's childhood from the lies his mother had to believe in order to remain sane: Mohammad is a kind person. I couldn't absorb it all as the Arabic poured in a steady stream. I turned to Mariam, then back to the family, then back to Mariam again, hoping that something synaptic would click and capture the conversation as accurately as the miniature tape recorder I'd left in my bag. I considered reaching for it, setting it upon the table and pressing "record." But this wasn't an interview. It was a reckoning. Or the prelude to one. I wasn't sure which.

Mariam continued to translate:

His mother says, "We visit him every month, and he tells us everything. He tells us nobody asks him about meeting you, that nobody has ever talked about it. He would agree if they asked him, I know he would agree. He wants to meet you –"

Samar says, "The leaders of Hamas in jail gave him the green light. He can meet with you. He has the green light –"

His mother says, "They don't let him touch the children. They kiss through the glass. He can't touch them. He wants to hold them. 'Why can't he hold me?' Sajidah asks –"

"Tell them that I can see this has been difficult for them as well," I said.

Mariam translated, listened to their reply, and turned to me, "They say that Mohammad is sorry for what happened. He's sorry for what he did, for the people who died. If he could, he'd take it all back, he would change everything he did if he could. They want me to tell you that he said so. That he is remorseful."

Samar leaned forward. Mariam spoke for him: "Samar does not understand how you have come here without a gun. 'Why don't you have a gun?' he asks you. If it were him, he would have a gun. He would be angry, and doesn't understand why you don't have one."

I looked at him, the knife tucked away in my pocket, hidden. "What Mohammad did changed our lives and the lives of others forever, changed them in unspeakably painful ways. I've been struggling ever since, trying to heal, trying to get beyond what he did. I've tried many things – nothing worked. Then I read in a newspaper that Mohammad expressed remorse when he was captured, and suddenly, I knew. I knew I needed to try and speak with him, with you."

Everyone was silent.

"I want to get past all this somehow. Past his murdering of my friends, his harming my wife. Past all the violence. I'm sick of violence. It may sound naive or clichéd, but I want peace. In my mind. Between us. And if coming here can help bring that, then, I don't know. It would be important. I think."

As Mariam relayed my words in Arabic, a smile crept across Samar's face. Then he began to speak again, his eyes shifting shyly to the floor. Mariam translated: "He says that he wants peace too. That they all do. And that he admires you for coming, and thinks what you have done is brave. That it means a lot to them, that you have come. He wishes there were more like you."

"There are," I said, nodding to Mariam. "I promise, I'm not alone."

I looked at Samar, looked at the family. Mohammad's mother said something to Mariam. "She believes you. She says 'I believe you,' " Mariam continued. "She says, 'Will you continue to try to meet with my son? Are you going to keep trying?' "

I looked at her and then at Samar, knowing I would never meet Mohammad.

"I will."

"Promise me you'll keep trying. Promise me."

"I promise. I will keep trying," I said, unsure whether I would ever make the attempt again.

"Good," said Samar. "This is good."

I wanted them to apologize, knowing they would not, knowing they could not stand in for Mohammad and apologize for that which they did not do.

A toddler, Samar's daughter, waddled over and plucked an album of photographs of my family from my backpack, an album Jamie had made for me before I left. The girl plopped down on the floor and began riffling through the pictures, giggling at images of my daughters as the pages flopped in clumps of twos and threes. The family leaned over and smiled at the pictures before squawking at the child to return my property. I reached into my bag and pulled out an orange rubber ball, an item I had been carrying with me during the trip, bouncing it against linoleum floors, concrete sidewalks, limestone walls. I got on the floor and presented the ball to the toddler, turning and twisting it between my fingers, a rotating offering, a negotiation. She reached out and slid the ball from my fingers as I pulled the album from her grasp, the book falling shut in my hand as she lifted the ball to her mouth. The family clapped. "We can tell you are a parent." And as I looked at their smiling faces, I knew that I would never get my ball back.

27

"Will you continue to try to meet with my son? Are you going to keep trying?"

"I will."

"Promise me you'll keep trying."

I had promised. And so, hoping action would be rewarded with an equal and opposite reaction, I followed through on the private meeting I had attained with the international spokesperson for the Israel Prison Service, Lieutenant Colonel Ian Dominitz. A South African immigrant and decorated Israeli military veteran, the Lieutenant Colonel had suggested for our meeting a coffee shop at Jerusalem's largest mall – hardly the location for official business. The name of the place he suggested: *Café Ne'eman.* Translation: Café Reliable.

I was hoping his choice would live up to the hype. Julie accompanied me – it was a coffee shop, after all, and such companionship didn't seem out of place. Two things soon became clear when the Lieutenant Colonel approached, dressed in military uniform: 1) he was only expecting to deal with me, and 2) nothing that came from his mouth could be trusted with any certainty.

There is an insincere trope achieved by many politicians which, to a trained ear, is immediately recognizable. Perhaps it's the focus on the projection of their words rather than on their meaning.

Or perhaps it's the practiced, mechanical phrases that seem as authentic as a choreographed smile for the cameras. I hadn't thought of the Lieutenant Colonel, as I spoke with him from abroad, as a political figure. But what was not internalized before my coffee date with him became clear the moment he took a seat and opened his mouth: spokesperson = spin doctor.

"David, it is a great pleasure to meet you. And this is?"

"Julie," said my partner-in-crime, decked out in a multi-colored, flowing skirt and a turquoise knit hat – business casual by her standards.

"She's a friend, here for support, so to speak."

"Well, it's my pleasure to meet both of you," he said, spreading out some folders on the table. Then turning to me, he said, "David, I am glad to finally have the opportunity to come here and speak with you. I want you to know that I am here, as a representative of the Prison Service, to do whatever I can to help you, in any way."

"Thanks."

"As you know, I have done everything in my power to follow up on your request to meet with the terrorist, Mohammad Odeh, a request that the Prison Service values and has acted upon in a most diligent fashion. And what I have learned is this: the prisoner has not agreed to meet with you, which is a precondition for the Prison Service before moving forward with such a request."

"He's only been asked once, right?"

"I believe this is correct. Now, I want you to know that the Prison Service wants to offer you whatever it can to help you achieve whatever it is you are looking for. I have brought some photographs of the prison where Mohammad Odeh is being held. Perhaps these will help you with your book?"

I looked at Julie, both of us understanding that this was going to be hopeless, that the Lieutenant Colonel couldn't possibly accept what it was I was looking for, much less understand it. Attempting to explain the psychology of it all would do nothing to help. There was nothing to say. So I said nothing.

"Or, perhaps you would like me to take you to the jail itself? You could view it from the outside, take some pictures, perhaps get a tour of the perimeter from the prison warden – "

"Ian, I appreciate it. I really do. But this isn't about a book. This is about something entirely different – "

"You only want to meet with the prisoner."

"That's right. This is all I'm seeking. I ask nothing else."

"I understand. Let me tell you. What I can do is this: there is a high-level meeting in a few days. If you like, I can press this again and have those in charge of making such decisions look into it again."

"I'd appreciate that Ian, because, honestly, and I'm not saying anyone here is lying, but it's just that there are inconsistencies, you know. The Odeh family claims that Mohammad wants to meet. They have spoken with him, and have spoken with me. The Prison Service claims he has refused. So I just need this to be checked, because something is not right."

The Lieutenant Colonel appeared to be swallowing some rising frustration. "Yes, of course. Again, I will check on this and email you the result of further inquiry."

"Because something isn't right. You understand? I'm getting mixed signals, and just need to make sure that what I've been told is accurate. I just want to make sure that it is accurate."

He understood my non-accusation. "Yes, David. I hear exactly what you are saying, and will do everything in my power to see if it will be necessary to check with the prisoner again. This is as important to me as it is to you, I assure you."

He then asked about Jamie, about her recovery, and for a moment I felt the warmth of sincerity. But when I handed him the photo album Jamie had prepared for my journey, he lingered a bit unnaturally on each picture, smiling politely, shaking his head as he turned the pages slowly, commenting on my beautiful family – it was a performance. A bad one. I suspected there would be no further checking.

On the way home, I plucked Moshe the taxi driver's card from my wallet, having promised to call – having promised not to be a typical American – and dialed his number.

"Hallo?"

"Moshe? Hi, this is David. I'm the American who promised to call you after – "

"David? Yes, yes. I remember. *Ma koreh?*" – What's happening?

"Well. I went to visit the Palestinian family. The one I told you about. And – "

"The terrorist family, eh?"

"Yes."

"And so I was right, yes? Bad idea, eh?" Moshe's voice crackled on the line.

"Wait. You must buy me lunch first, Moshe. Remember? Then I'll tell you about it."

"Ah, David. I'm sorry. I'm stuck in Tel Aviv – family thing."

"Oh, that's too bad. Do you come back soon?"

"Next week. Will you still be in *Ha-aretz*?" – The Land?

"Nope. I'm leaving soon."

"Back to America?"

"Yep."

There was a pause on the line. "So I buy you lunch next time you come, yes?"

"Okay, Moshe."

"So David, tell me. I was right, yes?"

"About?"

"About visiting the family. That it was not a good idea. It is worse for you, right?"

"You were wrong, Moshe."

"Eh," he grumbled.

"You were wrong. They were kind. Our talk was good."

"Give it time. You'll see. They are not good – you'll learn their words are all lies, and then you'll feel worse."

"And what if you're wrong, Moshe? What then?"

"Eh."

A single, guttural syllable. That was his only response to this possibility, which seemed to him, and, I imagined, a significant number of Israelis, utterly implausible. Palestinians could not be good. Could not be kind. They were the ones who taught children to sing songs of murder and martyrdom. They were the ones who blew up cafés and danced in celebration. They were the ones who would push all Jews into the Mediterranean, if given the chance. They were the repository for the fears of a historically traumatized people – a traumatized country.

While Mohammad's murderous plot had brought me face-to-face with an undeniably barbarous element woven into the fringe of Palestinian society, I had also been brought face-to-face with his family. And what I saw was a normal people. A kind people. A broken people. I saw a people who feared military uniforms, feared casual bureaucratic encounters, feared a knock on the door telling them that a child had been taken to prison.

I saw a people who feared helicopters and the sky in which they hovered.

I saw a people who feared midnight raids and indefinite detentions.

A people who feared armed, uniformed teenagers.

A people tired of the fear.

Tired of the suffering.

Tired of the shame.

And I saw that seeing all of this wasn't enough. Meeting them wasn't enough.

The next morning was chilly and misting with rain as I proceeded past cement barriers to the Jerusalem District Court, the location of Mohammad's trial in 2002. After weaving through temporary concrete walls to the court's security entrance, I came to a giant steel box set one hundred yards from the judicial building's vaulted face.

I had arrived after a decision:

Me: What is it you still want?

Me: I'm not sure.

Me: Was meeting the Odeh family not enough?

Me: It was good – it was helpful. But I want more.

Me: You want to speak with Mohammad.

Me: That's not happening – I think I've resigned myself to that. And the truth is, I'm not even sure I want it anymore. Like I said, meeting with the family was good. It really was. But I feel like there's more to be done.

Me: Maybe you just can't let go. Can't let go of the need for further seeking as a way to occupy yourself.

Me: That's not it.

Me: Whatever.

Me: Fuck you, it's not escapism. You don't travel to Israel and do all this for escapism.

Me: What then?

Me: I don't know. I think it's understanding. A lot of this has been about trying to understand how this happened in order to absorb it, soak it up and empty it somewhere else.

Me: So visiting the family did nothing?

Me: No, it did. I get them, I think. It helped. There was some sort of reconciliation between us, and a healing element accompanied that. I can feel it. Feel a shift within. But here's the thing: it didn't help me to understand Mohammad's derangement, to understand the chain of moments and influences leading up to his violent act. And even though I may never understand, there's still a need to try.

Me: So what's left?

Me: Maybe just an understanding of how the event happened. The pieces. Something to put together. Then at least I'd have a puzzle completed. Would have something to look at and say, "There it is."

Me: You want information.

Me: It's all that's left.

I knew that there was detailed information about the attack and the terror cell that had orchestrated it, copious amounts of information accumulated from the police investigation. And I knew most of this information must have come out during the terror cell's trial, must have been typed up by a court reporter into the public record. It existed. It was just a matter of securing it. And since Mohammad had been tried at the Jerusalem District Court, this seemed to be the natural place in which to dig. One last time.

The previous evening, preparing for a visit to the court, I had sipped nana tea at a local café while searching for names I could lean on if things didn't go smoothly at the courthouse. From journalistic accounts of Mohammad's trial, I learned that the state's lead prosecutor for the case was named Orit Blubstein. The presiding judge Ya'akov Tzaban.

I asked the waitress for a Jerusalem phone book and scanned for the name Blubstein, not expecting to find her listed, given her position. She was a woman whose job it was to prosecute politically and ideologically driven murderers. I certainly would not have listed my name and address in the public phone book. But there it was: *Blubstein, Orit – 2365 Weikovski Street – 02-4853945.*

I could not believe it.

What are you thinking? I said silently, looking at her name, speaking to the book. The name shrugged back. In a country hypervigilant about matters of security, I wondered how the equivalent of a United States district attorney could be listed in the local phone book. Shaking my head, I began to consider that perhaps I understood very little about the underlying logic driving the way things worked in Israel, if such a logic even existed.

I picked up my cell phone, thinking, *What the fuck*, and dialed her number. A woman answered.

Me: *Efshar l'daber eeym Orit?* – Could I speak with Orit?

Her: *Mi zeh?* – Who's this?

I explained, sputtering in Hebrew, thrown off by having to speak on the phone, handicapped by not being able to look at her lips as she spoke, my brain unable to process the visual formation of the words. So I stuttered. *Wife. Hebrew University attack. You were lawyer.*

After I finished rambling, her first question was: "How did you find my number?"

How did I find her number? "It was in the White Pages, Orit."

"Eh. Call me at my office tomorrow. Not now."

She gave me her number and hung up while I was still scribbling it down on a coffee-stained napkin, which I filed officially in a pocket.

At the courthouse, a small line of people had formed, waiting outside the steel security box as police combed through the belongings of those already inside. I approached its door and tried the handle, being the type who, coming to an elevator with people already waiting, presses the illuminated button. I've never trusted the masses. The handle was locked.

I backed away and filed into the queue as an officer poked his head out and said, "*Ode dakah.*" – One minute. When the door finally opened, we were ushered in. I placed my cluttered backpack on a counter as a middle-aged security guard pulled out its contents. It looked as though he was pulling a continuous stream of colorfully-tied handkerchiefs from a magician's top hat – not delighted, simply waiting for the trick to end. Small black notebook. Dell laptop. Tape recorder (miniature). Altoids (cinnamon). Pocket English-Hebrew dictionary. Cell phone charger. Woven knit hat. Loose change (American and Israeli). Then: something that elicited shouting.

"*Ma Zeh?*" – What's this?

It was the knife I'd taken with me to Silwan.

"And you wonder why we have to check all these bags?" he projected to everyone else in the small cell while looking at me, holding up the knife. "Why do you have this?"

"I forgot. I'm so sorry. I didn't remember it was in there."

"Why do you have it?"

"It's just something I carry. I forgot. I'm sorry. Please – "

He waved it in the air, showing it to the other security guards as people sighed and tapped their feet, anxious to get to their destinations.

"Do you have anything else?"

"No. That's it. I promise."

He turned my backpack upside-down and began shaking, then slid it down the counter as another guard took the knife and filled out a form.

"Sign here. You can have it back when you leave."

After scribbling my name in Hebrew, I was motioned to pass through a metal detector. I prayed it wouldn't go off. It didn't.

"Thank you," I said, scooping up my backpack and its contents and scurrying up the court's stone steps and into the main hall. Scanning the signs, I saw an arrow for the *mazkirut* (secretarial office) and followed its lead until coming upon a long room full of file-stuffed shelves. A beautiful, red-headed twenty-something woman with green-framed glasses and blue eyes was seated beneath a sign reading "Secretary."

I approached, placed my hands on the counter, and smiled. "Hi, I'm trying to find court records for a particular trial from 2002."

"Were you one of the parties involved?" Her voice was sharp, tough.

"Um. No. Well, yes, kind of." Then the sympathy-producing song-and-dance, feigning shyness, uttering the words "my wife was injured" and "terrorist attack" and "I've traveled all this way."

"So, you're not a citizen?"

"No."

"I'm sorry. You'll need someone involved in the case to sign off. Otherwise, we can't help you." The secretary looked past me, ready to help the next person.

I had no intention of backing down. "What if I *were* a citizen?"

"You're not."

"I know, but what if someone who *was* a citizen requested the documents. Would they get them?" I punctuated the question with raised hands, as though I were ready to catch a cheerleader I'd just thrown into the air.

"No, you have to be a party involved or an official organization able to access such information."

"Wait. So why'd you ask if I was a citizen, then?"

"*Staam*" – just because.

"Just because? Okay, tell me what I can do. Is there anyone I can contact who could give me permission or help me with this?"

"Do you know any of the lawyers? Or anyone else involved?"

I pivoted toward the door. "Thanks for your help," I said, already heading to the main hall with my phone in hand. Pulling out the coffee-stained napkin, I dialed Orit Blubstein's office.

"Hallo?"

"Hi. I'm trying to call Orit Blubstein."

"This is Orit."

"Hi Orit. This is David. I called you at your home last night. I'm the American whose wife was injured in the Hebrew University bombing."

"Um. What do you want?"

"Well, you were the prosecutor for the case against the terrorists. And I'm at the Jerusalem District Court right now trying to get documents from the case."

"Yes? So?"

"They say I need someone who was involved to help me get them. Could you help?"

"Me? No. I cannot help you. I am not who you want. Ask the judge, maybe."

"But they said you could – "

"This is wrong. They give you wrong information."

"Oh."

"Is that all?"

I thought for a moment. It wasn't. "Orit, I've traveled all this way. I'm trying to learn more about Mohammad Odeh – he was the one who perpetrated the Hebrew University bombing. Can I meet with you?"

"What? Meet with me?"

"Just to get some of your memories. Could you meet me for coffee – just a half hour – and maybe talk with me about what you remember about Mohammad? What he might have said during the trial?"

"I do not remember anything."

"You don't remember anything? It was a huge trial."

"No, I cannot be of any help to you. I'm sorry."

"Did Mohammad express remorse?"

"I'm sorry. I do not remember many details. This was a long time ago. There have been many cases since then."

"So you won't meet?"

"I can meet if you like, but it will be no use. A waste."

"Oh. Okay."

"I'm sorry."

"Okay."

"Is that all?"

I hung up the phone. Two judges wearing black robes shuffled down a marble staircase bisecting the main hall. Looking up and past them, a second floor revealed itself, a floor which contained a wrap-around balcony and private offices and chambers for court officials. It was off-limits.

I retrieved my backpack, sat down, and waited patiently for the space to clear. When the security guard stationed in front of the central entrance stepped away from his position for some reason, I scurried up the stairs and found the directory to the private offices bolted on the stone wall. *Find the judge*, I thought, and scanned for the name, Ya'akov Zaban, hoping five years later he would still be sitting on the Jerusalem court. Room 204, it showed.

When I approached the appropriate door, three men in suits were arguing before it. Unable to understand the contents of their heated back-and-forth, and unsure whether Judge Zaban was among them, I waited for a lull, standing by idly. At a break in the conversation, I asked, "Judge Zaban?"

"Inside," said a lawyer, pointing to a closed door as everyone turned to look at me. "But you can't go in just yet."

I gripped my backpack and squeezed past them, turning the handle and pressing myself into what looked like a miniature courtroom. *His chambers.* Two columns of polished wooden benches stood five rows deep before the judge's raised bench, which was empty. Below it, a blond woman squinted up from her typing and said, "Can I help you?"

I took a breath. "Hi. Yes. This is a long story, but my wife was injured in the bombing at Hebrew University in 2002 and Judge Zaban presided over the trial of the Hamas cell tried in December of that year and I'm just looking for – "

The stenographer stopped me. "You know this is not a public office, yes?" she said, her stern face shadowed by a hint of mischievousness.

"I know. I'm sorry. It's just that – "

"How did you find it?"

"This office?" I couldn't believe this question again. "From the directory outside."

"You're American, yes?"

I was a rare specimen, it seemed. This was good. "Yes."

"Come here," the stenographer said, beckoning me to her side with an outstretched finger. "Tell me again what you want."

"Court documents, I'm hoping. That's what I'm trying to get. I traveled all this way to learn more about what happened.

Anyway, I was just in the secretarial office, hoping to acquire some documents from the trial, and was told I can't have them."

"Why can't you have them?" said another woman who magically appeared, seated in the first row, this one brown-haired and young, wearing sleek glasses, her lip gloss shining as the words formed, her skin liquid. *Sirens*, I thought. The lip gloss woman leaned her elbows on the railing separating us.

"They said I have to be an official party involved with the trial. I'm not, I guess." I replied.

"Huh. Do you remember the date of the trial?" asked the stenographer. I realized that she was Judge Zaban's secretary.

"I think, December 15, maybe?"

"I'll help you. Don't worry, my sweet," she said, opening up some internal court database.

"You're lucky. Normally, people can't just walk into chambers like this," said the woman with lip gloss. "But she's the nicest assistant in this entire building. An angel. She's an angel. And she's also the best. You're in good hands."

But this angel was unable to locate the trial in the database. She stood and said, "Excuse me a moment," before floating up a side staircase, past the bench, and toward a curtained room in the back.

"Judge Zaban is here. He's in a meeting."

I nodded.

When the stenographer returned, she smiled and slipped a note gently into my hand. "Judge Zaban remembers the trial clearly. He wishes you good luck. The note has the trial's archival number and the judge's signature." Then she took the note back and scribbled her number on the other side. "Tell them to call me if they give you trouble."

"Tell who?"

"The secretarial office. They have what you need."

When I handed the stenographer's note over to the red-haired secretary, she looked at it and then looked up. "What's this?"

"It's a note from Judge Zaban. You said I needed something from somebody involved, so here's a note from him. He was the judge presiding over the trial I'm seeking documents for. It's got his signature right there below the case number."

"And?"

"Excuse me?"

"So what do you want from me?"

"What do I want? Um. Records from the trial, please."

"I'm sorry, but I can't help you."

"Why not?"

"They're not here."

"How do you know?"

"We don't have any files here from that long ago. They'd be in the archives at the prosecutorial office downtown."

"Where's that?"

She gave me the address, which was across town. Two hours later, after trekking to the prosecutorial office and learning that they had no such documents, I was referred back to the courthouse. Back to where I started.

"I'm back."

"Hello."

"You sent me to the prosecutors' office, but they sent me back. They said the documents I'm looking for are here."

The secretary picked up the phone and began yelling, "Why'd you send him back? You have all the – they are? – Okay – Fine."

She hung up and stared through me. "Go see the Secretary for Criminal Records next door. She has them."

I handed this new secretary, a large-boned Ethiopian woman, my note from Judge Zaban and explained the situation.

She nodded. "Sure. No problem. Just fill out a request and it should be here in about a month."

"A month? But I'm leaving the country soon. I don't live here. Is there any way I can get it sooner?"

"I'm sorry. It's in the archives, and it takes time. They have to retrieve it, send it over. You know. It's a process."

"But I can't wait that long. There's no way I can pay for a fast service or something?"

"I'm sorry."

A woman next to her, listening to our conversation, took the note and began pecking into her computer, after which a printer began spitting out pages. She grabbed the stack and slapped it on the counter.

"Here's what you need."

"What?"

"It's what you're asking for. Here. Take it."

"What is it?"

"It's the closing arguments and the sentencing. About fifty pages. Can't imagine it doesn't contain what you're looking for – all the details of the case will be covered."

"How did you do that? I don't understand."

"It's in the system. Nothing to it."

"In the system?" I looked at the other woman, who looked back and shrugged sheepishly. "Do I owe you anything?"

"No."

"Not even for the printing?"

"No."

I picked up the pages, the weight of information almost unbearable. I knew it would take time, knew that I would take the pages back to America and work many nights on a good translation. I knew that the work would be slow, navigating through legalese, through thirteen indictments and all the evidence contained within, looking for some small mention of remorse, looking for any word as to how Mohammad had become involved with Hamas, looking for something, somewhere, to explain Jamie's scars.

Months later, at home in North Carolina, with Hebrew–English dictionaries strewn across an oak desk, I would learn many things:

I would learn that the attack was meant to have happened on July 28, three days prior to when the bomb went off – that Mohammad had placed the bag on a table in the cafeteria, similarly to the way in which he did so on July 31, then got in the getaway car with Kassam. Called the bag. And then retrieved it after nothing happened. After no ambulances rushed to the scene.

I would learn that Mohammad took the bomb to Ramallah for repair. For another attempt. The malfunction just a stumbling block. An obstacle around which to maneuver.

I would learn that he was born in 1973, a year before me.

That he returned home after successfully bombing Hebrew University on July 31 to his family and ate dinner.

That he was captured at his home three weeks later, dragged away by police in front of his wife and son.

That he had planned to bomb a supermarket in downtown Jerusalem and had helped scout locations for other attacks, including the bombing of Café Moment, where he and an accomplice cased the streets, gauging traffic and escape routes.

I would learn that Mohammad was recruited by the terror cell's leader, Abu Moaz.

That Abu Moaz was impressed by Mohammad's determination, his creativity, his Israeli resident status.

That Mohammad was convicted because of such determination. "He wasn't deterred by the difficulties which stood in his path," the judge had said.

I would learn that Mohammad was a dedicated killer, and that he was rewarded for such dedication with 9 counts of murder, 84 counts of attempted murder, 124 counts of providing aid for attempted murder, 5 counts of aiding the enemy during a war, 2 counts of giving information to the enemy, and 1 count of connection to the execution of murder.

And I would learn other things. I would learn that Mariam was organizing peace initiatives amongst her East Jerusalem students – basketball games between Israeli and Palestinian children.

I would learn that the Odehs had asked after me and my family, had extended an invitation to visit anytime.

I would learn that these people were now my friends. That I would expand the definition of "friend" to include them. And in including them, I would feel finished. Feel done. Feel that it was over. *It was over.* The journey, at least. The traveling backwards, trying to unravel everything. Somehow, meeting them, meeting the other side, the side responsible for what had happened – along with the impersonal information coldly reflected in the court documents – had helped close a door ripped open by the attack.

And though it was a door I couldn't lock – never learning first-hand if Mohammad's words of remorse were true – just closing the door was enough.

Reconciliation. It had happened, to some degree. And in happening, had impressed upon me the force of restorative dialogue. Its capacity for release, for unclogging the synaptic pores and letting loose all the filth which was contained within.

I had not picked up a gun. I had not involuntarily sought revenge, nor had I succumbed to any form of demonic violence as a way to exact justice. I just got on a plane, sat on a couch, and provided an opportunity for my subconscious voice to say, as

Mariam translated streams of Arabic, *My god, they are not monsters. They are not monsters.*

And in understanding this – they are not monsters – I understood that maybe, maybe there is hope for this world. For this land. For my people.

28

The evening before leaving Israel, I walked through the old neighborhood where Jamie and I had lived. I walked our old street, Rachov Yehoshuah bin Nun, stopping at our old building, 28א (28A), the front bordered by the same low, stone wall, the same wood-stained fence embedded into the stone wall, the same cactus-sprinkled garden bordered by cobblestones and tended in the same courtyard by the same Dutch woman who, years before, had been responsible for gathering the building's maintenance fees and collecting our mail when we went abroad.

I ascended the interior stairs and flipped a red light switch, timed to stay on for twenty seconds, just enough time to conquer four floors when hustling. I hurried to the sky blue door of apartment 8. The door was closed. I pressed my ear to the metal surface just as the light went off. Silence. The same silence we left years before.

I could have stayed there, concentrating, my ear flush against the metal, listening for the voices of our friends – our past lives – echoing off the linoleum and plaster within. But I didn't stay. Chose not to stay. It was enough. Just knowing it all still existed was enough.

Outside, the air was cool. I headed south on Kovshei Katamon. Then the phone rang. It was Lieutenant Colonel Dominitz.

"Hello?"

"Hello, David, this is Ian from the Prison Service."

"Hi Ian."

"I want to let you know that I checked with your request one last time. I'm sorry to say that, unfortunately, the prisoner has again refused."

"Thank you for calling. I understand."

"If there is anything I can do, please let me know."

"Of course, Ian. Of course. Thank you for your help."

"It is no problem."

"Well, that's it, then."

"Have a safe trip."

I hung up the phone and glanced over to see a young boy, while helping his mother unload groceries from the back of a van, pause from the task to toss a pomegranate into the air playfully. As it rose, slowly arcing in the night sky, I thought of my family. Of my love for them. I imagined squeezing my girls and holding Jamie as the pomegranate fell into the boy's hand, his mother saying, *Maspeek* – Enough. The boy reached the pomegranate out to her pleadingly, a gesture of forgiveness. The fruit rolled into her cupped palm. She placed it in a bag, kneeled down, and kissed him on the forehead, his arm reaching round her neck, her palms gently pressing the small of his back as he lifted his body to hers, standing on his toes.

And I knew. Knew everything needed was contained in feet lifting onto pointed toes, was contained in kisses on foreheads and arms reaching. Knew it was time to go back, time to live the life we'd been granted by chance.

The boy looked over at me as the van's door closed and smiled, waving. I waved back. "Goodbye," I said. "Goodbye."

Notes

Part I. The Bombing

1 **Three weeks before ... over his shoulder.** – From a transcription of the sentencing of Mohammad Odeh and three others on December 15, 2002. The documents, procured from the Jerusalem District Court, were in Hebrew – a transcription of the final arguments, which entered into the record all indictments and evidence pertaining to them before the sentencing. For posterity's sake. About sixty pages' worth of posterity. And so I translated all of them, to rid myself of posterity. Or to rid it of me.

2 **"passed time"** – Exact words used by the prosecutor when relating during final arguments the time spent by Mohammad Odeh before striking. I found the words so casual, so normal – so perfect in expressing the callousness of it all – that they were irreplaceable.

3 **Mohammad Odeh lived ... The phone ringing.** – Most of this is again from the Jerusalem District Court's sentencing documents, though supplemented by a few news articles:

1) "Handyman is Arrested in Bomb Blast" by Laurie Copans, Associated Press, August 21, 2002;

2) "Arrests in Hebrew Univ. Bombing" from CBS News, August 21, 2002;

3) "HU Bomber Worked on Campus" by Etgar Lefkovitz, *Jerusalem Post*, August 21, 2002.

4 **The voice of the blood ... from the ground.** – Genesis 4:10. Much of rabbinic commentary on this verse focuses upon the word blood due to its plural construction in the Hebrew: "קול דמי אחיך –The voice of your brother's bloods." This construction leads Rashi to conclude that "blood" is pluralized to indicate that not only was Cain killed, but so too all future descendants. However, it has always been the word "ground" that has most sparked my interest in this verse. Perhaps it's the writer, the metaphor-seeker within who gravitates toward striking images, toward

an image of the ground, soaked, emitting screams: "צועקים אדי מן האדמה – Yelling to me from the ground."

5 Genesis 2:22.

6 Genesis 12:1.

7 **Many answers have been given … points as well.** – This is my understanding of Nachmanides' comment on the verse, which I read in the original Hebrew from a volume entitled *Torat Hayim*, published by Mossad Harav Kook, which is a multi-volume set covering the books of the Torah with accompanying rabbinic commentary.

8 **For several months … Palestinian cabinet ministers.** – This is from a July 21, 2002 Associated Press article entitled "Israel, Palestinians Plan Talks" by Nicole Winfield.

9 **Activists from Fatah's … sealed since June,** – From two July 18, 2002 Associated Press articles: 1) "Israel Suspends Palestinian Talks" by Mark Lavie; 2) "Israel Keeps Restrictions After Bomb" by Jason Keyser.

10 **But first, July … the terrorists out.** – Ibid.

11 **Here is what … struggle for independence.** – From a July 20, 2002 *Ha'aretz News* article entitled "Report: PA Discusses Suicide Bombing Halt with Hamas, Jihad" and a July 25, 2002 *New York Times* article by James Bennet and John Kifner entitled "Palestinian Cease-Fire Was in Works Before Israeli Strike."

12 **According to a … a moral mistake.** – From a July 25, 2002 *Times* (London) article by Stephen Farrell entitled "Agreement Was to End Attacks Immediately."

13 **However, an anonymous … the Palestinian people.** – From *Ha'aretz News,* "Report: PA Discusses Suicide Bombing Halt with Hamas, Jihad."

14 **Those in the … and the Palestinian Authority.** – From Bennet and Kifner, "Palestinian Cease-Fire."

15 **In their three … A start.** – From Winfield. "Israel, Palestinians Plan Talks."

16 **Few things were … the Palestinian people.** – From a July 21, 2002 BBC News article entitled "Israel, Palestinians Resume Talks."

17 **Immediately, funds Israel … million it owed.** – From a July 22, 2002 Reuters article by Danielle Haas entitled "Israel Says Releasing Withheld Palestinian Funds."

18 **Much of this … to succeed.** – From Bennet and Kifner, "Palestinian Cease-Fire."

19 **Ninety minutes after … entire families.** – From a July 22, 2002 Associated Press article by Ibrahim Barzak entitled "Israel Air Strike Kills at least 10" and Bennet and Kifner, "Palestinian Cease-Fire."

20 **Here is what ... the targeted bombing.** – From a July 24, 2002 *Times* (London) article by Stephen Farrell entitled "Palestinian Ceasefire Plan Lies Buried in the Rubble of Gaza" and Bennet and Kifner, "Palestinian Cease-Fire."

21 **Israeli officials acknowledged ... on terrorist activities.** – From Bennet and Kifner, "Palestinian Cease-Fire."

22 **According to media ... its suicide bombings.** – From a July 24, 2002 United Press International article by Saud Abu Ramadan entitled "Hamas Halts Palestinian Authority Talks."

23 **Shahada had been placed ... began in 2000.** – From a July 23, 2002 *Ha'aretz News* article by Amos Harel entitled "Israel Kills Hamas Founder in Gaza in Air Strike."

24 **Having founded ... over ten years.** – From a July 23, 2002 BBC News article entitled "Profile: Sheikh Salah Shahada."

25 **A span during ... hundreds of attacks.** – From a July 23, 2002 *Independent* (London) article by Justin Huggler entitled "Ten Killed in Israeli Air Strike on Home of Hamas Chief."

26 **After escaping one ... conducted or not.** – From BBC News, "Profile: Sheikh Salah Shahada."

27 [**Shahada**] **had grown close ... next in line.** – From Harel, "Israel Kills Hamas Founder" and BBC News, "Profile: Sheikh Salah Shahada."

28 **Shahada's death sent ... the other victims.** – From a July 23, 2002 *Ha'aretz News* article by Amos Harel entitled "100,000 Attend Funerals of 15 Fatalities of Gaza Bomb Strike."

29 **Retaliation is coming ... of our operations.** – From a July 23, 2002 CBS News article entitled "White House Scolds Israel for Attack."

30 **But it wasn't ... area like this?** – From a July 24, 2002 *Times* (London) article by Stephen Farrell entitled "'Would the British Attack like This to Kill Adams?' Civilian Rage after the Attack on Gaza."

31 **This time was ... contribute to peace.** – From CBS News, "White House Scolds Israel for Attack."

32 **Critics cynically going ... ceasefire talks.** – From Bennet and Kifner, "Palestinian Cease-Fire."

33 **Diplomats intimately involved ... is now gone.** – From Farrell, "Palestinian Ceasefire Plan."

34 **Even though ... "the biggest successes"** – From Harel, "100,000 Attend Funerals."

35 **Which proclaims itself … in the world**. – http://www.ict.org.il/AboutICT/AboutUs/tabid/55/Default.aspx

36 **What wasn't reported … and desirable targets.** – From an article by Dr. Ely Karmon, Senior ICT Researcher, entitled "Israel's War on Terrorism," which was previously published as an Op-Ed in the *Jerusalem Post,* found on ICT's website at: http://www.ict.org.il/Articles/tabid/66/Articlsid/74/currentpage/9/Default.aspx

37 **And in the winter … for future attacks.** – From an article by Matthew Levitt, previously published in *Peacewatch*, the Washington Institute's Special Reports on the Arab-Israeli Peace Process, entitled "Hamas: Toward a Lebanese-style War of Attrition?" It can be found on ICT's website at: http://www.ict.org.il/Articles/tabid/66/Articlsid/77/currentpage/10/Default.aspx

38 **And absent from … in the territories.** – Karmon, "Israel's War on Terrorism."

39 **Israel was following the best intelligence available at the time.** – Though Karmon's last assessment – that targeted assassinations could prevent Hamas's rise to political prominence – turned out to be woefully wrong, demonstrating that "intelligence" is often little more than a network of informed guessers uniformed in sophistry.

40 **It reaches back … in the 1980s.** – Obviously, one could go back even farther, principally to the British Mandate and the colonial history of Palestine. But this will be visited in part IV.

41 **In the 1960s … social welfare services.** – From a 1999 ICT article by Dr. Boaz Ganor entitled "Hamas – The Islamic Resistance Movement in the Territories."

42 **The Brotherhood's desire … gave "tacit consent"** – From a paper by Shaul Mishal and Avraham Sela, originally published by the Tami Steinmetz Center for Peace Research at Tel Aviv University and reprinted by ICT under the title "Hamas: A Behavioral Profile."

43 **To its actions … even encouraging them.** – From an ICT article by Reuven Paz entitled "Sleeping with the Enemy – A Reconciliation Process as Part of Counter-Terrorism. Is Hamas Capable of 'Hudnah'?"

44 **Islamic Jihad was formed ... by the Brotherhood** – Ganor, "Hamas – The Islamic Resistance Movement in the Territories."

45 **"claim for exclusive ... Islamic law.** – Mishal and Sela, "Hamas: A Behavioral Profile."

46 **We promise … on every street.** – From a July 23, 2002 Reuters article entitled "Condemnation, Vows of Revenge Follow Israel Attack."

Part II. Disconnection

1 ***The Lord giveth. The Lord taketh away*** – This is from the Book of Job, 1:21. It's Job's response after learning he has lost everything, including his children.

Part III. Recovery

1 **It took nearly … the Potomac River** – I checked with the U.S. Geological Survey (USGS) at http://md.water.usgs.gov/publications/press_release/2003/2003-10/index.html to make sure my remembrances aligned with the documented timeframes and geological reports from the hurricane. Sometimes memory works. Sometimes it fails. In this particular instance, it half-worked, and the USGS helped the other half.

2 **We first considered … until he falls asleep.** – The block quote is from page 127 of *The No-Cry Sleep Solution,* published by McGraw-Hill (2002). I paused before deciding to cite this book properly, for I'm convinced of its innate evil, and wouldn't wish to unleash the book's manic suggestions on any struggling parent, much less one suffering from existential traumas unrelated to parenting, which itself is an existential trauma. A trauma I'd never trade in, understand. (Yes, N & T, I wrote that for your benefit. One day you'll be reading this, say, in twenty years. I think ahead.) As for the book, it sucks. Plain and simple. Oh sure, it gets 4 ½ out of 5 stars on Amazon.com from 726 reader reviews, which is a staggering number on Amazon, comparatively speaking. And it's the 233rd best-selling book on the site, another very impressive statistic. And the reviews? Take the title of this one from a self-proclaimed "Childbirth Educator" (she capitalized it) – whose review was rated as the most helpful by fellow readers: "A Practical (and effective!) Guide for sleep-deprived parents." My response? There is nothing less practical for sleep-deprived parents than asking them to rip pacifiers from the mouths of their sleeping infants and then chronicle in detailed logs, for weeks, every movement that infant makes through the night. No, that is not practical. That is self-fulfilling. That is torture, literally. Sleep-deprivation being a known torture technique, long recognized by the Convention Against Torture and the Geneva Conventions as a form of psychological torture. Here's an interesting found fact: "After World War II, the US military successfully prosecuted several Japanese soldiers who had subjected American prisoners to sleep deprivation" (http://www.hrw.org/en/news/2007/08/21/psychological-torture-and-bush-administration).

3 **tested it on trauma victims … emotional abuse** – One of Shapiro's early papers was "Efficacy of the eye movement procedure in the treatment of traumatic memories," published in the *Journal of Traumatic Stress,* vol. 2, no. 2, April 1989,

pp. 199–223. According to Shapiro, "The results of the study indicated that a single session of the EMD procedure successfully desensitized the subjects' traumatic memories and dramatically altered their cognitive assessments of the situation, effects that were maintained through the 3-month follow-up check." The study involved twenty-two people suffering from "intrusive thoughts, flashbacks, sleep disturbances, low self-esteem, and relationship problems" related to memories of traumatic events.

4 **Kathy** – It needs to be noted that "Kathy" is actually a composite of two separate therapists I saw consecutively during this time. I created this composite therapist for two reasons: A. In my memory, I can't separate what was said or discussed with each one. The conversations have blended together, the demands they made have blended together. To separate them would itself be an exercise in inaccuracy. So I created "Kathy," who allows me, as a composite, to accurately and truthfully relate some experiences I had in therapy. B. Forgetting for a moment reason A., which made the composite "Kathy" necessary, I felt that such a composite character would be cleaner for the narrative. I mean, did you really want me to go on for pages about how I couldn't remember who was who, and do that song and dance for each scene? I didn't think so. Thus, this note, in the spirit of full transparency and a commitment to the truth. And "Kathy," in the spirit of narrative integrity and clean storytelling.

5 **I decided to research … on wrapped mattresses.** – As indicated, this information was culled from www.cotlife2000.com, Check it out for all your mattress-wrapping needs.

6 **Not a word.** – Actually, this is not true, though it's not a lie. I published in the summer of 2005 a poem about the attack called "On Being Anchored" in *Pebble Lake Review*, though, unlike my other published pieces, I never thought about it after its publication, never re-read it when the customary contributor's volume came in the mail, wrapped in plastic. So when I wrote the words "Not a word," they were written with sincerity, for I thought them to be true. Because, in essence, they were. Though I had written once about the attack, written a poem about the attack, and had even published it, the experience of writing had made no impression, had been compartmentalized, erased. It was as though it hadn't happened. The experience of writing, in my mind, had never happened. So consider "Not a word" as psychic truth.

7 **Research … sure thing** – Sitting in the computer lab, the following articles are those I first read:

1) "Hamas bomb suspect arrested" by Ross Dunn, *Times* (London), August 22, 2002;

2) "Arrests in Hebrew Univ. Bombing" from CBS News, August 21, 2002;

3) Lefkovitz, "HU Bomber Worked on Campus."

I know this because these are the articles I initially emailed myself, beginning the process of building a research database from which to work.

8 **It was embedded … put on him."** – The AP article in question, from which both quotes came: Copans, "Handyman is Arrested."

9 **And so I … was growing within me** – As my wife pointed out while reading the manuscript, mention of South Africa in this context always evokes what she called "the Jimmy Carter red flag." I want to make clear that mention here of South Africa is only in relation to my own journey in discovering the impulses that were gaining momentum within myself. There is no equivalency between Israel and apartheid South Africa being made here, obviously. I don't believe the two are comparable. But Jews are sensitive, and many, I'm sure – particularly those who might falsely claim to love Israel more than I – would like nothing more than to point toward this text and say, "Ah, he's just like Jimmy Carter."

10 **This is what I learned … back to Jerusalem** – For my initial crash-course on the history of South Africa, I went to the government's website (http://www.info.gov.za/aboutsa/history.htm#apartheid) and found a relatively clear historical summary.

11 **The adoption … conflicts of the past** – From the introduction of Antjie Krog's *Country of My Skull* (New York: Times Books, 1998), p. x.

12 "**Truth recovery process"** – Ibid.

13 **Would give victims … suffering and loss.** – ibid., p. xi.

14 **Initially, she was … them from silence.** – ibid., p. 32.

15 **Your voice tightens … after all** – ibid., p. 50.

16 **Jamie could hang … self or others."** – I referenced the PTSD diagnostic criteria at behavenet.com, which reproduced the material with permission from the American Psychiatric Association.

17 **Then I … of spring rain."** – This is from "Understanding the secondary traumatic stress of spouses" by Kathleen Gilbert from *Burnout in Families: The Systemic Costs of Caring* (Figley, Charles R.; Boca Raton, FL: CRC Press, 1998) pp. 47–74.

18 "Watermelon" from Billy Jonas' album *What Kind of Cat are You?!* (2002).

19 **We prick up … one-way flood.** – Krog, *Country of My Skull*, p. 74.

20 **Some people got … hi to me.** – From *Encounter Point.*

IV. Collective History

1 **It was a thought … To live.** – This from Benny Morris' *Righteous Victims* (New York: Vintage Books, 2001), pp. 14–17.

2 **But when … to redeem it.** – ibid., p. 38.

3 **Palestine was far … region being Jews** – Rashid Khalidi, *The Iron Cage* (Boston: Beacon Press, 2007), p. 96.

4 **Dear Lord Rothschild … any other country.** – http://www.yale.edu/lawweb/avalon/mideast/balfour.htm

5 **What was remarkable about … as a people.** – Khalidi, *The Iron Cage*, pp. 32–33.

6 **There was no … did not exist.** – Khalidi, *Palestinian Identity*, New York: Columbia Univeristy Press, 1997, p. 147.

7 **The historical connection … in that country.** – http://www.yale.edu/lawweb/avalon/mideast/palmanda.htm

8 **The sudden introduction … as a nation.** – Khalidi, *Palestinian Identity*, p. 149.

9 **Palestinian leaders … representation and self-determination.** – Khalidi, *The Iron Cage*, p. 33.

10 **Recognition of the … legally subordinate position.** – ibid., p. 33.

11 **Fully-fledged representative … the mandatory state.** – ibid., p. 37.

12 **Zionism, be it … that ancient land.** – ibid., p. 36. Now, some might argue here that I am ignoring the restrictions the British placed upon the Jewish community, restrictions which were rebelled against (via violent resistance). These restrictions came later, and do nothing to mitigate the truth of Balfour's statement or Britain's priorities vis-à-vis the two peoples. And besides, the point, again, of this section is to understand the suffering of Palestinians. To understand them. Not to diminish Jewish suffering. History – true history – is not a zero sum game.

13 **After the First World War … of state power.** – ibid.

14 **In the end, we won.** – After our own struggles with the British, of course.

15 **Overnight … in camps elsewhere.** – Khalidi, *The Iron Cage*, p. 1.

16 **If I was ... they accept that?** – Nahum Goldmann, *The Jewish Paradox* (Grosset & Dunlap, 1978), p. 99. This was translated by Steve Cox.

17 **Allon's desire … without national rights.** – Gershom Gorenberg, *The Accidental Empire* (New York: Times Books, 2006), pp. 16–17.

18 **As long as … Zion and Jerusalem** – http://www.mfa.gov.il/MFA/Facts%20About%20Israel/State/The%20State

19 **The logic of … unconnected to defense.** – Gorenberg, *Accidental Empire*, p. 36.

20 **The reasons weren't … land of Israel.** – ibid., p. 37.

21 **There were minority … mainly Arabs live?** – ibid., p. 51.

22 **The situation today … presence on you.** – ibid., p. 83.

23 **While these … each passing car.** – Khalidi, *Iron Cage*, pp. 200–201.

24 **The quintessential Palestinian … as a people**. – Khalidi, *Palestinian Identity*, p. 1.

25 **Checkpoint story … used to it.** – From The University of Minnesota's Center for Restorative Justice, http://rjp.umn.edu/dialogue.html.

V. Reckoning

1 **The first entry … a misstep.** – Yes, I'm lazy. The definitions came from dictionary.com, http://dictionary.reference.com/browse/trip.

2 **Dr. Mordechai Kedar … on Israeli Arabs.** – http://www.biu.ac.il/Besa/mordechai_kedar.html

3 **I'm "Why Does" … Daniel Bar-Tal.** – This is the title of Daniel Bar-Tal's article appearing in *Political Psychology*, vol. 22, no. 3, 2001.

4 **It's because fear … creativity and flexibility.** – Bar-Tal, "Why Does Fear", p. 601. This piece of "dialogue" is a quote from Bar-Tal's article, adjusted slightly. The full quote reads: "fear is an automatic emotion, grounded in the perceived present and often based on the memorized past (also processed unconsciously) ... Hope, in contrast, involves mostly cognitive activity … and thus is based on creativity and flexibility."

5 **Oh, sorry … the theoretical future.** – ibid., pp. 604–605. This piece of "dialogue" splices the following quotes from Bar-Tal's article with supplementary text to make the dialogue work in context: "Hope is an emotion" and "resembles a state of mind."

6 **More or less … interference of fear.** – ibid., p. 601. This piece of "dialogue" is formed with connective text and the following direct quote from Bar-Tal's article: "is based on thinking, it can be seriously impeded by the spontaneous and unconscious interference of fear."

7 **And this fear … it is invoked.** – ibid., p. 604. This piece of "dialogue" is adapted from the following quote: "which bypasses the thinking process. It's a mechanism of adaptation that automatically protects life and homeostasis, but may operate irrationally and even destructively at the moment it is invoked."

8 **You've got it … a lingering flaw.** – ibid., p. 604. This piece of "dialogue" uses the following quote from Bar-Tal's article: "when in fear, human beings sometimes tend to cope by initiating a fight, even when there is little or nothing to be achieved by doing so."

9 **This is "Psychological ... and Clark McCauley**. – This is the title of an article by Ifat Maoz and Clark McCauley which appeared in *Political Psychology*, vol. 26, no. 5, 2005.

10 **Negotiation research has ... sides better off.** – This quote, minus the word "now," appears in ibid., p. 793.

11 **In every generation ... for this.** *Haaretz*, April 27, 1987 – Bar-Tal, "Why Does Fear," p. 617.

12 **In Israel, we ... are better off.** – The "dialogue" in this section from the pages are adapted from information gleaned throughout Maoz and McCauley's article.

13 **Everlasting shrug** – I love this phrase, which I plucked from Claudia Rankine's *Don't Let Me Be Lonely.*

Author's Note

When I began writing this book, many people asked, *Don't you think your wife should be the one to tell this story? Why do you think this is your story?*

At first, I had no response other than guilt. After all, Jamie *had* been the one directly impacted by the bombing, the one who had been targeted, the one who nearly lost everything. And in this context, the question – *Why do you think this is your story?* – became a debilitating one.

However, I eventually came to understand that this book, at its core, wasn't about the bombing. It was about a personal attempt to overcome the psychological horrors that haunted me after the attack. It was about those horrors that have haunted both Israelis and Palestinians in the land where this attack occurred. And it was about how those horrors can be transcended by reconciliation – about its power to soften both our internal and external conflicts.

It was then that I knew this story was mine to tell – a story that certainly belongs to so many others as well. Obviously, one such person is my wife, Jamie, who I want to thank for her uncommon support and strength throughout this entire process – a process which has not been easy for either of us.

I also want to thank the amazing writers who helped me with this book during my time in the MFA in Creative Writing program at the University of North Carolina, Wilmington. Namely: Philip Gerard, Rebecca Lee, Sarah Messer, David Gessner, Wendy Brenner, Karen Bender, Robert Anthony Siegel, Clyde Edgerton, Haven Kimmel, Peter Trachtenberg, John Jeremiah Sullivan, Jason Mott, Tim Conrad, Adam Petry, Douglass Bourne, Lukis Kauffman, Kate Sweeney, Joe Bueter, Kara Norman, Jarvis Slacks, and so many more.

Special gratitude is owed to my editor at Oneworld Publications, Robin Dennis, for her advice and direction. I also want to thank the marketing and publicity teams at both Oneworld Publications and 45th Parallel Communications, specifically: Henry Jeffreys, Lamorna Elmer, Alan Bridger, and Jennifer Abel Kovitz. Additional thanks go to Jessica Papin at Dystel & Goderich, who was one of the first people to believe in this book, and to Adam and Lori Simon, who read this book in its infancy and offered valuable feedback.

My meeting with the Odeh family could not have happened without the selfless help and support of countless people, particularly Leah Green of the Compassionate Listening Project, Julie Seltzer, and a number of Israeli and Palestinian activists and individuals who helped behind the scenes, including Mariam and Fakhree. I am grateful to the Odeh family for having the courage to invite me to their home and for warmly welcoming me.

Most of all, we will forever be grateful for the loving support of our family, our friends, and our Pardes community. There are no words to express the journey we have been through together and how much their support, in ways large and small, has meant to us.

Finally, I want to acknowledge the Blutstein and Bennett families, who never left my thoughts during the writing of this book. The memories of Ben and Marla will forever be with us.